'This book probes deeply into the methodological and theological obstacles to understanding the spiritual experience of people with profound intellectual disability to discover we have to ask even more primordial questions about how God reveals Godself at all. The result is a wide-ranging scriptural, philosophical, and theological inquiry into the God who would be perceived by human flesh despite the limitations of cognition. What was intended as an intervention in the arena of intellectual disability has ripple effects in Christian theology as a whole.'

— *Amos Yong, Professor of Theology & Mission, Fuller Theological Seminary, and author of* Theology & Down Syndrome: Reimagining Disability in Late Modernity

D1333642

GOD BEYOND WORDS

Christian Theology and the Spiritual Experiences
of People with Profound Intellectual Disabilities

Jill Harshaw

Jessica Kingsley *Publishers*
London and Philadelphia

First published in 2016
by Jessica Kingsley Publishers
73 Collier Street
London N1 9BE, UK
and
400 Market Street, Suite 400
Philadelphia, PA 19106, USA

www.jkp.com

Library of Congress Cataloging in Publication Data
Names: Harshaw, Jill, author.
Title: God beyond words : Christian theology and the spiritual experience of
   people with profound intellectual disabilities / Jill Harshaw.
Description: Philadelphia : Jessica Kingsley Publishers, 2016. | Includes
   bibliographical references and index.
Identifiers: LCCN 2016011849 | ISBN 9781785920448
Subjects: LCSH: Church work with people with mental disabilities. | Mental

   illness--Religious aspects--Christianity. | People with mental
   disabilities--Religious life. | Experience (Religion) | Spiritual
   life--Christianity.
Classification: LCC BV4461 .H36 2016 | DDC 261.8/322--dc23
LC record available at https://lccn.loc.gov/2016011849

British Library Cataloguing in Publication Data
A CIP catalogue record for this book is available from the British Library

ISBN 978 1 78592 044 8
eISBN 978 1 78450 302 4

For Rebecca

One day…

CONTENTS

ACKNOWLEDGEMENTS

There are many people to whom I am indebted for the opportunity to undertake this work. Here I wish to acknowledge the many disability theologians whose work is discussed below. All of these (including those with whom I sometimes disagree) have stimulated and fuelled my own academic reflection on the subject of intellectual disability. Two of these scholars in particular have had a profound influence on my thinking and on this work.

The first is Jean Vanier, whose life has been inspirational on both an academic and personal level. In Jean's writings, and especially in my personal encounters with him, I have found someone who has helped me understand that my daughter Rebecca's life, while often difficult, is not a source of tragedy but a continual cause for wonder, celebration and thanksgiving. The second is Professor John Swinton, whose tireless passion, courage and innovation in the task of challenging the Church to value and respect the lives and contributions of people with intellectual disabilities has left an indelible impact on those of us who take this issue seriously and want to see not just understanding but transformation. My engagement with John's work, both in person and through his writing, has been invariably challenging and thought-provoking.

Special thanks to Dr Natalie Watson, who inspired me to dare to believe that I have something to contribute to the field of intellectual disability theology and who has been supportive through periods of personal difficulty during which this book has been written.

I am deeply indebted to my friend and colleague Dr Ian Dickson, who was the superv᷉____ ᷉___ ᷉__ doctoral research. Ian has worked alongside, encouraged _____ s well as intellect on my journey into ⟨ _____ ⟩ my dear friend Agnes Hamilton for _____ his project – and with life in general!

Above all, I want to _____ ___ ₂ contribution of my family. My husband, William, has been unendingly encouraging, despite the other pressures and demands of life at home which might have detracted from my capacity to complete the work. And finally, to

Rebecca, my deepest love and thanks. You have opened my eyes, in a way that no one else could, to what is truly important both in life and in faith. I am so very proud to be your mother.

INTRODUCTION

In the spring of 2014 I was invited, on the basis of my experience as a teacher and researcher, by the Irish Churches' Council for Healing to speak at their Annual Conference. This year's subject was to be 'disability'. I initially (politely) declined, explaining that there were two reasons for my sense of ineligibility to take on the task. First, I was uncomfortable with any attempt to speak about 'disability' as if it were a homogeneous condition, and I did not have a robust background in thinking theologically about disability in general – my focus has always been on intellectual disability. Second, and more pivotally, I could not conceive of discussing intellectual disability in the context of 'healing', as if a person would be better off without it, and God, if he were asked, would confirm this perspective by removing it. In response, the Council members graciously reiterated their invitation and gave me free reign to address the subject of intellectual disability in whatever way I felt was appropriate. I addressed the Conference on issues of social and theological oppression and marginalization, and the importance of inclusion and meaningful participation in faith communities and of advocating for the rights of people with intellectual disabilities, including challenging a culture that would even deny their right to exist. The reception to the plenary addresses was surprisingly positive – given that I had not mentioned the word 'healing' at all! During a discussion in one of the break-out groups, however, a member of the clergy came to seek me out because, as group leader, he had been asked a question that he felt inadequately equipped to answer. The question was about whether it is possible for a person who cannot understand the Bible to encounter God or 'be saved' (in the terminology of some participants)?

The fact that those present were deeply exercised about this question and yet had no theological framework within which to address it did not surprise me, but it did disturb me. It did not surprise me, because I am increasingly hearing it articulated in conversations with parents (like me) whose children have profound intellectual disabilities and for whom the voice of the Church has not yet been able to offer satisfactory and robustly faithful answers to their questions, thus contributing to their sense of isolation and uncertainty. Sadly, I continue to encounter it in academic theology both within and beyond the currently small and discrete (though not for much longer, I hope) area of disability theology. Decades after the burgeoning of disability theology as an academic discipline, this perceived conundrum remains alive, and it is my hope that this book, which represents the outcome of many years of research and rumination on what seems to me to be a hugely significant question, goes some way to addressing it.

The subtitle of this work highlights two core terms which should be defined in order to set the context for the discussion that follows. The first, 'spiritual experience', requires a brief explanation; the second, 'profound intellectual disabilities', a more lengthy one, for the identification of the distinct group of people who are the precise focus of the work is vital to an understanding of the issues to be discussed.

What do I mean by 'spiritual experience'?

The argument presented in this book is constructed within the framework of the Christian faith tradition. The term 'spiritual experience' here is used to connote a human being's encounter and relationship with the Christian God, initiated and sustained by his gracious approach to human beings, and in many ways an indefinable, mysterious entity, albeit that its reality is often indisputable for the one who is its recipient. The term is used in preference to others used elsewhere in disability theology, of which 'spirituality' is the most common, although there is no intended difference in meaning.[1] 'Spirituality', despite its relatively straightforward biblical roots in Old Testament (*ruach*) and New Testament (*pneuma*) presentations of the presence and activity of the Spirit of God in creation and in transformative divine–human encounter, has become a less closely defined concept in the journey of the Church from the New Testament to the present day. The twists and turns of the term's pedigree have, over two millennia, demonstrated a range of expressions including, at times, a disengagement from the theology that underpins it, a privatized and eliticized, often ascetic, lifestyle and a concept confined to what McGinn describes as 'inner dispositions and inner states of the soul' (1991, p.3). It was often marginalized by suspicion, and the

---

1   See, for example, Swinton, J., Mowat, H. and Baines, S. (2011) 'Whose Story Am I? Redescribing profound disability in the Kingdom of God.' *Journal of Religion, Health and Disability* 15:1, pp.1–19.

term has at various points been ascribed to a set of practices frequently disdained by some as theologically ungrounded.[2]

Even within the contemporary resurgence of interest in the subject, spirituality continues to appear a somewhat nebulous and ambiguous concept, attracting a plethora of possible definitions and meanings, both religious and non-religious.[3] These include a focus on the essential human condition: in his excellent discussion of the subject through the lens of the history of Christian mysticism, McIntosh, for example, describes spirituality as 'the discovery of the true "self" precisely in encountering the divine and the human other' (1998, p.5). Others, like Schneiders, place emphasis on a more active response to God's approach on the part of human beings: 'Christian spirituality is a self-transcending faith in which union with God in Jesus Christ through the Spirit expresses itself in service of the neighbour and participation in the realization of the reign of God in this world' (2002, p.134). The widely acknowledged and much-lamented (at least by some) divorce of the experiential encounter with the person and mystery of God from theology as a set of beliefs, exemplified in the way in which Western academia came to regard detachment as essential to academic integrity, has given birth to fresh understandings of spirituality as an intrinsic and indispensable aspect of a comprehensive theological education. Consequently, 'spirituality' has also become used as a descriptor of an academic discipline, albeit one that deserves its place within the wider enterprise of the study of theology. Scholars and writers are quick to caution, however, against potential divisions which this recognition of the value of studying spirituality might precipitate. Merton (1972, p.255) warns that '[w]e must not separate intellectual study of divinely revealed truth and contemplative experience of that truth as if they could never have anything to do with one another. On the contrary, they are simply two aspects of the same thing.' This complexity-ridden provenance of the term 'spirituality' sets the backdrop to my preference for 'spiritual experience' to connote a life-giving encounter and ongoing relationship with God. This term has potential to evoke a simple clarity, in tandem

---

2   For a comprehensive discussion of the various manifestations and interpretations of the phenomenon, see Sheldrake, P. (1991) *Spirituality and History: Questions of Interpretation and Method*. London: SPCK; and Waller, R. and Ward, B. (1999) *An Introduction to Christian Spirituality*. London: SPCK.

3   For evidence of the plethora of definitions, see Cobb, M., Puchlaski, C. and Rumbold, B. (eds) (2012) *Oxford Textbook on Spirituality in Health Care*. New York: Oxford University Press.

with a non-prescriptiveness that lends itself to an open dialogue with some of the theological propositions with which this book will engage. Consequently, a deeper explanation of what is meant here by a Christian 'spiritual experience' will inevitably unfold as the discussion progresses.

What do I mean by 'profound intellectual disability'?

The term 'intellectual disability' is the most recent in a long line of descriptive language used to connote that subgroup of the population that is the most cognitively impaired. Previous terminology over the last 200 years has included 'idiocy, feeblemindedness, mental deficiency, mental disability, mental handicap, and mental subnormality' (Schalock, Luckasson and Shogren 2007). New terminologies have been introduced to replace earlier versions which have acquired a pejorative status over time. A brief explanation of various nomenclature and of the rationale for the particular terminology used here is offered below, but it is acknowledged that while medical and psychology 'experts' debate the appropriateness of various expressions, it is evident in the rise of self-advocacy movements that some people to whom these are being applied are asserting their right to define their own classification (Goodley and Rapley 2000, p.137).

The current term of usage within the United Kingdom health and social services domain is 'learning disability', while the World Health Organization's *International Classification of Diseases* (ICD-10) employs 'mental retardation'.[4] However, a growing consensus is building, and it is anticipated that the forthcoming ICD-11 will adopt the term 'intellectual disability'. This is the emergent term in current disability theology.

With respect to the criteria that give rise to an identification of the condition, it is broadly agreed across the range of sources and disciplines that engage with the subject that intellectual disability comprises three discrete and essential criteria. The first of these is a significant impairment of intelligence; intelligence involves such general cognitive abilities as reasoning, problem-solving, abstract thinking, planning and learning from experience (Schalock *et al.* 2010, p.31). The second criterion is a significant impairment of social functioning, which comprises a range of

---

4   World Health Organization (WHO) (2010) *International Statistical Classification of Diseases and Related Health Problems, 10th Revision (ICD-10)*, Chapter 5: 'Mental and Behavioural Disorders, F70–F79 Mental Retardation.'

conceptual skills (including language, reading, writing, money, time and number skills), social skills (including interpersonal, social responsibility and social problem-solving skills) and practical skills (including personal (Schalock *et al.* 2010, pp.43–4). The third is an age of onset prior to adulthood (that is, before the age of 18 years). Both intelligence and social functioning are assumed to be 'normally distributed' throughout the population, such that most people function in or around an average level and the further one deviates from that average, in either direction, the smaller the numbers of people encountered (Bartholomew 2004, pp.87–8). Intelligence, for example, is typically measured by the 'IQ' (Intelligence Quotient),[5] where the population average is set at 100. Half the population (50%) would be expected to have an IQ of between 90 and 110, 68% between 85 and 115, and 95% between 70 and 130. Only just over 2% will be considered extremely 'gifted' with an IQ of over 130, although in what sense this is understood as a gift, and who its giver might be, raises some interesting issues. A similar 2–3% will be particularly limited, with an IQ of less than 70 (Herrnstein and Murray 1996, p.582). It is this level of intelligence (an IQ of approximately 69 or below) – in association with a commensurate level of social functioning and an age of onset prior to adulthood – that defines intellectual disability.

Just like intelligence in general, intellectual disability constitutes a continuum in terms of ability. Historically, this has been represented by a number of 'levels' of intellectual disability. The United Kingdom Mental Deficiency Acts of 1913 and 1927, for example, distinguished between 'idiots', 'imbeciles' and 'feeble-minded persons'. Interestingly, the World Health Organization (2010) makes comparable distinctions, albeit couched in more contextually acceptable language, between those with 'profound', 'severe', 'moderate' and 'mild' mental retardation. The group categorized as having 'profound mental retardation' equates to fewer than 1 in 1,000 approximately of the general population, with IQ and corresponding social functioning levels of approximately 40 or below, for whom there is little if any agential capacity or consciousness of self as distinct from the world around them.

In education contexts, this group tends to be referred to as having 'profound and multiple learning difficulties', while the commonly

---

5   The three most commonly employed tests of individual intelligence are the Wechsler Adult Intelligence Scale (Wechsler 2008); the Wechsler Intelligence Scale for Children (Wechsler 2003); and the Stanford-Binet Intelligence Scales (Roid 2003).

used term in health service provision is the briefer 'profound learning disabilities'. In order to avoid a specific alignment with one or other of the approaches associated with these differing perspectives, an alternative label, 'profound intellectual disabilities', will be employed in this work.[6] To the extent that the people at the heart of this discussion may generally be expected to lack such cognitive capacities as would facilitate the use of language or other communicative tools as a means to understand, receive and convey information about their own lived experience and the world around them, the term 'profound intellectual disability' conveys well both the nature and the extent of the difficulties they might be supposed to encounter in accessing the traditional means of divine revelation that are believed to provide at least some of the keys to such a spiritual experience.[7]

Challenges and tensions inherent in this work
Labels and categorization

Before we proceed any further, I need to acknowledge that while identifying the degree of cognitive deficit of the people who are at the heart of this research is vital to presenting an understanding of its subject, doing so inherently creates personal reservations as to its appropriateness. I continually struggle with the fact that assigning what might be perceived as 'labels' means an inevitable degree of alignment with medical and individualized models of disability (to be discussed below), whose prejudicial and restrictive effects on people with disabilities has been a prevalent aspect of their experience over many decades. The imposition of classifications of disability on people with profound intellectual disabilities, and consequently on all people with intellectual disabilities, sits uncomfortably with me on many levels. Davis (1995, p.xiii) importantly points out that such terms 'are all hopelessly embroiled in the politics of disability, or ability'. Moreover, to enact a process of constructing a definition intrinsically involves presenting disability as 'a lack, a deficit...a problem experienced by an

---

6   The term is employed to delineate an equivalent level of intellectual disability by prominent disability theologian Professor John Swinton in 'Known by God' in Reinders, H. (ed.) (2010) *The Paradox of Disability: Responses to Jean Vanier and L'Arche Communities from Theology and the Sciences*. Grand Rapids, MI: Eerdmans, p.143.

7   I am indebted to my friend and colleague Dr Ivan Bankhead, Clinical Psychologist, for his expertise in relation to this material.

individual…a deviation from a state of normality' (McCloughry and Morris 2002, p.9). The implication is that 'you are disabled; I am not', and questions arise with regard to the basis on which 'I' assume the authority to make such a distinction. Moreover, as Newell importantly highlights, 'where concepts of normality seem to function as the abiding definition for treatment and intervention [it is] difficult to allow for more tentative and paradoxical conclusions and who disables them' (2007, p.325).

While acknowledging this reluctance and the ambiguity that exists in the ensuing critical references to the consequences of such an approach, it should become clear that my work is permeated by a consistent disavowal of any lack of respect for the value and equality of any person whom I, and society as a whole, have categorized as disabled. Moreover, it is intended that this book will address some of the seemingly intractable barriers to uncovering the paradoxical conclusions as to who disables people with profound intellectual disabilities in relation to understandings and assumptions concerning their potential for spiritual experience.

Nonetheless, inextricably linked to this difficulty is the fact that to write or speak in terms of 'people with profound intellectual disabilities' seems to imply that they are a homogenous group, for the most part the same in many respects, rather than individual persons. Any implication that people with profound intellectual disabilities lack such individuality is both patently ridiculous and entirely contrary to the Christian theology that this book explores. Its underpinning ethos is that neither cognitive impairment nor any other aspect of the human experience has any power whatsoever to undermine the theological foundation of human personhood. Accordingly, while reference to 'people with profound intellectual disabilities' is a necessary feature of this work, I want to affirm at the outset that such categorization attaches no stigma or implication of loss of value, dignity or individuality of any kind. Referring to such people collectively in this context is no more a pejorative act than it would be if the subject of this research was the spiritual experience of the very small group of people whose IQ score exceeds 150. It is ultimately the case that any discussion of disability, theological or otherwise, involves some degree of identification of impairment and, as Susan Wendell comments (1997, p.32), '"people with disabilities" is not a meaningless category as long as there is social oppression based on disability'. If the ending of social repression can indeed negate such categorization, then, sadly, almost two decades following her statement, the term is not yet redundant.

Intellectualism

Another of the primary tensions inherent in this discussion is intellectualism. I concur with Walmsley that 'there is a long tradition, to which I and other [academics] belong, of non-people with disabilities taking up the pen to address injustice and to speak for people who lack the confidence and means to speak for themselves' (2002, p.34). This tension is, of course, an aspect of all theological discussion with regard to people with profound intellectual disabilities, and there is always the potential for work of this nature to sit uneasily with writer and reader alike. The further danger is that the work might appear patronizing, if not rife with pretensions of superiority. While it is important to identify the presence of such challenges, in the end we face a choice between speaking about (although not on behalf of)[8] people who cannot speak for themselves and excluding them from our consideration altogether. It is this that overcomes Haslam's reluctance to speak about the humanity of people with profound intellectual disabilities (2011, p.17), and, notwithstanding the reservations expressed, I also prefer the former option.

The 'right' to speak

Nonetheless, this book will consistently emphasize the dangers of assuming that any of us has the right to speak from a position of certainty of the spiritual experience of people who cannot speak for themselves. The claim to specialist human-based knowledge of the details of what is an unarticulated, inner experience, occurring in a mysterious and ultimately indefinable encounter between God and people with profound intellectual disabilities, is heavily scrutinized in this work. The authenticity of 'knowledge' of their spiritual lives gained from external observations of those close to these people, and the feelings of those observers about them, is challenged, as are purportedly consequent theological insights. It might then be argued that I am guilty of the charges I am alleging, by indulging in a similar practice of assuming

---

8   The dangers of such an approach will be highlighted later in the book.

'knowledge' about the spiritual experience of people with profound intellectual disabilities. Again, while this argument is acknowledged, the intention throughout is to avoid speaking *for* these people but to invite the voice of Christian theology, rather than mine or others' who draw conclusions from their behaviour, to speak *about* them. Ultimately, while the description of people with profound intellectual disabilities as 'others' or 'another' is implicit in this work, and discussion will take place to which they are not party, it is in the spirit of Bevans' comments that the discussion is conducted:

> [O]ur first task in approaching another people, another culture, another religion, is to take off our shoes, for the place we are approaching is holy. Else we may find ourselves treading on men's dreams. More serious still, we may forget that God was here before our arrival. (2002, p.127, first published 1992)[9]

Personal experience

Finally, I am cognisant of the significance of my personal experience in relation to disability which differently but critically impacts the lives of two members of my immediate family. I am continually at pains to encourage my theology students to become intentionally attentive to the 'me' who is a party to their theological conversations – *my* past and present experience, *my* underlying assumptions and preferred outcomes. Thus I acknowledge that, as the parent of a woman who has profound intellectual disabilities, I (perhaps understandably) hold a preferential option for a positive view on whether any person with profound intellectual disabilities can experience God in a personal way. I hope that this tension is mitigated by the rigour with which the boundaries of Christian theology are both explored and respected, and I believe that in many respects a personal passion for the subject has potential to be an additional incentive to apply concerted effort to establishing a sustainable argument. As Newell writes (2007, p.324) in relation to his own experience of illness and disability, 'the context in which disabled theologies are explored is one in which theological engagement is an ongoing process in which disabilities within one family and the reflection on those disabilities continues to raise real concern and challenge'. This

---

9   A combined paraphrase of Exodus 3.5 and W.B. Yates' famous poem 'I have Spread My Dreams Under Your Feet'. Bevans refers here also to Warren (1963, p.10).

is perhaps the reason why so many contemporary theologians working in the area of intellectual disability are, like me, in close familial, social or professional relationships with people with intellectual disabilities.

1

A BRIEF CONTEXTUAL SURVEY OF DISABILITY IN CHRISTIAN THEOLOGY AND SOCIETY

A comprehensive history of theological perspectives on the existence and experience of disability is to be found in Swinton and Brock's excellent *Disability in the Christian Tradition* (2012); accordingly, I do not attempt to offer any broad historical survey of the subject. The primary focus at this point, following an initial brief acknowledgement of some of the complexities in current biblical scholarship on the human condition of disability, is an exploration of relevant developments from the second half of the twentieth century to the present day – a period within which the treatment, rights and equality of people with disabilities have become significant issues within wider Western social, political and, eventually, theological agendas.

Recent scholarship on biblical motifs of disability

It would be something of an understatement to say that disability has a mixed profile in biblical sources. Weiss Block describes the predominant climate of biblical studies' limited engagement in this area to date as one in which 'scriptural exegesis of the disability passages begins with a "hermeneutic of suspicion"' (2002, p.101). As a contributor to one of the most comprehensive collections of biblical scholarship on the subject to date, *This Abled Body: Rethinking Disabilities in Biblical Studies* (2007), Wynn articulates one of the core challenges emerging from scriptural references to disability. With particular reference to what appear to be the most problematic Old Testament presentations of the human experience of disability in which connections are routinely made between various disabling conditions and spiritual and physical impurity, sinfulness, curse and ineligibility to be found in the priestly service of God, she comments (2007, p.91), for example, that the understanding expressed in texts such as Leviticus 21.17–23 – the 'Priestly perspective' – is 'that disability is primordial chaos breaking into God's created order'. John Hull identifies the broad problem inherent in a three-stage biblical eschatology of perfection, fall and restoration, from the first and second of which, he claims, people with disabilities are excluded:

> Men and women, boys and girls with disabilities become the concrete instances of a general phenomenon of disability which itself is part of the imperfect world. It is because of associations such as these that many people with disabilities have come to believe that far from being a power for their emancipation, Christian faith is a major source of the social and economic disadvantage that they suffer. Christian faith, to put it more bluntly, is not seen as part of the answer but as part of the problem. (Hull 2003, p.10)

The pertinence of his claim becomes increasingly apparent as this book unfolds.

In seeking to address some of these issues as well as the ways in which they are being confronted in biblical and disability theology studies, Avalos, Melcher and Schipper identify three important and distinct hermeneutical approaches to the majority of disability texts which he clearly construes in a negative light. The first is a 'redemptionist' approach, which 'seeks to redeem the biblical text, despite a negative stance on disabilities, by recontextualizing it for modern application'. The second, 'rejectionist' approach 'would argue that the Bible has negative portrayals of disability that should be rejected by modern society'. The third, 'historicist' approach 'undertakes historical examinations of disabilities in the Bible and its subsequent interpretation, sometimes in comparison with neighbouring ancient cultures, without any overt interest in the consequences of the conclusions for modern application' (Avalos, Melcher and Schipper 2007, pp.4–5).

While it is possible to trace Avalos' designations across a range of theological scholarship in the area of disability, it is difficult to conclude that hermeneutical approaches taken by disability theologians fall neatly and exclusively into these categories. Some scholars have adopted a less defensive stance, choosing instead to place the exegetical spotlight on texts that demonstrate a more positive perspective on disability. Among a number of such instances, McCloughry and Morris, for example, highlight aspects of the Levitical code in which mistreatment of people who are deaf or blind is stated to be offensive to God and cite, among other narratives, Jacob's disabling encounter with the Angel of the Lord as a favourable portrayal of disability (2002, pp.40–6).

For the most part, however, preference has been demonstrated for the first and second of the approaches of Avalos *et al.*, given the overall ambiguity and potential prejudice evident in perspectives on the condition of disability within and beyond theological and ecclesial contexts. In *The Disabled God* (1994), widely regarded as the most catalytic work in disability theology of the late twentieth century, Eiesland comments that 'the persistent thread within the Christian tradition has been that disability denotes an unusual relationship with God and that the person with disabilities is either divinely blessed or damned' (1994, pp.70–1). It would then be surprising if there were to be no attempt to apply the conclusions of the interpretive task to the construct of disability which most commonly portrays it as a manifestation of a fallen and corrupted creation, powerfully illustrated in Betcher's ironic expression of the oppression and spiritual and social unacceptability she experienced following the amputation of her leg as her 'fall from grace' (2007, p.25). Indeed, grappling with the implications of such oppressive influences is part of the process by which disability theology is developing its own identity and status as a genre of contextual theology, similar, if not yet equal in status, to that of other liberation and feminist theologies.[1] It is to be hoped that this inequality will soon be redressed through the continuing development of scholarship in the field.

Highlighting some typical expressions of the use of one or a merger of more than one of Avalos *et al.*'s approaches may serve to further expound the backdrop of current use of biblical texts. Black highlights (1996, p.22) some of the tensions inherent in the contemporary quest for appropriate hermeneutical approaches to disability biblical texts by identifying continuing inconsistent interpretations in which '[d]isability implies punishment for sin or lack of faith but…also…obedience to God's will in being a courageous witness to the world'. Adopting what might be termed a 'redemptionist' approach, she argues that a contextually authentic understanding of Jesus' healing acts requires the reader to focus on the reinstatement of people with disabilities within the wider community. Jesus' allowing the touch of the woman deemed impure because of persistent haemorrhage, his addressing her as 'daughter' and healing her, for example, brought about not only a physical remedy but a remedy of the elements of her lived experience that kept her in a state of social exclusion. On this basis, Black advocates a homiletic approach to the healing narratives that challenges a contemporary church

---

1   The catalyst for this development is frequently attributed to Eiesland's The *Disabled God*.

community's 'unwritten purity codes…[and]…boundaries…established to protect themselves from those considered unclean' (1996, p.184). Tataryn and Truchan-Tataryn endorse a similar interpretation: 'the actions of Jesus confuse previous distinctions between the sacred (pure) and profane (impure)' (2013, p.43). They too prioritize the inclusionary nature of Jesus' miraculous acts of healing, describing the 'prevailing message of the miracle stories [as] the presence of the Kingdom – not by Jesus' performance of supernatural wonders but by his refusal to allow social constructions of human worth to obstruct the sacred power of relationship' (2013, p.100).

Wynn's work in exposing a contemporary 'normate hermeneutic.'[2] which she claims is employed by biblical scholars ranging 'from traditional white males to feminist interpreters' (2007, p.92) and which mirrors social prejudice and discrimination by interpreting incidences of disability in the Yahwistic texts as inextricably related to death, powerlessness, diminished value and tragedy, also seems to represent a redemptionist approach. In her alternative interpretations of selected Old Testament texts,[3] she argues (2007, p.101) that 'disability is not a reason for loss of status and indeed can be a mark of status'. Basing this argument on contextualization of ancient Near Eastern cultural influences, in line with Avalos *et al.*'s 'historicist' category of interpretation, she demonstrates that it is possible to identify the use of more than one of Avalos *et al.*'s approaches within the same work. Graham Monteith's argument seems to fit more easily within the 'rejectionist' designation, as it presents a direct challenge to the miracle motifs in the gospel narratives which, he insists, have contributed to discriminatory stances being taken against people with physical disabilities. Nonetheless, he does not refuse to engage entirely with the text but, like Black, seeks to find an authentic alternative reading that does not negate the value of the original narratives but affirms the right of people with disabilities to understand themselves and be understood by others as whole persons, without need of a cure (2005).

A number of scholars prefer to place particular emphasis on the metaphorical aspect of the miracle cures – that Jesus was acting in material ways to demonstrate a deeper reality in terms of his ultimate

---

2   Wynn is adopting the term 'normate' introduced by social scientist Rosemarie Garland-Thomson who describes it as the socially constructed ideal image 'through which people can represent themselves as definitive human beings' (1997, p.8).

3   Wynn cites, for example, the blindness of Isaac and the blessing of Esau in Genesis 27.1–45.

mission to heal human beings of their estrangement from God. Fuller comments (1963, p.125) that Mark's account of the miracles functions on two levels: 'as stories of actual physical miracles and as symbolic constructs to emphasize the inability or refusal of the disciples to understand who Jesus was'. Young highlights the deeper truth behind the healing of the blind man in John 9.1–12, describing it as 'an acted parable. Jesus gives sight to the blind man as he gives light to the world' (1990b, p.73). Such symbolic, metaphorical or parabolic interpretations are, however, rejected by those who insist on the legitimacy of a literal reading both of what Jesus did and of his self-declaration as the one sent to proclaim 'recovery of sight for the blind' (Luke 4.19), for example, in addition to his specific citing of his miraculous healings acts as evidence that he is who John the Baptist had hoped he might be (John 11.4–5). Interestingly, Yong's emphasis on the power of Jesus' touch is not, like Black's, placed on its inclusionary impact but on its association with the 'life-transforming and transcending power of God, [which]…combined with his spoken word to bring about healing or a bodily resuscitation' (2011, p.77).

On different grounds, Black contests a kind of symbolic interpretation of the healing miracles in which conditions of disability become inextricably connected with ignorant, wilfully disobedient or sinful responses to God (1996, p.54) when aligned with other texts where blindness and deafness, for example, are used metaphorically to describe an inability to perceive, understand or respond obediently to what God is doing or saying (see Isaiah 42.18–21; 42.8). Indeed, it is important that we pay attention to the impacts of such metaphors on people whose physical blindness and deafness is integral to their experience of the world. Making a comparison between the contextual ramifications of the use of words such as blindness or deafness and black or white, she comments that 'the use of language is always a symbolic act and when words or symbols are always used in negative terms, the language contributes to the oppressive way people view and treat those who have blindness or blackness as part of their essential identity' (1996, p.188). Young, on the other hand, argues that, when viewed through a semi-literal lens, the relationship between suffering and judgment cannot be totally discounted because while:

> it is not punishment for sin…disability does bring about judgment, a *krisis*, because it's a kind of test. It discriminates between those who rise to the occasion and those who fail to do so… It shows up people, their

relationships, their values, for what they are. Society is judged by the way it treats people with disabilities. (2014, p.105)

She may be correct, and a reading of Matthew 25.31–45 might indicate that it is not only society but the individuals who comprise it who will ultimately face an even greater judgment. Nonetheless, she is referring here to an entirely different relationship between disability and sin to that which places sin and disability in some kind of causal relationship, and it is surely the latter that precipitates most problems for people who can and do recognize themselves to experience disabilities, as well as the families of those who cannot.

While healing miracles continue to be recorded, albeit to a lesser extent, within the book of Acts,[4] the primary biblical narrative of the burgeoning Church in relation to those who are socially marginalized in general is an emphasis on the Church's obligations to embody God's care for the poor and the outcast and to prioritize the weakest within the new ecclesial communities.[5] In the prevailing Graeco-Roman context in which these communities took shape, attitudes towards infants born with disabilities were, as Caspary (2012, p.25) explains, entirely negative and literally destructive.[6] Thus, while there is no specific reference to people with disabilities within records of the New Testament Church's caring activity, its compassionate approach to those deemed to be of low social status – presumably people with disabilities among them – was radically counter-cultural. Commenting on the continuation of such ecclesial practices, Caspary writes (2012, p.26):

[W]hile the Church Fathers of the late third and fourth centuries showed little if any theoretical interest in physiological origin or moral nature of physical differences, they adamantly recommended pastoral care and philanthropy as…responses to social exclusion as enjoined in the New Testament.

Gates, writing from an academic health and social care (rather than theological) perspective, affirms this assessment, commenting that 'with the dawn of Christianity emerged a compassion and concern for those who had a learning disability' (1997, p.11).

---

4   The book of Acts contains 13 healing narratives.
5   See also James 1.27; 2.14–17.
6   See also Yong 2007, pp.79–116.

Other aspects of the life of Christ, from incarnation to ascension have been variously positively interpreted as a source of theological insight into the subject of human disability. Disability theologians have argued that Jesus' engagement with social outcasts, people with disabilities among them, and his personal identification with the marginalized, exemplified in his discourse on the final judgment in Matthew 25.31–46, locates him firmly on the side of those whom society disdains,[7] a viewpoint to which further reference will be made at a later point in this work. Similar arguments pertain to Jesus' further promise to 'set the oppressed free' (Luke 4.19), which aligns with the many Old Testament texts portraying God taking the side of the poor (Psalm 103.6, for example), and others emphasize the radically counter-cultural nature of the inclusive kingdom of God.[8] Perhaps most prominent among these positive readings of the life of Jesus is in Eiesland's *The Disabled God* in which she proposes that the incarnation and the portrayal of the post-resurrection Christ as wounded and scarred, a demonstration of his self-identification with people with disabilities, has potential to obliterate their biblical and ecclesial discrimination. In a penetrating challenge to seemingly intractable theological perspectives, she writes: 'disability not only does not contradict the divine–human integrity, it becomes a new model of wholeness and a symbol of solidarity' (1994, p.101) – an argument with which Wynn's Old Testament exegesis seems to concur.

Pauline theology has been a further fertile ground for those concerned to redress negative interpretations of biblical sources on disability. His somewhat ambiguous teaching on the body is to some extent indicative of the fact that the concept of 'body' and interpretations of the term and its relationship to other elements of the human person – mind, soul, spirit – within Scripture are complex and have been continually influenced by and contextualized in wider philosophical contexts.[9] Parsons, for example, emphasizes the dangers inherent in a broader social and cultural context dominated by physiognomy – a philosophy that describes physical traits as indicators of the character of the inner soul (2005, pp.295–312).

---

7   This idea has been variously explored in recent disability theology and perhaps most notably in the hugely insightful articles by John Swinton, 'Building a Church for Strangers: Theology, Church and Learning Disabilities' and 'The Body of Christ has Down syndrome.' See also my own work in (2010), 'Prophetic Voices, Silent Words: The Prophetic Role of Persons with Profound Intellectual Disabilities.'

8   See McCloughry and Morris 2002, especially Chapter 5: 'Jesus and the Kingdom.'

9   This cannot be explored here, but an excellent examination of the subject is found in Creamer 2009.

With particular attention to 1 Corinthians 12, Yong (2011, pp.91–6) stresses the necessity and giftedness of all and the honouring of the weakest or least presentable argues that a 'disability hermeneutic can help us re-read St. Paul toward a more disability-inclusive theology of church (ecclesiology)'. The conclusion of his exegesis of the 'body of Christ' text here is that 'people with disabilities are by definition embraced as central and essential to a fully healthy and functioning congregation in particular and to the ecclesial body in general' (2011, p.95). Hull also engages with the body of Christ imagery, arguing (2003, p.23) that 'when we start our thinking [about disability] from the body of Christ, rather than from the image of God, we discover a theology of disability which is supported by various elements within the Christian faith'. Indeed, we might add that the passage in which those who are deemed 'least presentable' – in the apostle's context, those who were weak and of low social class and education; in ours, those who have for too long been kept out of sight in society and sadly also in the Church – are to be afforded the greatest honour establishes a kind of Orwellian perspective on the Church in which everyone is equal but some are more equal than others! With Ford (2005), Yong further expounds the Apostle Paul's prioritization of weakness over strength and exposure of the folly of human wisdom (1 Corinthians 1.20–31) to similarly support the case for valuing and respecting people with disabilities and especially viewing those with intellectual disabilities as possessing characteristics that afford them a particular place within the kingdom (2011, pp.97–104).

It is clear from the preceding discussion that the biblical pedigree of disability is a complex one and that the Christian theological tradition has been far from value-neutral in its dealings with the subject. What biblical texts reveal about the subject of disability is enormously important, but it is not the aim of this book to mitigate what seems to be a preponderance of prejudicial perceptions of disability within the biblical canon; many others are engaged in this specific task. Inevitably, such discussions lead not only to the experience of disability but to important questions of theodicy and the nature of God. Such themes permeate all three of Young's personal and theological reflections on life with her severely disabled son, Arthur (1985, 1990b, 2014), and Black is most concerned with 'what…we as communities of faith believe that reconciles the reality of disability with our faith in a loving compassionate God' (1996, p.32). Yet to perceive the function of biblical studies' engagement with issues of disability as primarily that of establishing a defensive approach to problematic biblical texts and theological concepts is to underestimate the potential of disability theology to generate a positive contribution to the wider body of theological knowledge and to minimize the value of contextual theology in its various forms. Although there is considerable work to be done to redress the balance of a prejudicial past, Yong's presentation of the need to 'attempt to redeem disability for contemporary theology' (2011, p.35), while not untypical as Avalos *et al.*'s assessment on relevant sources demonstrates, seems to suggest such an unnecessarily defensive stance. While my own work here offers an exploration of biblical sources as one aspect of a journey to potential fresh understandings, a broader approach to the impact of aspects of the Christian tradition on how people with profound intellectual disabilities are perceived and treated in academic theology and the Church, rather than specific hermeneutical approaches to disability texts, will be its primary focus. Davis rightly insists (1995, p.2) that 'disability is not an object – a woman with a cane – but a social process that inevitably involves everyone who has a body and lives in the world of the sense' (for which we must surely read, everyone). Yet neither can disability exist outside of an embodied experience. Not surprisingly, then, the contextualization of recent embodied theologies has been a significant contributor to contemporary disability theology. In a critique and expansion of McFague's embodied theology (1993), Creamer rightly stresses that 'it is embodied creatures, not disembodied ones, who do theology. Knowledge is necessarily related to the experience of embodiment' (2011, p.61). In a similar context, Tataryn and Truchan-Tataryn emphasize that 'all of creation participates in the radical effect of Christ's embodiment and therefore all bodies, in their limitless variety, are equally valuable icons of God' (2013, p.111).

The most potent reality for this work is not that disability exists, but that it exists as an embodied experience. The ways in which theological reflection on embodied experience is used to generate fresh understandings of the biblical texts and of the experience of disability is of huge importance, as the brief summary above demonstrates. Further similar reflection in relation to the wider Christian tradition has potential to offer equally significant insight. Focussing specifically on people with profound intellectual disabilities, this book explores the reciprocal impact of the Christian tradition on perceptions of their spiritual experience and of that experience on the Christian tradition.

Diverse roots or recent academic engagement with disability

It is significant for an understanding of the impetus for the trajectory of disability theology, on whose increasingly strong foundations this book builds, that the most recent theological debate in this area initially surfaced in the context of physical disability, coinciding with or, perhaps more accurately, following in the wake of the campaigns by the largely Western-based[10] secular disability movements[11] that led the outcry against the widespread inequality and exclusion which, it was argued, had been the experience of people with disabilities up to that point.[12] The genesis of these recent movements can be traced to the civil rights protests of the early 1960s, emerging primarily in the United States. Progress was initially slow; as late as 1995, for example, Davis described disability as 'the missing term in the race, class gender triad' (1995, p.1). Eventually, however, socio-cultural discrimination began to be addressed by a series of legislative initiatives.[13] In the United Kingdom, these culminated in the Equality Act 2010, replacing the Disability Discrimination Act of 1995 and bringing the rights of people with disabilities within wider equality policies pertaining to gender, race, ethnicity, religion and sexual orientation. In the global context, the 2006 United Nations Convention on the Rights of People with Disabilities states: 'The purpose of the present Convention is to promote, protect and ensure the full and equal enjoyment of all human rights and fundamental freedoms by all persons with disabilities, and to promote respect for their inherent dignity.'[14]

At the heart of the issues being challenged by disability rights campaigners were what are most frequently termed medicalized and individualized models of disability which, it was claimed, resulted in the identity of people with disabilities being defined by and filtered

---

10 Pakistan is among a small number of non-Western countries to adopt policies that promote equality for people with disabilities in its 'National Policy for Persons with Disabilities' (2002).

11 For example, the Union of the Physically Impaired Against Segregation and the Disability Alliance.

12 This argument is epitomized in a document produced at a 1975 meeting of the Union of the Physically Impaired Against Segregation and the Disability Alliance, 'Fundamental Principles of Disability', www.leedsac.uk/disability-studies/archiveuk/UPIAS/UPIAS.pdf.

13 See, for example, Australia, Disability Discrimination Act 1992; Canada, Ontarians with Disabilities Act 2002 (only in Ontario – no other province has disability protection); United States of America, Americans with Disabilities Act 1990.

14 While thus far (2016) over 140 countries have signed the convention, thus indicating their intention to ratify and implement its terms, fewer than 60% have actually done so.

through the lens of medical or physical impairments; hence the term, 'medical model'. A radically different perspective was introduced by Oliver[15] in what was subsequently widely referred to as the 'social model of disability'.[16] Oliver's foundational point hung on a differentiation between impairment and disability – a distinction that precipitated a debate which is ongoing. He was essentially redefining disability as a social construct resulting from discriminatory processes and practices, rather than an individual, impairment-based experience. Consequently, it was society's responsibility to make the necessary adjustments to facilitate the opportunity for people with disabilities to experience in actuality their inherent equality and right to participation at every level of society.

Under the social model formula, in order to be counted as a disabled person, three criteria must be fulfilled: he or she must (1) have an impairment, (2) experience discrimination and (3) identify him or herself as disabled (Oliver 1996, p.5). Goodley, however, correctly argues that the question of identification as a signifier of the condition of being disabled is much more complex than Oliver's criteria suggest (2010, p.30), and McCloughry and Morris (2002, p.16) specifically highlight the difficulties for people with intellectual disabilities who might lack the capacity for such self-identification. We might also ask whether a person who has an 'impairment' but does not consider him or herself to have experienced discrimination should not be considered disabled. As Barnes points out, 'many people with impairments do not consider themselves [to be] members of an oppressed group' (2004, p.49, first published 1993).

Oliver's argument inspired and was developed by academics[17] and activists in the UK, the US and other Western countries. Although it was eventually extended to include all people who have disabilities, including those who have intellectual disabilities and those who are deemed to have emotional, mental health or behavioural problems,[18] Goble (2004,

---

15   First articulated in Oliver, M. (1983) *Social Work with Disabled People*. Basingstoke: Macmillan.

16   For a comprehensive articulation, see Oliver 1990. 'The Individual and Social Models of Disability.' Paper presented at Joint Workshop of the Living Options Group and the Research Unit of the Royal College of Physicians, http://disability-studies.leedsac.uk/files/library/Oliver-in-soc-dis.pdf.

17   Yong (2007, p.100) notes that around this time disability became 'conceived of both as a subject of inquiry and as a methodology and category of critical analysis…positioned as part of the liberal arts curriculum, as an academic discipline in its own right'.

18   Controversy exists regarding perceptions of determinable social norms which support the theory that people with intellectual disabilities can be appropriately described as having 'behavioural problems'.

p.45) comments that 'the people with disabilities' movement [is] not a place that people with intellectual impairments have always found very welcoming'. This absence of welcome is clearly exemplified in Winter's assertion that 'from the standpoint of the disability rights movement, the right and ability to exercise autonomy over one's own life is the basic, defining, characteristic of what it means to be human' (2003, p.37). Since it is patently the case that some people with intellectual disabilities have no capacity to exercise recognizable autonomy over their own lives, it is important that the disability rights movement, in rightly and successfully advocating for the respect that is due to all human persons, does not construct definitions and issue statements that stigmatize those whose disabilities are intellectual in ways that exclude them from the category of human-ness, thus condemning such persons to further exclusion. This important issue is one of many with which recent disability theology has sought to engage.

Despite the significance it continues to assume in some areas of academic theological reflection on the experience of disability to be further explored below, there has been an increasingly refined critique of the social model within the broader academic field. On an international political scale, as a way of understanding disability, it was to some degree superseded by the International Classification of Functioning, Disability and Health in 2001, which sought to find a new approach to the question, with the focus on participation and on the universality of varying levels of functioning.[19] Indeed, many general disability scholars argue that 'the social model is now considered to have outgrown its usefulness within disability studies' (Barnes and Mercer 2010, p.93) and that 'the original challenge of the social model of disability no longer provides an effective dynamic model' (Shildrick 2012, p.15).

It is significant that some sociologists have drawn attention to the dangers of generalization and simplification, which excludes the importance of the diversity of forms of impairment when constructing disability theories and practices. Specifically with regard to intellectual disability on the one hand, Goodley and Rapley's emphasis remains on the overall impact of social constructivism: 'phenomena frequently understood as being an essential feature of "intellectual disability" are better understood as *aspects of social interaction*...the notion of intellectual disability as a given form of being in the world is unsustainable' (2000, p.127). In contrast,

---

19   For more detailed analysis, see McCloughry and Morris, 2002, pp.20–4.

however, Thomas and Corker argue that while there are some implications common to all disabilities, 'people with impairments such as learning difficulty...have specific kinds of encounters with disablism more closely bound up with the features of the impairment itself...impairment does matter' (2000, pp.24–5). I strongly endorse this position.

Although refuted by Oliver (2004, p.8), Thomas' analysis parallels that of disabled feminists who accuse the social model of a lack of attention to personal experience (Morris 1992). For my work, the issue of at best minimizing and at worst ignoring the impact of particularities of impairments assumes huge significance, because not only do the specifics of individual impairment matter when considering the general subject of disability, but they also matter enormously *within* the broad spectrum of experiences and conditions of intellectual disabilities. Consequently, when disability theology ventures into explorations of the spiritual experience of people with intellectual disabilities, some of whom *can* articulate their relationships with God and some of whom cannot, it must tread carefully and in a manner that respects differences between degrees of cognitive capacity.

Society and theology: recent points of connection

It is impossible to overlook the fact that the development of anti-discrimination movements was energized and directed by people with disabilities, rather than by able-bodied people acting on their behalf,[20] and that although gaining the recognition sought has been an uphill struggle, they have been highly, though not completely, successful in influencing and effecting social change. Given the degree to which theology's interest has paralleled the wider social agenda, it is hardly surprising that the primary contributors to the emergent theological debate in this context were stimulated by a personal experience of physical disability of one kind or another.[21] In succeeding years, the question of the 'right' or appropriateness of people who do not have disabilities to participate in the theological exploration of the issues has been a matter of increasing scrutiny. Creamer, for example, notes that during a session of the Religion and Disability Studies Group at the American Academy of Religion in 2003, 'delegates...questioned the legitimacy

---

20 Oliver, for example, has physical disabilities.
21 Eiesland is perhaps the most prominent example.

of those who presented papers or asked questions as outsiders, (those without "sufficient personal experience with disability") or as "affiliates" (those who are the parent, partner or child of a person with a disability)' (2009, p.5). Given the fact that presenting papers or asking questions at such a gathering is beyond the competence of a significant proportion of people with intellectual disabilities, it seems clear that even at this point when disability theology was advancing apace, there remained some degree of reluctance or inability to locate such persons on the theological radar.

While theological voices might also assess the progress achieved since their initial attempts to engage the Church in a theological conversation about its treatment of people with disabilities with some, if limited, degree of satisfaction, for example, in relation to improved physical accessibility, the origins of advances in this area are of a more complex nature than might superficially appear to be the case. Of course, the influence of secular impulses on church practices is not automatically or inherently detrimental. On the contrary, the revision of the role of women in the Church which, to some extent at least, parallels progress on the issue of female equality in wider society, exemplifies the positive impact of social development on ecclesial practice. Nonetheless, the probability that it was legislation-propelled compulsion rather than fresh theological perspectives that provided the catalyst for the recent adaptations to church buildings betrays a continuing paucity of theological self-examination which requires to be addressed. Any complacent belief that recent and limited change in practice is adequate to address underlying prejudices has potentially serious repercussions for the authenticity of theology's voice in this hugely important area. Narrow doorways are more easily rectified than narrow mindsets.

As a case in point, questions of what constitutes 'acceptable behaviour' in church services attract radically contrasting views, exemplified by a debate between Ramshaw and Newell. The former claims (1987, p.79) that 'retarded children and adults may not catch on to standards of appropriate behaviour...but most of them can learn these standards if clearly taught'. In a direct response, Newell adamantly refutes such a view.

> There are clearly...'standards of appropriate behaviour' to which retarded...children and adults must conform. Standards set by those who have been deemed appropriate to enter into the public discourse as to the nature and expression of worship...that has excluded from

participation those who will be still subject to its rules. We do not seem very far from the Temple Purity Code of Leviticus. (2007, p.335)

While there seems to be little awareness of a public debate on this matter, the continuing experiences of individuals and families who are impelled to strive, if not fight, for the inclusion of children and adults who have intellectual disabilities in local faith communities underlines the pertinence of Newell's point.

It is further contextually significant that theological engagement is taking place in the context in which the United Kingdom socio-political debate (which parallels that of other Western societies) demonstrates that disability remains something of a 'hot potato' for successive governments. The relationship between disability and the economic climate fuels the political nature of the discussion. Whether or not action taken in the UK to decrease the number of people in receipt of government support on the basis of their incapacities[22] is appropriate is an issue ridden with practical and ethical complexities. Nonetheless, as Priestly contends, in this atmosphere and as economic pressures mount, there is a tendency to 'define people with disabilities simply as a financial "burden" to society, while failing to address their potential contributions' (2003, p.51). He is right to make the point but might be accused of inadvertently engaging in a 'balance sheet' argument which requires him to justify the lives of people with disabilities by setting their potential contribution against their potential drain on resources.

Smith further argues (2011, pp.18–99) that perceptions of disability have been subsumed within the political atmosphere surrounding action to reduce public health costs in, for example, the promotion of anti-smoking and anti-obesity campaigns, with the insidious effect of creating a prejudicial climate, in which parents are encouraged to believe that the decision to terminate a pregnancy in which the risk of the child having Down syndrome is 'high' is normal and expected. The universality of prenatal testing for the condition, and when a positive test result is

---

22 The roll-out from April 2013 of the replacement of Disability Living Allowance (DLA) with Personal Independence Payments in an attempt both to reduce government spending and incentivise people with disabilities to find employment is one such initiative, www.gov.uk/pip/overview. A 2014 survey of more than 4,500 people with disabilities, carried out by a coalition of 90 campaign and support groups of people with disabilities, claimed that losing DLA will drive 8 in 10 people 'into isolation', www.bbc.co.uk/news/education-19963608. The same applies to the new Capacity for Work Assessment to which, at the time of writing (2016), my profoundly disabled daughter is being subjected on the basis of her 'employability skills'.

the subsequent abortion rates,[23] provide further evidence of increasing prejudicial and potentially dangerous political attitudes. Highlighting the perilous position of people with intellectual disabilities, Goble (2004, p.45) comments that 'eminent philosophers promote the argument that the likelihood that an infant will never become the self-sufficient and autonomous individual so idealized in Western culture and society as a reason to warrant killing him at or near birth'. Shakespeare resists the professionalized power relationships and lack of 'provision of positive information about disability alongside the clinical material' (1998, p.681), which influence decisions to terminate, and Murray comments (1996, p.132) that:

> there is an implicit message within the goals of prenatal testing that society believes that raising a child with disability is such a grave burden that it is both morally correct and medically appropriate to take expensive measures to ensure that such children are not born.[24]

From a more complex and even paradoxical perspective, Brian Brock importantly highlights that when parents of disabled children are presented or understood as being extraordinary or heroic, cultural perceptions are created which imply that the care of such children can be undertaken only by extraordinary or heroic people and is so 'out-of-the-ordinary' as to be undesirable or even virtually impossible. Indeed, the attribution of 'special-ness' not only to children who have intellectual disabilities but to the parents who love them is a common experience of those with whom I have worked over many years. One parent of a child who has autism recently asked me: 'Why am I special? Because I love my son?' Brock comments that 'the use of supererogation…fuels trajectories in Western medicine that seek to eliminate human vulnerability and with it those human beings who are characterized as "defective"' (2010,

---

23   UK and US statistics vary widely from as high as 92% (www.abortionreview.org/index.php/site/article/963g, ww.downsyndromeprenataltesting.com/from-the-news-page-prenatal-testing-to-explode-98-termination-rate-reported) to 67% (Natoli *et al.* 2012). It is, however, undisputed that the recent availability of less invasive diagnosis methods are significantly are resulting in a significant decrease in the number of live births (https://lozierinstitute.org/new-study-abortion-after-prenatal-diagnosis-of-down-syndrome-reduces-down-syndrome-community-by-thirty-percent). See also Swinton and Brock 2007.

24   See also Williams 2007; Bridle, L. (2014) 'Confronting the Distortions: Mothers of Children with Down Syndrome and Prenatal Testing', www.intellectualdisability.info/diagnosis/confronting-the-distortions-mothers-of-children-with-down-syndrome-and-prenatal-testing.

p.128). In the climate in which such genetic screening develops, Hubbard (2010, p.200) accuses scientists and physicians of reconstructing a 'Nazi past by making the decisions about what lives to "target" as not worth living by deciding which tests to develop'. It seems clear that Shildrick's question continues to be relevant, even, as she points out, in the twenty-first century:

> What is it about the variant morphology of intra-human difference that is so disturbing as to invoke in the self-defined mainstream not simply a reluctance to enter into relationship, but a positive turning away and silencing of the unaccepted other? (2012, p.1)

As this challenge continues to elicit a response from sociological, medical and political sources, it must also fall within the responsibility of both the Church and academic theology to develop strategies to confront such alarming realities.

Of course, such trends must be addressed alongside a recognition of more positive developments in a number of spheres including, for example, the progress towards de-institutionalization of people with intellectual disabilities in a number Western societies,[25] fresh multi-disciplinary approaches to their care and efforts to promote integration. Concomitant opportunities for dialogue between sociological and theological ideologies are emerging in relation to the expansion of understandings of authentic holistic care. While the UK *Space to Listen* report in 2002, commissioned by the Foundation for People with Learning Disabilities, identified a gap in provision of spiritual care in Church and society, Narayanasamy more recently comments (1996, pp.204–5)[26] that 'in the caring professions a focus on individuals as psychosocial–spiritual beings is gaining recognition' and advocates the need to 'understand the concept of spirituality if we are going to offer it as a component of holistic care to people with learning disabilities' (1996, p.205). In such an atmosphere of openness, theology is finding a window of opportunity to contribute to wider discussions of the holistic needs of such people, evidenced by the inclusion, for the first time in its history, of a theological contribution at the World Down Syndrome Congress in Dublin in 2009.[27]

---

25 There are, however, concerns relating to the provision of adequate community resources to make such de-institutionalism sociologically healthy for people discharged from state-run institutions.

26 See also Cobb *et al.* 2012.

27 Dickson 2009.

Recent developments in intellectual disability theology

Specifically within the theological arena, perhaps nothing has been of greater recent significance in motivating an exploration of the spiritual lives of people with intellectual disabilities than the work of Jean Vanier and the *L'Arche* movement.[28] It is difficult to overestimate the catalytic effect of Vanier's work in the developing attempt to identify theological insights from the lives of people with intellectual disabilities and those who are in relationship with them.[29] The impact of Vanier's work and that of his contemporary Wolf Wolfensberger[30] has been subsequently documented, explored and developed by prominent theologians and this work continues to expand in a number of directions.[31] It should also be acknowledged that, alongside academic theologians, other significant voices of practitioners in health and education sectors who share a commitment to see the Church appropriately include people with intellectual disabilities have significantly influenced this conversation. In the global forum, Jeff McNair (Professor of Special Education at California Baptist University and Founding President of the US-based National Association of Christians in Special Education) has been a tireless advocate for such an engagement.[32]

Theological use of the social model

As has been emphasized above, a belief in the continuing presence of God in the world creates the expectation that his influence and action are to be found beyond the doors of the Church and the academic theology departments of the universities. The impact of socio-political perspectives, including the use of the social model in intellectual disability theology, has in recent decades been a significant stimulus to the expansion of theological perspectives. Nonetheless, while serious engagement with the specialisms and expertise of other areas of enquiry is absolutely vital, theology must retain the confidence to subject the

---

28   While there is an enormous body of writing on the subject of *L'Arche*, the history of the movement is most comprehensively expressed by its founder in Vanier 2012 and 2013.

29   A wide-ranging collection of individual responses is in Reinders 2010.

30   See, for example, Gaventa and Coulter 2001.

31   In addition to those already cited above, see, for example, Hauerwas 2001; Swinton 2004; Gillibrand 2010. It is, of course, impossible to do justice to the depth of any of these contributions within the confines of my work and those that are selected for further comment relate specifically to the subject of this book.

32   See McNair 2010.

knowledge to be gained from other disciplines to the critical light of its own unique framework of reference. If, therefore, we are to ensure that the drivers for ongoing development are theological as well as or, perhaps when appropriate, *instead of* secular, the ongoing use of the model merits further assessment.

It is undoubtedly the case that insightful and creative theological use of the social model is evident across a range of contributions to disability theology and intellectual disability theology specifically. Weiss Block (2002, pp.122–3) uses the social model to expose and challenge the theological and consequent practice-based contradictions between an inaccessible (in a literal and ideological sense) exclusionary Church and the God who is both accessible and inclusive. Swinton and Mowat advocate its usage 'to enable the analysis of the life situations and experiences of people with learning disabilities' (2006, p.232). When academics such as Rumbold, for example, continue to promote models of health and spiritual care whose 'key strategies are supporting, normalizing [and] resourcing' (2012, p.179), it is important that the concept of normalizing in this context is effectively challenged and the social model has undoubtedly provided a framework for such an endeavour. Yong's argument that the social model of disability serves to illuminate how disability is a social and cultural construct, and how historic notions of 'freakery', 'monstrosity' and 'disability' (2007, pp.84–6) combined to produce notions of 'normalcy' that have not only been socially, politically and economically but also theologically oppressive to people with disabilities (pp.79–116), represents such a challenge. He is correct in arguing that 'whatever else disability is, it is also the experience of discrimination, marginalization, and exclusion from the social, cultural, political and economic domains of human life' (p.99). It is clear, then, that the lens of the social model has been one factor among many others that have precipitated the highlighting of the imperative to include people with intellectual disabilities within ecclesial communities and the identification of ways in which people with intellectual disabilities can and do contribute to the Christian community. Foundational issues of inclusion must remain on the agenda, and not only in the practical action of the Church but in critical reflection on underlying attitudes and theological perspectives. The cynicism with which Shakespeare and Raymond-Pickard highlight the dangers of complacency in relation to this matter does not invalidate the sentiment: 'Inclusion can become the patronizing gesture of those who consider themselves to be insiders, inviting in those poor unfortunates who languish at their gates' (2006, p.33). Their perspective is affirmed by John Gillibrand's comment on his experience that his autistic son Adam's 'full participation in the realm of being…as with other people with disabilities, is so much more conceded in theory than in fact' (2010, p.98).

Nonetheless, as the contemporary secular debate recognizes a need to move beyond social model approaches, questions need to be asked concerning whether a section of disability theology is in danger of becoming entrenched in the limited success for which the social model has been a catalyst. Is it really adequate to address the foundational theological imperatives at stake here? The problem with adapted social model approaches being inculcated within ecclesial practices is that many issues may remain unaddressed. Even some of the most highly developed arguments for the rights of people with intellectual disabilities to respect, inclusion and participation within faith communities might be accused of falling short of an adequate perception of their lives. I acknowledge here that the contributions of Yong and others constitute an example of the enormous steps being taken in the direction of fully appreciating what disability theology argues is the God-given value and role of people with intellectual disabilities within and without the contemporary Church. Yong rightly and powerfully argues that:

> in the post-modern, post-denominational, and even post-Christian world of the twenty-first century, the Church is fully the charismatic fellowship of the Spirit only insofar as she is an inclusive community of hospitality wherein the disabled and non-disabled together welcome, befriend and embrace the stranger, the marginalized and the disenfranchised. (2007, p.225)

In my view, however, there is considerable ground left to explore and potential, where necessary, to de-couple theological investigation from social theory – even if this might lead us to confront an uncomfortable reality that theological prejudice towards people whose intellectual disabilities are profound runs at a much deeper level which neither the exposure of the exclusionary practices of the past that aligned themselves with individual models of disability and subsequent ecclesial contextualization of the social model nor theological exploration of the essential humanness and ministry of such people has yet fully addressed. In this light, Newell (2007, p.327) pertinently asks whether the social model 'goes far enough in challenging exclusion, in confronting models of normality… It may well challenge the boundaries and contexts by which we define disability but it may well set broader and more flexible boundaries.' McCloughry and Morris offer a timely warning that 'in an attempt to address the view that perceives disability as a tragedy… the social model discounts impairment as a physical, emotional, psychological or sociological reality' (2002, p.17).

Creamer's alternative model

Such dissatisfaction has served as a catalyst for Creamer's recent insightful work in *Disability and Christian Theology* (2009) which proposes an alternative model for theological discussion in the general context of disability. Here she exposes the inadequacies of the medical model, for which she uses the term 'deficit model' (pp.93–4), but insists that disability theology's use of the 'social/minority group model' is also not immune to criticism: '[t]he attempt to normalize or contradict the specific analysis of the experience of disability as a deficit captures much of what has been said to date in disability theology. This response is not adequate for disability theology' (p.95). Creamer's thesis has much to commend it. Her subtle refocus from being 'limited' to 'experiencing limits', leading to her 'limits model', highlights the fact that 'disability is not something that exists solely as a negative experience of limitation but rather that it is an intrinsic, unsurprising and valuable element of human limit-ness' (p.96), thus affirming McCloughry and Morris's earlier comments (2002, p.22) that 'we are all involved, rather than just people with disabilities. Everybody functions well in some ways and not others.' She offers a helpful perspective on the importance of holding a balanced position on wider disability issues, on both a personal and communal level: 'acknowledging of limits means neither defining ourselves in terms of perfection and thinking of ourselves too highly as an individual/nation…nor defining ourselves on the basis of what we lack and thinking too lowly of ourselves as an individual/nation' (Creamer 2009, p.111). As part of this new 'limits model', Creamer rejects the 'signifier "disabled" [which] attempts to hold a wide variety of bodily experiences in one designated category' (p.96) and specifically refers to cognitive disabilities as 'a different difference' (p.103). In this regard, her position implicitly supports my own view that any attempt to explore the spiritual lives of people with profound intellectual disabilities will necessarily involve affording attention and respect to the particularities of their embodied experience. It is precisely such attention that creates a potential catalyst for uncovering the theological insights that are being sought here.

While Creamer's alternative model offers insightful and stimulating material for further reflection on the inclusivity of human limitations which mitigates against the 'them/us' divide that has plagued so much of the experience of people with disabilities, politically, sociologically and ecclesiologically, it raises interesting and complex questions for theology. In advancing her limits model, Creamer advises (p.112), that 'as it tells us in Genesis 1 that human beings are created in the image of God, we must then ask what it tells us about God that human beings are limited'. The implication of Creamer's argument is that God's being is, to some extent at least, in our image as ours is in his, and we are recommended (p.113) to 'try this lens on' alongside other possible lenses. She claims that 'a notion of God that includes limits' is consonant with the facts that 'traditional anthropomorphic notions of God suggest that God took limits willingly – for example, by creating or allowing free will or by taking on personhood and death through Jesus' and that 'contemporary science and post-modernism include claims about limits' (p.112). Creamer's argument here raises significant issues in relation to the important dialogue between human experience and the traditional sources of the faith tradition. Particularly here, questions arise as to what weight is to be attached to either the self-limitation of God under the terms Creamer outlines or to contemporary cultural understandings of finitude in the light of, for example, the doctrine of the Trinity, and the wider divine–human dynamic. Do the voluntary limitations of the God–man Jesus extend completely and eternally to the fullness of the Godhead? While Hull argues that God's perfection is a perfection of vulnerability (2003, p.22), this is not the same as attributing human-like limits to who God is and what God can do. Specifically in relation to the crucified Jesus, Young, while affirming the significance of the nail marks on his resurrected body, points out the danger of talking about God as if he were 'a being like other beings… God [is] transcendent and immanent, personal and not limited as all persons we know are' (1990b, p.62). Here, perhaps, it might appear that Creamer's proposal of a 'limits model' as a new *theological anthropology* becomes something of an *anthropological theology* in which the limitations of human beings are reflected in the being of God. Creamer is rightly and importantly concerned to defend the equality of people with disabilities. She is understandably opposed to any inference that 'if God is unlimited, then the less limited are more like God' (2009, p.112), yet the hermeneutical subtleties between 'likeness' and 'exact representation', the latter being something that Scripture recognizes only in Christ (Hebrews 1.1–2),[33] cannot be ignored. Although she finds that 'imagining God as having limits has a number of positive benefits' (p.112), questions remain as to the theological basis of the position she adopts. As Gillibrand cautions, 'one should not allow one's desire to make a text applicable to a contemporary situation to transform the text itself' (2010, p.105).

Creamer goes on to propose (2009, p.112) that 'such characteristics as perseverance that come when one seeks to live with limits might… be characteristics we would find in God or wish to attribute to God'. Deeper complexities permeate her argument here. First, theological tensions arise with respect to the idea of human beings attributing to God the characteristics we might choose him to possess. Second, if God's characteristics are to be are reflective of human beings', why should we not afford him some of our worst as well as some of our best? Further developing the argument that God might be conceived of as mirroring some of the more positive human attributes, Creamer claims that:

> the existence of limits also speaks to creativity, as we all, (whatever our limits) develop alternatives and work to compensate for what we cannot do, whether designing a new wheelchair or developing a satellite. The human proclivity toward creatively adapting to our limits might be a characteristic represented in a limits God. (2009, p.113)

It seems clear that such human capacity for creative problem-solving is not universal and thus despite her aversion to a perception of the more able being more like God, her argument seems to imply that this is the case. She offers more examples (p.113): 'Limits also speak to strength, as people with disabilities are often stronger in at least some ways than "normal" (as anyone who has used crutches can attest).' Again the danger is of stereotyping or idealizing the experience of people with disabilities. Might prioritizing positive human qualities demonstrated through the experience of disability and claiming that a 'limits model… allows us to imagine new possibilities focussing on characteristics such as perseverance, strength and creativity' (p.118) lead to the kind of hierarchical view of disability she explicitly disavows? Nonetheless, despite some of the concerns noted above, her development of a theology of embodiment adds an additional layer to this important perspective and opens up fresh ground from where she rightly proposes further reflection should emerge.

---

33   See also Young 2014, p.151.

Common themes
Instructive capacity and vulnerability

In terms of the breadth of perspectives that emerge from the many individual contributions to theological engagement with intellectual disability, Young's *Arthur's Call* (2014) – a reflection on her personal experience, her engagement with the L'Arche communities and the insights of wider theological scholarship – helpfully summarizes a significant degree of the content of current scholarship. The reciprocal fruitfulness of her dialogue with Vanier over recent decades is perhaps most graphically expressed in Vanier's striking comment that it is possible that 'the whole of the history of Christianity is culminated in [Young's son] Arthur'.[34] Arthur, and others similarly disabled, Young argues (2014, pp.141–58), 'have a vocation to be a "sign" in the biblical sense: a prophetic sign, pointing beyond themselves' (p.157). They are a sign in illuminating the mystery of grace and the often-shrouded and enigmatic scriptural truths about where Christ is to be found; about truly honouring the weakest; about what it means to be in the image of God (p.158). They are a sign in exposing universal human vulnerability (p.144); in summoning us to:

> deeper self-knowledge and true humility in the presence of God… offering a model of contemplative appreciation…bear[ing] witness to the Christ who had no beauty…was despised and rejected, ensuring that that image is included as one facet of the body of Christ; speaking to us of a wholeness which incorporates our impairments…of a transcendence that does not negate the cross…of an hour of glory in which all our 'gone-wrongness' is embraced, entered and borne and so transformed…showing that worship is more about the grace and love we receive than anything we do. (pp.157–8)

On the pervasive prioritization of vulnerability, which lies at the heart of much of the reflection of which Young's statement is typical, however, Morris persuasively makes the point that there is a danger that identifying such vulnerability as something to be fully embraced by those who cannot possibly experience its full ramifications can idealize an experience that is often far from desirable. 'Being vulnerable and wounded is no constant rose garden of discovery of what it means to be human. It is often tough, it is often painful, it is often frustrating,

---

34   Conference at the L'Arche Community, Trosly-Breuil, December 2002, cited in Ford 2005, p.154.

and it often causes anger, for all concerned, disabled and able-bodied.' Thus, he insists, reflection on 'being vulnerable to one another can only enhance our lives if it is accompanied by a commitment to justice and a resistance to any abuse of human vulnerability' (2013, p.242).

Furthermore, championing the cause of people with profound intellectual disabilities in terms of praising their inherent potential for awakening the wider faith community to the reality of human dependency (Young 2014, p.144) is not without its tensions and, as, McCloughry and Morris caution, can 'pander to a false patronage' (2002, p.30). While, as Morris acknowledges (2013, p.240), Reynolds, for example, despite his focus on human vulnerability, rejects any notion that people with profound learning disabilities are 'instructive tools' (2008, p.117) for able-bodied people, much of the focus of theological enquiry with respect to people with profound intellectual disabilities has a tendency to present them as such. Indeed, the revelation attributed to people with intellectual disabilities that not only they but all human beings live in a state of dependence and interdependence is not particularly new, nor has it emerged in an exclusively theological context. On the contrary, it represents a theme that runs throughout the history of philosophical and social anthropology. Contemporary sociologist Garland-Thomson argues along with disability theologians that 'disability challenges the cherished cultural belief in the individual and…our fantasies of stable, enduring identities' (2002, p.20), and Shepherd (1966) questions the notion that any of us is an autonomous being, insisting that we are all interdependent. It is not surprising, then, that Reinders asks what he terms 'the obvious question about why we need theology for something that philosophy and social theory have established long ago' (2008, pp.250–1).

Theological anthropology and the image of God

Specifically in relation to the focus of my work, there are additional important concerns, some of which are insightfully identified in Haslam's *A Constructive Theology of Intellectual Disability* (2011). She specifically draws attention to some of the underlying anthropological understandings that emerge in this kind of theological reflection, specifically in relation to *imago Dei*, which many disability theologians define in terms of capacity for relationship. While applauding the contributions that have been made thus far, Haslam rightly points out that 'each in various ways betrays a bias towards a level of intellectual disability unavailable to individuals with profound intellectual disabilities'

(2011, p.5). Reynolds' interpretation of *imago Dei* as the capacity for relationship, including 'the freedom to self-consciously acknowledge and enter into relationships' (2008, p.182), for example, inherently excludes people with profound intellectual disabilities who lack the 'agential self…the intellectual capacity to conceive of the self as distinct from the world around us' (Haslam 2011, p.4). This problem is also highlighted by Hull who, from a different angle, argues that 'if the image of God is conceived of as residing in relationality, then those whose human relations are damaged are at a disadvantage' (2003, p.6). In a further respect, Yong's anthropology of interrelationality or interdependence is also problematic. He, to some extent at least, attributes the dignity of personhood of the individual who has an intellectual disability to that of her caregiver: 'she is a being who has become who she is through the loving care of a mothering person – a person who herself embodies intrinsic worth' (2007, pp.184–5), and Swinton *et al.* make a similar point (Swinton, Mowat and Baines 2011). While Haslam has limited sympathy with this view, I cannot align myself with it in any respect whatsoever. The existence of theological justification for the principle that any human being's dignity or ability to be one's self is predicated on another's, and that this is necessary because of the disparity in intellectual disability and capacity for self-consciousness between the two, must be questioned.

Similarly, while these differing theological lenses on the nature of human interdependence shed varying rays of light on the subject, Tataryn and Truchan-Tataryn's perspective that 'we need relationship to be human…[and] sharing, interrelating is a human imperative' on the basis of the Trinitarian imprint of the 'God who goes beyond self in order to be whole' (2013, p.111), leaves those who are without meaningful relationships in a precarious position. In response to such viewpoints, Orye (2014, p.1) wonders whether such arguments indicate 'a projection of social ideals onto the trinity'. On the other hand, with strong emphasis on the suffering of Christ, Moltmann argues that it is possible to conceive of the image of God as inherent in the disability itself: 'having a disability, whatever form it may take, is a gift of the Holy Spirit, if through and in the disability, one is called to be the image and glory of God on earth' (1996, p.107).

In advocating an anthropology of relationship or friendship, Reinders' particular focus is not on a theology of disability, but on what people with intellectual disabilities reveal of what it means for all human beings to be made in the image of God (2008, p.244). He acknowledges the difficulties for people with more severe intellectual disabilities if the essence of *imago Dei* and humanness resides in a person's capacity for self-conscious response to the loving approach of God and others. In an alternative perspective, he proposes that the relationality inherent in being human is 'inaugurated by divine action, not human action' (p.244) and is therefore accessible to all of humanity. Human beings find their humanity in being drawn into the communion of the triune God – something which God alone accomplishes (p.15). Haslam, however, sees a potential gap in Reinders' argument, in that fully locating the humanness of a person in an understanding of God as the sole relational agent raises the question of in what way human beings image God and she further disputes an errant 'cosmological dualism' that she believes to be implicit in his theory (2011, p.8).

Haslam's particular objective is to construct a 'theology anthropology for people with profound intellectual disabilities that is life-giving' and promotes their flourishing (pp.6, 9). Her work is insightful, not only in her critique of others' but in her robust confrontation of exclusionary conceptions of *imago Dei* in terms of rationality.[35] Drawing specifically on the work of Martin Buber, she offers a different perspective which 'locate[s] the understanding of the human being in the realm of "the between"... We find our humanity in relationships of mutual responsiveness' to God and others in which 'people with profound intellectual disabilities participate as responders, albeit in a nonsymbolic way' (pp.9, 14). Thus she claims that the concept of the human she presents is 'broad enough to recognize the full humanity of individuals...for whom...objectification of and reflection upon that which exists outside of itself is not a possibility, but responsiveness to the other is' (p.112). Haslam further uses her observation of a man who has profound intellectual disabilities and his 'nonintentional communication' expressed in bodily behaviour (here in reaction to a sports event) as evidence of the responsiveness that is intrinsic to the state of being human (p.111), although we might ask why such behaviour needs to be identified in light of her assertion of the non-necessity and even irrelevance of intentional responsiveness. In a complex investigation of who or what God is, which, with Pseudo-Dionysius, she conceives in terms of 'yearning itself', she argues that people with profound intellectual disabilities 'image God, not because of some intellectual capacity they possess, but because their participation as responders in relationships is expressive of the longing that God is'

---

35   See especially Chapter 5.

(p.110). She makes it clear, however, that the quality of the relationship is pivotal here: abusive relationships are not included among those that define our humanity, because in 'engaging with the Other merely as an object of my own perspectival, objectifying functions…not only am I sacrificing my own humanity but I am also substituting the humanity of another for the fulfilment of my needs' (pp.111–12). Yet it is worth considering whether, however heinous her action, a human being can actually sacrifice or detach herself from her humanity. Orye too (2014, p.1) highlights the ambiguity in interpreting the image of God in relational terms in which 'bad relations are not seen to be relations at all'.

Ultimately, by her evidently highly motivated and extensive efforts to set wide enough parameters for the purportedly essential condition of responsiveness to be identifiable in people with profound intellectual disabilities, is Haslam essentially inferring that being human is simply about being human? If this were what she is doing (and although this seems unlikely she does explain (2011, p.4) that this is the way in which people of all capabilities find their humanity), I would strongly endorse this view. The assertion of the humanness of people with intellectual disabilities in the face of secular forces which negate the value of their lives and even seek to eliminate them on the basis of their non-personhood[36] is hugely important, but here also we find dangers of adopting unnecessarily defensive approaches.

The anthropological argument seems to be two-sided. On one side, being human consists in some form of relationality (a perspective that pervades current disability theology but is a far from universal position on the subject in wider theological sources) and consequently we must find a way in which to understand people with profound intellectual disabilities as being capable of engaging in such relationality, in spite of their lack of cognitive ability or consciousness of self, so that we can assure ourselves or others that they are human. On the other side, people with profound intellectual disabilities *must* be human, and in order to confirm this we need to find something in their way of being that is common to all human beings and fundamental to being human. Both these approaches raise the question of why it should be necessary to construct a theological anthropology that is 'life-giving for and promotes the flourishing of people with profound and intellectual disabilities'.[37] Is their humanness not 'a given'? Might the complexity of the arguments

---

36   See Hauerwas, 'The Retarded and the Criteria for the Human' in Swinton 2005.
37   See above.

being presented provide some evidence of a, perhaps sub-conscious, belief that intellectual capacity *is* a definitive issue for humanity after all? Is the search on for a life-giving theological anthropology for any other group of people?

People with profound intellectual disabilities are surely to be understood as inhabiting their human being-ness in the way that everyone else does, in that they *are* human beings, *created as* human beings by God. As Haslam acknowledges (2011, p.9), 'rarely will the mother of a profoundly intellectually disabled child wonder if her child is a human being', and Reinders insists (2008, p.283) that 'the widest possible variety within humankind can be acknowledged because the differences do not matter at the most fundamental level'. The question Haslam is explicitly addressing 'of whether these individuals participate in being human' (2011, p.17) is difficult to reconcile with the basics of Christian theology, unless it is necessary to ask whether every individual participates in being human. As Reinders, reflecting on the life of Kelly who has profound intellectual disabilities, insists, 'if the humanity of human beings like Kelly is to be affirmed at all, it must be affirmed *unconditionally* [thus] only by the One who affirms the humanity of human creatures unconditionally' (2008, p.246).

Potential for expansion in intellectual disability theology

Undoubtedly, there have been enormously fruitful outcomes of the debate about what people with profound intellectual disabilities contribute to an understanding of *imago Dei*. Nonetheless, inclusion must continue to be pursued both within the practice of the Church and in disability theology, in an authentic recognition of the theologically indisputable fact that 'we are all without exception created in the image of God' (McCloughry and Morris 2002, p.26). While the contribution that theological reflections on the vulnerability and dependence of people with intellectual disabilities have made to the subject is widely acknowledged, and there is no attempt here to dispute the experience of those who have found the presence of people with intellectual disabilities to be healing and transformative,[38] there is growing impetus to push beyond them. Does the discussion of their theologically instructive potential go far enough in adequately respecting and engaging with

---

38   See Nouwen 1997, for example.

their spirituality? Is there still some distance to be travelled before the last vestiges of what was once penetrating theological prejudice against people with intellectual disabilities, and those with profound intellectual disabilities in particular, is eradicated from our thinking and practice? Creamer suggests (2011, p.108) that 'within a discourse dominated by intellectual and academic rigour, it is difficult to know where an entry point for the cognitively disabled might appear'.

In light of the scholarship highlighted above (and below), it is clear that such an entry point has already been identified. Nonetheless, there still remains a need for people with intellectual disabilities and those with profound intellectual disabilities in particular, to be invited further towards a place of full recognition in academic theology. The theological discourse to date has perhaps inevitably, and certainly beneficially, focussed on the reciprocal human relationships between people who have profound intellectual disabilities and those of us who do not, and of *their* influence on *our* understanding and our behaviour. Genuine inclusion, however, means recognizing and valuing their relationships not only with *us* but with *God*. Asserting their equality as those who should be included within and contribute to the life of ecclesial communities is vital, but it does not go far enough. Valuing and reflecting on their humanity intrinsically requires us to give attention to their capacity to enjoy a meaningful relationship with God in the face of those who would deny it.[39] While an adapted social model might seek to include them, even learn from them, my contention is that respecting their capacities for spiritual experience as individuals in their own right might require something more and perhaps even something essentially different: a reflection not on *our* relationships with them but on *God's*. In this regard, although the subject of the spiritual experience of people with less severe intellectual disabilities is taking place, it is still remarkably limited in comparison with the growing body of work in other areas. Even more limited is reflection on the spiritual experience of people whose intellectual disabilities are profound and complex, although some signs of practical theological work in this area are beginning to emerge. This book advocates the importance of the task of addressing any residual theological discrimination of which the paucity of engagement in this area might be evidence.

Given the pitfalls highlighted above, however, in the ongoing journey towards a fuller academic embrace of the spiritual experience of people

---

39 See below.

whose intellectual disabilities are profound, it is vital that appropriate models and methods of reflection are employed, especially in light of the inadequacies of social model approaches to move the discussion forward. Creamer's implication that the dominance of intellectual and academic rigour might bar the way to genuine engagement with the subject is paradoxical. It is surely only by approaching the subject of the spiritual experience of people with profound intellectual disabilities with intense academic rigour that disability theologians can attain the authentic progress and genuine understanding to which they aspire. The spiritual experience of people with profound intellectual disabilities is indeed an emergent area of enquiry to which particular challenges pertain. Thus it is important to ask questions about the robustness of our methods of reflection in this discrete area. How effective are they? Are there possible alternatives? Addressing these questions will require an analysis of one of the most innovative methods being used to explore the spiritual lives of people with intellectual disabilities and, more recently, people with profound disabilities: qualitative research.

2

THE ROLE OF QUALITATIVE
RESEARCH IN INTELLECTUAL
DISABILITY THEOLOGY

While self-advocacy and theological reflection on personal experience
has been a driving force for disability theology by and with respect
to people with physical disabilities, the dilemma for those who have
intellectual disabilities in relation to making their voice heard is obvious.
Nonetheless, a notable development in intellectual disability theology
has been facilitated by the use of empirical and, for the most part,
qualitative methods of theological enquiry. The data generated from
this early empirical work has provided valuable source material which
has been used to offer insight and direction for transforming praxis
in the spiritual care of people with intellectual disabilities and their
place within faith communities. Such progress owes much to a small
number of theological pioneers, whose determination to draw people
with intellectual disabilities away from the margins into the centre of the
Church's attention is beginning to bear some fruit.[1]

Although it has been hugely theologically enlightening to use
qualitative research approaches to listen to people with intellectual
disabilities who *are* capable of articulating aspects of their own lives,
understandings and experience of God and of their faith communities,
acquiring empirical data in relation to the experience of people with
profound intellectual disabilities is inevitably more problematic. Indeed,
for those whose intellectual disabilities are of such a nature as to preclude
them from any verbal and more than extremely limited non-verbal means
of expressing themselves, the challenges are particularly acute, if not
insuperable. Yet, despite the inherent difficulties involved, a small number
of influential practical theologians are attempting to utilize qualitative
research methods which are largely, if not exclusively, linguistically

---

1   See, for example, Swinton, J. (2002) 'A space to listen: meeting the spiritual needs of
     people with learning disabilities.' *Learning Disability Practice* 5:2.

based, to extrapolate information and theological knowledge of the spiritual lives of people with profound intellectual disabilities; to 'listen carefully and transformatively to those who have no words' (Swinton *et al.* 2011, p.7) and to use what is heard to generate wider theological insights. The motivation for such attempts is clearly a positive one, given the limited attention such people have received in academic circles, both theological and beyond. It is vital, however, that an earnest desire to uncover information and generate knowledge of a subject which has for too long been neglected does not permit the by-passing of questions of theological rigour in relation to whether a method is appropriate to the task to which it is assigned. It is therefore important to probe the issue of whether it is justifiable to assume that people with profound intellectual disabilities who have no capacity for verbal communication are capable of expressing their own spiritual experience; whether there really is a way in which they can be listened to on this subject; and whether the integrity of practical theology's use of qualitative research is maintained when employed in this context. Lying beneath the methodological discussion that follows is the more fundamental question of whether any form of self-expression on their part, actual or imputed, is a necessary component of any attempt to identify the existence and foundations of their spiritual experience. I propose that there are more reliable sources of information that can guide this quest. First, however, it will be useful to trace the origins of practical theology's relationship with social science research methods.

The development of practical theology

In recent decades, practical theology has made considerable progress in establishing its academic credentials among the more historically recognized fields – systematic, biblical, historical and philosophical, for example – of theological studies. The achievement of such progress has involved making the gradual and difficult journey on the path of divesting itself of its earlier so-called 'Cinderella' status.[2] Affirming such progress, Swinton and Mowat rightly insist that:

---

2   The Cinderella metaphor first emerges in the work of Farley, E. (1983) *Theologia: The Fragmentation and Unity of Theological Education.* Philadelphia, PA: Fortress Press, and reiterated in Duce, P. and Strange, D. (2001) *Keeping Your Balance: Approaching Theological and Religious Studies.* Leicester: InterVarsity Press, pp.76–7.

contemporary developments in the field have shown it to be a rigorous theological discipline which, while retaining a unique approach to theology and theological development, continues to offer a significant contribution to the wider field of theology and the practices of the Church and the world. (2006, p.v)

In promoting the parity of esteem of its particular field, the ensuing increase in practical theology's self-confidence has had a catalytic effect on the development of more widely established and highly respected research approaches as practical theology has developed a fruitful dialogue with other academic disciplines, most notably the social sciences. Thus the use of qualitative research has become increasingly prominent. As a practical theologian, I welcome these developments and their potential for facilitating innovative, challenging and insightful research that often offers a platform for previously absent contributors to the theological debate and that can become a means of empowerment – even liberation.

Nonetheless, two qualifying factors need to be highlighted here. First, I strongly endorse Pattison's instructive and insightful warning about the dangers of an over-commitment to empiricism in practical theology (PT) as a whole. In this context he warns that:

[i]f PT becomes too narrowly preoccupied with empirically understanding small parts of the ecclesiastical and theological firmament, we may have succeeded in making our activity more 'doable', finite and explicit. However, we may lost the very elements which make our discipline of the greatest value to humanity, e.g., understanding and interpreting what is of ultimate significance for existence, but which cannot easily be treated of in propositional as opposed to metaphorical and creative terms. (2007, p.278)

This point will become increasingly prominent as my work progresses. Second, the undeniable benefits of empirical research in practical theology does not make the appropriateness of the ongoing use of qualitative research methodologies in theological contexts immune to scrutiny of the same rigorous nature as is inherent in their applicability to other areas of enquiry. The discussion that follows will subject the use of qualitative research in profound intellectual disability theology to such a process of scrutiny, but, first, a few preliminary comments arising out of wider social science theory about the nature of qualitative research.

Qualitative research: definitions and characteristics

While definitions of the qualitative methodology proliferate, the summary of its characteristics articulated by two of its most prominent theorists, Denzin and Lincoln, provide a helpful basis for the discussion which follows:

> Qualitative research is multi-method in focus, involving an interpretive, naturalistic approach to its subject matter. This means that qualitative researchers study things in their natural settings, attempting to make sense of, or interpret phenomena in terms of the meanings people bring to them. Qualitative research involves the studied use and collection of a variety of empirical materials – case study, personal experience, introspective, life story, interview, observational, historical, interactional and visual texts that describe routine and problematic moments and meanings in individuals' lives. (1998, p.3)

Crucially, and particularly pertinent in our context, the beginning point of the researcher's task in any field of empirical research is the choice of methodology. As Hawkesworth comments, however, 'the appropriate methodology for any particular inquiry is a matter of contestation, as scholars often disagree about the "way to truth"'. Summarizing its etymology, she explains that the term 'methodology':

> arises from the conjunction of three Greek concepts: *meta, hodos,* and *logos*... Bringing the three Greek terms together opens possibilities for a variety of interpretations of methodology: 'a shared quest for the way to truth', the action thought takes en route to being 'a shared account of truth' or 'the way a group legitimates knowledge claims'. (2006, p.28)

Consequently, the specific choice of methodology to be adopted in a particular academic community is, she stresses, of some consequence. 'Strategies that are accredited as legitimate means to acquire truth gain their force from decisions of particular humans working within particular academic communities; thus there is a power element in the accreditation of knowledge' (2006, p.28). Her comment provides an early alert to the potential dangers of a 'one-size-fits-all' methodological approach to research undertaken in what is perhaps wrongly perceived to be a common subject area. For Silverman also, the question of whether methods of research are appropriate to the nature of the question being addressed is the first criterion for the evaluation of any qualitative research work (2005, p.228), and he particularly alerts researchers to the fact that 'qualitative research is not always appropriate to every research problem' (2005, p.7).

Qualitative research: a tool for practical theology

Silverman's comments in relation to the importance of methodological appropriateness to some extent illuminate the backdrop for a consideration of contemporary practical theologians' preferences for using qualitative research in intellectual disability theology. Denzin and Lincoln's (1998) synopsis highlights the significant overlap between the qualitative research methodology and the core values of practical theology, particularly with respect to the perspective that sees theology emerge from 'below' within human experience. This, according to Swinton and Mowat, (2006, p.5) is 'one of the things that marks practical theology out from other theological disciplines'. It is a foundational precept of theologies of liberation in which, while the biblical story provides the blueprint for Christian living, it is also 'read through the lens of the experience of the present, thereby enabling it to become a key to understanding that to which the text bears witness – the life and struggles of the ancestors of the faith' (Rowland 2007, p.645). The understanding of the theological significance of the 'living human document' has been fruitfully developed by prominent practical theologians.[3]

It is also important to note, however, that the use of qualitative research by practical theologians has not been without its critics. Swinton and Mowat (specifically citing Milbank's work) acknowledge that 'the relationship between theology and the social sciences has always been tense…some argue that the social sciences are wholly incompatible with theology and that social science methods are therefore inappropriate tools in the task of doing theology' (2006, p.vi).[4] Whether this is an entirely justified reading of Milbank's view is a matter of debate, but he does emphatically attack those he describes as:

> contemporary 'political theologians' [who] tend to fasten upon a particular social theory, or else put together their own eclectic theoretical mix, and then work out what residual place is left for Christianity and theology within the reality that is supposed to be authoritatively described by such a theory. (1990, p.2)

---

3   See 'The Living Human Document' in Graham, Walton and Ward 2005, Chapter 1.
4   They refer to Milbank, J. (1990) *Theology and Social Theory: Beyond Reason.* Oxford: Blackwell.

Milbank seems most concerned to refute the view that theology *must* be mediated by the social sciences (a view he attributes in particular to Boff): 'the question is much more fundamentally, can there be theology, *tout court*, without mediation by the social sciences? Because only if the answer is yes (as I hold) can one go on upholding the fundamentally historical character of salvation: in other words, orthodoxy' (pp.251–2). Arguing that, on the contrary, there is no incompatibility between theology and social sciences, Swinton and Mowat's work, *Practical Theology and Qualitative Research* (2006), referred to above, offers perhaps the most comprehensive explanation of the theory that underpins the significance of creating contextually relevant qualitative research methodologies for theologians. As an example of the importance and effectiveness of multi-disciplinary scholarship, standing alongside and engaging with parallel work in sociology studies, it has become a core text for practical theology researchers. A number of examples of actual research projects recorded in the book demonstrate the highly effective use of qualitative methods in the search for theological understanding emerging from human experience.

Specifically enjoining the debate on the dangers articulated by opponents of theological qualitative research, they insist that 'theology's significance is…prior to and independent of research data' (2006, p.87). Consequently, a process of 'conversion' of social sciences' qualitative research methods is required, by which 'God "converts" the field of intellectual enquiry outside theology…and uses it in the service of making God's self known within the Church and from there on into the world' (p.92). Such 'conversion' involves, for example, an adjustment of social sciences' assumptions relating to the impossibility of attaining truth-full knowledge of the world so that the reality of God can be a guiding principle of theological use of the methodology. This adjustment is largely agreed to be central to ensuring that those aspects of qualitative research that might unacceptably conflict with theological perspectives on the world are addressed The implementation of the process of adjustment is inherently complex and alertness to the challenges involved is an ongoing requirement. Yet it is clear that, in recent decades, qualitative research has become a major piece of the practical theology armour, as it has sought to forge new perspectives on the task of the people of God to live out the gospel in the world and has further added to the case for understanding practical theology to be of wide-ranging, unique and indispensable significance within the discipline of theology a whole.

Prominent qualitative research in intellectual disability theology

In 1993, Webb-Mitchell highlighted the fact that 'first-person narratives of people with mental retardation have not been collected, heard and understood by others' (1993, p.5). In recent years, however, the Centre for Spirituality, Health and Disability at the School of Divinity, University of Aberdeen, under the direction of Professor John Swinton, has been particularly active in undertaking and promoting theological research in the field of intellectual disability, as well as in a number of other areas of health and social care. In a variety of ways, research linked to the Centre founded on the principles and practices articulated in *Practical Theology and Qualitative Research* (Swinton and Mowat 2006) has significantly advanced the work of educating the Church in how it might appropriately learn to value and support people with intellectual disabilities.[5] Swinton specifically defines the relationship between practical theology and disability theology in the following terms: 'If practical theology pushes towards faithful discipleship, disability theology pushes us to think of the broad range of possibilities that there are for being human and living faithfully' (2012, p.260). The work of the Centre demonstrates determination and commitment to countering the failure to address the obstacles, previously perceived as almost insurmountable, to addressing negative assumptions about the spiritual lives of people with intellectual disabilities, consequent upon what Swinton and Mowat identify (2006, p.233) as 'the way in which society in general and religious communities in particular define "spirituality" [which] implicitly exclude and marginalize people with learning disabilities'. The work pioneered by Swinton and others has gone a considerable way to redress Webb-Mitchell's earlier concerns. It has provided the catalyst for these small yet important beginnings in addressing the shortage of 'descriptive, first-hand information available to the disability community and service providers as they seek to work out effective forms of theological reflection, and political and ecclesial action, and effective policy and support services' (p.229). Yet, while projects of

5   See, for example, collaboration in the establishment of the Kairos Forum for People with Intellectual or Cognitive Disabilities (KFICD), which 'seeks to highlight and respond to the spiritual and religious needs of people with disabilities', http://thekairosforum. com; 'Knowing "how" but not "why"; knowing "why" but not "how"' (Research Report 2012); Swinton, J., Gangemi, C., Tobanelli, M. and Vincenzi, G. (2013) 'Enabling Communities to meet People with Learning Disabilities and respond effectively to their expressed Spiritual and Religious Needs: A Participatory Action Research Approach', http://thekairosforum.com/content/resources; also Swinton, J. (2012) 'Reflections on Autism and Love: What Does Love Look Like?' *Practical Theology* 5:3, pp.259–78.

this type represent a significant and welcome challenge to the reluctance to engage with the spiritual lives of people with intellectual disabilities highlighted previously, it is my view that important aspects of the subject, and some of the people they are intending or purporting to include in their research, remain inadequately acknowledged or untouched.

The search for 'voices'

Across the range of disability studies, the continuing existence of what some perceive to be the 'lost voices' (Atkinson and Walmsley 1990, p.204) of people with intellectual disabilities remains a matter of serious concern (Walmsley and Johnson 2003, pp.64–70). In the theological context, Swinton and Mowat express similar dissatisfaction: 'the voices of people with learning disabilities have frequently been excluded from research approaches which assume them to be *objects* rather than the subjects of the research' (2006, p.229). This concern provides impetus for committed attempts to include people with intellectual disabilities within any theological discussion of their spiritual lives. It is nonetheless the case that significant challenges pertain to qualitative research in the area of intellectual disability and profound intellectual disability in particular. It seems clear to me that there *are* people whose profound or complex intellectual disabilities are such as to genuinely preclude them from expressing their 'voice' on this subject at all, given their severely limited or complete lack of verbal communication skills. Despite attempts to overcome or disguise this reality, its negative impact on the possibility of undertaking qualitative research in which such people can genuinely be deemed as participants has been acknowledged in wider empirical research methodologies scholarship.[6]

In this context of using qualitative research methods to allow participants the opportunity to be heard, it is particularly significant that the majority of the small number of research projects providing the basis of theological reflection in this field are focussed primarily on the lives of those who, while having intellectual disabilities, either have some capacity to articulate their own experience verbally or have had their experience interpreted and articulated by those closest to them.[7] Returning to the controversy identified above concerning whether those

---

6   See above.
7   See Swinton and Powrie's two-year project (beginning in 2004) outlined in Swinton and Mowat 2006, Chapter 4; also Swinton, Mowat and Baines 2011, and Chi-fung Sarah Shea, 'What does it mean to be saved? Evangelicalism and People with Severe Intellectual Disabilities' (Unpublished thesis, University of Aberdeen, 2014).

who reflect and speak theologically about disability are entitled to so do if they themselves are not directly affected by the experience, current research approaches demonstrate a general assumption that, with respect to offering knowledge-generating data for practical theology research projects, those who have some kind of a meaningful relationship with people with profound intellectual disabilities do have a capacity to speak authoritatively of and for them. This assumption implies the possession of some particular understanding of the spiritual experience of those to whom they are closely related or for whom they care. Undoubtedly, in the absence of such expression, there would be no *personal verbal* articulation of the spiritual experience of people with profound intellectual disabilities of any kind.

Nonetheless, recent attempts to push the qualitative methodology into the context of profound intellectual disability in ways that present such persons as first-hand participants in the research are beginning to emerge, and it is here that I think we need to apply caution. The outcomes of a notable example of a research project of this nature (cited above)[8] carried out through the Centre for Spirituality, Health and Disability were published in the *Journal of Religion, Disability and Health* in 2011.[9] The authors, John Swinton, Harriet Mowat and Susannah Baines, describe the piece as 'a series of extended meditations on the lives of some real people and the issues they bring to the table as theological conversations develop' (p.6). The real people whose lives are the subjects of these extended meditations are persons with 'profound disabilities with high support needs' (p.6),[10] and the issues they bring to the table relate specifically to their identity and to their spiritual lives and experience (p.5). The primary issue that the researchers seek to address is that, because of what they present as an intrinsic link between a person's story and his or her identity, people with profound intellectual disabilities

8   The title of the research project, funded by the UK Arts and Humanities Council, is 'Understanding the Spiritual Lives of People with Profound and Complex Intellectual Disabilities – A Community Orientated Action Research Approach', www.abdn. ac.uk/sdhp/intellectual-disabilities-a-community-orientated-action-research-approach-195.php.

9   The article which presents the findings of this research is Swinton, J., Mowat, H. and Baines, S. (2011) 'Whose Story Am I? Redescribing profound disability in the Kingdom of God.' *Journal of Religion, Health and Disability* 15, pp.5–19.

10   In line with the definition employed in this book, Swinton's definition of this terminology is 'a profound disability, which includes high support needs and communication difficulties that present major challenges to having one's views and preferences heard and understood' (2011, p.6).

who cannot tell their own stories easily fall victim to prejudicial narratives being constructed about their lives, which in turn have a negative impact on how they are perceived and treated. This, they claim, happens not only in wider society but within the Church, thus making people with profound intellectual disabilities subject to theological as well as social discrimination, in that little if any attention is paid to their spiritual lives – a proposition with which I wholeheartedly concur.

Swinton *et al.* are clearly and rightly concerned by the inability of people with profound intellectual disabilities to 'narrate their own stories without the assistance of others, *all* of whom may misunderstand their stories and who frequently tell stories about the person that are different, contradictory and sometimes untrue'. They warn (2011, p.6) that they 'can easily become the victims of constructions of their own stories that they do not own'. Because the identity established by such negative stories cannot be accepted, such people require other stories to be told in order that a more positive identity might be established. For this to be achieved, we must 'work towards developing…counter-narratives of resistance' (pp.6–7). Consequently, the difficulty lies in identifying who is appropriately qualified to create these counter-narratives and what these narratives are to be. This challenge is to be averted by 'explor[ing] what it might mean to listen carefully and transformatively to those who have no words' (p.7) through a process of qualitative research, and the implication is that if we learn to do this, it will be their own story that we hear. The researchers present a way for this to happen: a series of case studies in which stories that resist societal prejudice are created and narrated by their parents and 'caretakers and various other support workers' (p.7).

This project will be further examined below as an exemplar of some of the challenges inherent in using qualitative research with people with profound intellectual disabilities, but I should emphasize again that I fully respect the motivations that fuel attempts to access an understanding of the spiritual experience of those who do not use words, and there is authenticity in the efforts to find a way to listen to people with intellectual disabilities when the people concerned *do* have some verbal or clear alternative means of communicating aspects of their experience. Difficulties arise, however, in the vacuum that is created if and when nothing is or can be said, or, perhaps more accurately, in the apparent discomfort of some disability theologians precipitated by an encounter with that vacuum and their consequent efforts to fill it. I want to consider whether an unwillingness to accept the inability of some people with intellectual disabilities – namely those whose are profound – to articulate aspects of their spiritual experience justifies attempts to present them as intentional participants in ways that are at best unconvincing and potentially unsustainable. In the course of such consideration, questions will inevitably be raised concerning whether practical theologians' use of such methodologies in this context is legitimate and capable of eliciting the genuine theological insights they seek. Of more fundamental importance, however, is the question of whether any form of self-expression, actual or imputed, is even a necessary component of any attempt to identify and acknowledge their spiritual experience.

Potential advantages of using qualitative research methods to explore the experience of people with profound intellectual disabilities

In order to offer a balanced assessment of the efficacy of using qualitative research to uncover insight into the spiritual experience of people with profound intellectual disabilities, it is essential to identify potential advantages as well as disadvantages that might be offered by such an approach. Immediately, it becomes apparent that since the objective of this book is to provide a lens through which to focus on the spiritual experience of a discrete group of human beings, employing qualitative research methodologies might offer particular benefits, particularly in the light of their potential to identify and articulate aspects of complex human experience within a theological framework, as well as their intention to assist in the epistemological aspect of theological research.

Potential for creating ideographic source material

The interpretive paradigm of qualitative research inherently provides encouragement to any researcher attempting to establish and adhere to epistemological assumptions in relation to truth and knowledge in an ideographic rather than a nomothetic context. Crucially for qualitative research, uncovering objective truth, if it exists, is not the aim; it may indeed not even be achievable. Rather it is the attainment of understanding and meaning that are the desired results of its quest (Bogdan and Knopp Biklen 2007, p.7). Writing specifically of a narrative-based process to qualitative research, similar to that employed by Swinton, Bailey and Tilley explain that:

researchers who analyse stories identified in interview data recognize the primacy of stories as meaning-making strategies. They are interested not so much in the facts or truth of these accounts, but rather in the meaning portrayed in story form... Storytellers reconstruct their stories to convey a specific perspective of an event: it is meaning not truth that is conveyed in the form of stories. It is the truth of their experience, not an objective, decontextualized truth. (2002, p.581)

This is a highly positive aspect of the qualitative research method in a theological context; attaining nomothetic knowledge is arguably neither possible nor desirable when the ultimate source of such knowledge is transcendent and infused with mystery. This is not to argue, however, that there is no such thing as truth or reality. In their discussion of the subject, Swinton and Mowat, for example, are careful to stress that reality does exist but that 'our ability to understand and define [it] is always filtered through a process of interpretation and constructivism that is influenced by a number of social, cultural, spiritual and interpersonal factors' (2006, p.36). In a non-theological context, Yanow makes a similar point, commenting that 'the social world we inhabit and experience is potentially a world of multiple realities, multiple interpretations' (2006, p.12).

Potential for interpretation of experience to elicit genuine understanding

It is important to acknowledge that non-necessity of objectivity has rendered qualitative research vulnerable to attack from those who advocate the superiority of scientific and quantitative research methodologies, which are claimed to be capable of producing more reliable knowledge on the basis of the possibility of such research outcomes being falsified, replicated and generalized.[11] There is, however, an increasing amount of scepticism in relation to the extent to which knowledge produced by quantitative methodologies can universally be assumed to be objectively obtained and unassailably reliable, epitomized in Willis' comment (1981, p.194) that the world 'cannot empirically present itself'. As Webber explains in relation to what he refers to as 'the scientific revolution', 'because matter is in perpetual movement, post-moderns

---

11   This trifold description of the essential characteristics of quantitative research and the nomothetic information it purports to produce is helpfully explored in Swinton and Mowat 2006, pp.40–2.

argue that we cannot arrive at rational and scientific facts' (1999, p.21). Thus, post-modern approaches to qualitative research reject the idea of a 'stable, consistent and coherent self…you can only know something from a certain position' (Bogdan and Knopp Biklen 2007, p.21). Haraway (1991, p.584) characterizes such approaches as a rejection of 'the view from nowhere'. Specifically in relation to the supposed 'risk' of subjectivity inherent in qualitative approaches, Gadamer argues that it is wrong to assume that any researcher (quantitative or qualitative) can ever be totally detached from the object of her interpretation. In fact, pre-understandings, he argues, can be beneficial rather than detrimental to the research enterprise. In qualitative research contexts, 'to interpret means precisely to use one's own pre-conceptions so that the meaning of the text can really be made to speak for us' (1981, p.358). Bogdan and Knopp Biklen (2007, p.4) go further, claiming that 'the researcher is the key instrument'. Nonetheless, as Swinton and Mowat specifically emphasize (2006, p.59), it is imperative that the researcher enact a continuous process of critical self-reflection throughout the course of the research in order to maintain ongoing awareness of her own constructive and interpretive contribution to the research process. Walmsley and Johnson make the same point: 'a recognition of the researcher's attitudes and values is integral' (2003, p.38). Corbin and Strauss stress the reciprocal nature of such reflection (2008, p.11): 'we must be self-reflective about how we influence the research process and, in turn, how it influences us.' In the act of interpretation, however, striking a balance between one's personal experience and that of the research subjects is an inherently difficult task and perhaps more so when the quantity of the first-hand information being interpreted (for example, in the case of people who lack a capacity to clearly articulate their own experience) is of lesser volume than that which forms the basis of the researcher's own preconceptions. It must also be acknowledged that 'a method that focuses on lived experience – such as participant-observation, ethnography, interviewing with that focus and so on, is phenomenologically inflected' (Yanow 2006, p.28) in that it is inevitably enacted within a particular framework or way of seeing the world. The qualitative researcher must thus proceed with a degree of caution when it comes to engaging with and seeking to establish meaning and knowledge from the source material.

One further challenge concerning the relationship between the researcher, those whose experience is being researched and the data to be interpreted is worth noting – that of the potential for information to be influenced by the power dynamic which may lie unnoticed and unintended beneath the surface of the engagement. Yanow raises this as an issue that demands serious attention: 'asked directly to explain their acts and/or beliefs, research-relevant publics are likely to report what they think the researcher wants to hear, or what they believe is socially acceptable, or simply what they think they believe or value' (2006, p.19). Swinton and Mowat also acknowledge the significance of this possibility, warning that:

> situations are complex and complexing entities that are filled with hidden values, meanings and power dynamics. The task of the Practical Theologian is to excavate particular situations and to explore the faithfulness of the practices that take place within them. Such an exploration of situations and practices enables the Practical Theologian to inhabit a unique and vital role within the process of theological reflection. (2006, pp.vii–ix)

In light of this perspective, the practical theologian's hermeneutic approach to achieving understanding of human behaviour and experience seems to have much to recommend it when applied in a quest for an understanding of the spiritual experience of people with intellectual disabilities. Yet it is also the case that the more challenging the human behaviour is to interpret, as in the case of those whose intellectual disabilities are profound, the greater care must be taken to test the interpretations being made. When, owing to the difficulties of interpreting their behaviours, this kind of research further involves gaining data which has its source in one who is adjudged to have some basis on which to speak about a person who has a profound intellectual disability, the researcher must also be aware of the fact that *this* data has already been subjectively interpreted by someone who has a pre-established relationship with the subject/participant. Thus the 'unique and vital' role of the practical theologian precipitates the need for intentional ongoing awareness of the complexities of the process and the underlying preferences and assumptions from which the data attained in the research emerges.

Potential for promoting academic and theological rigour

Those who advocate the use of qualitative research argue convincingly for its academic weight and solidity. Concurring with the view of McLeod on the onerous nature of the task (2001, p.3), Swinton and Mowat insist that 'qualitative research is rigorous, painstaking, exacting, complex and difficult' (2006, p.30). Such key characteristics offer potential to infuse a vital degree of robustness into the exploration of the subject of this book, as it investigates an area which might be regarded by some as speculative in nature and unlikely to lead to the uncovering of definitive conclusions. Swinton and Mowat specifically identify four elements of the practical theology method: it is hermeneutical, correlational, critical and theological (p.76). Despite his more sceptical, if not dismissive, approach to social science methods in theological exploration, Milbank's position on the absolute priority of the Christian perspective of human history is here consonant with that of Swinton and Mowat: 'The logic of Christianity involves the claim that the "interruption" of history by Christ and his bride, the Church, is the most fundamental of events, interpreting all other events' (1990, p.390). Similarly for Swinton and Mowat (2006, p.77), the theological element in their use of qualitative research element means that the method must 'locate itself in the world as it relates to the unfolding eschatology of the gospel narrative; a narrative that indicates that the grasping of truth is possible'. This inevitably, at times, brings it into conflict with the practice of qualitative research outside of theological contexts, often heavily nuanced by post-modern influences in which the possibility of uncovering of any such universal truth is hugely questioned, if not dismissed (Rorty 1980, p.23). Again, identifying and achieving an appropriate balance within the dialectical engagement of gathered knowledge from the lived experience of the objects or subjects of the research and the eschatological narrative of God is inevitably a complex and challenging task and assumes even greater pertinence when the data from which the knowledge is gained does not emerge directly from those with whose experience the research is concerned.

Potential for 'freedom' in scriptural interpretation

Nonetheless, from a specifically theological standpoint, the fact that qualitative research allows for and even assumes a degree of openness on the part of the researcher with regard to the interpretation of Scripture might be perceived as one of its core strengths. Swinton and Mowat describe this as a 'prophetic freedom [in which]…theological understanding is presumed to be emergent and dialectic rather than simply revealed and applied' (2006, p.82). In this respect, the appropriateness of the methodology and framework of qualitative research might seem particularly persuasive in relation to the enquiry of this book, which requires just such an enticing level of theological freedom, since it has as its central focus the uncovering of fresh ways of contextualized thinking in relation to biblical and theological propositions which might be perceived by some as being historically 'settled' within a range of aspects of the Christian faith tradition. While aspects of both Protestant and Catholic orthodoxy, for the most part, require evidence of intentional and rational adherence to theological 'givens' in their own areas of belief, to be explored at a later point in this work, my thinking probes beyond such intellectualized, cognition-dependent conditions for a divine–human relationship, and to envisage an alternative means by which people with profound intellectual disabilities might apprehend the presence of God as an internal experience. Interpretive freedom for this task is clearly required. Where 'truth' in this area might be considered by some to be already fully established, this work seeks to probe the reliability of such a view.

It is, however, important to consider the tensions in adopting the preferential option for the emergent in such a way as to add to, rather than detract from, the body of theological knowledge. Contextual theology has an inestimable role in developing rich theological insight by both taking into account 'the faith experience of the *past* that is recorded in Scripture and kept alive, preserved, defended – and perhaps even neglected or suppressed – in tradition…while taking account the experience of the present, the *context*' (Bevans 2002, p.5). When enjoying their 'prophetic freedom', qualitative researchers must continue to be attentive to the question of where the boundary lines are to be drawn. As Swinton and Mowat concede (2006, p.vii), 'left to its own devices, knowledge [from the social sciences] can easily subsume theology and orient the theological task towards goals and assumptions that are inappropriate and theologically unsustainable'. The challenges here are complex, for, as Ward explains, practical theology finds itself situated:

> within a variety of 'relations' that follow the modernist project. These include the relationship between theologies of revelation and human experience, the relationship between the social sciences and theology and the way empirical methodologies, both quantitative and qualitative, might relate to systematic or doctrinal theology. (2008, p.45)

These elucidations of the complex dynamics of the relationships in which practical theology must engage are highly significant. Ward's comments provoke questions of how and where practical theologians doing qualitative research might identify the checks and balances necessary to prevent the creation of theologies of their own particular preferences, or founded on inappropriate use of the method itself or the data generated by its use. It is a priority in all such work, however, to pay close attention to the way in which what Swinton (2012, p.264) refers to as a 'disability hermeneutic' engages with Scripture and the wider theological tradition. Naturally, my own work is not exempt from such challenges, and the issue will be further addressed at a later point.

Potential obstacles to using qualitative research with people with profound intellectual disabilities

Despite the various attractions of the qualitative research methodology noted above, it becomes apparent that there are significant and, in my view, insurmountable obstacles to proceeding by such means into an exploration of the spiritual experience of people with profound intellectual disabilities. None of these is a 'stand-alone' obstacle, but each contributes to and is interwoven with the others to create a cumulatively stultifying effect on the potential for the effective use of the methodology in this context. In identifying and highlighting these obstacles, the intention is not in any respect to attempt to discredit qualitative research as a legitimate methodology for 'doing' practical theology but to raise questions concerning the potential limits of its effectiveness in research in the specific area of profound intellectual disability, where first-hand accounts of the participants' experience are not available. The issues are many, but the primary concerns are noted below.

The central role of language

The essential difficulty of using qualitative research with people with profound intellectual disabilities is that the method relies largely, and in many cases entirely, on linguistic communication in order to be effective or of value in explaining the lived experience of another person. For Gadamer, qualitative research involves the process through which researcher and researched come to understand each other's frame of reference, with language playing the central mediating role in interpretation (1981, p.238). Chiovotti and Paran (2003, p.430) specifically list among their criteria for achieving academic rigour that the researcher must 'let the participants guide the process and use participants' actual words in the theory'. Indeed, Swinton and Mowat insist on the centrality of conversations which are 'necessarily deep, intense and rich'. It is the researcher's task to identify significant words in the linguistic responses to questions posed and to locate their importance in relation to the wider context of the answers given; the 'end-point is never clear until the verbal journey is over' (2006, p.64). Yet it seems legitimate to ask how one might make the verbal journey on one's own behalf without a means of communication adequate to the task of doing so? It is not only in the telling of the story that words play a central part, however. There are preliminary issues that need to be raised.

The challenge of consent

It is a fundamental and non-negotiable aspect of the qualitative method that the express consent of the objects, subjects or participants in the research is essential to the ethical validity of the project. Bogdan and Knopp Biklen advise researchers that:

> the subject should be told of your research interests and give you permission to proceed…[and you should] be particularly sensitive and diligent in explaining yourself and getting consent when studying people who are vulnerable to manipulation, such as people labelled mentally disabled. (2007, p.50)

Walmsley and Johnson agree that consent is of primary importance in research with people with intellectual disabilities, but are uncomfortable with the reality that 'confining research only to those who can give truly informed consent may well exclude large numbers of people with learning disabilities from being involved at all'. Thus they argue that 'the use of guardians who can give informed consent is one way to ensure that exploitation of people who are unable to give informed consent can be avoided' (2003, p.159). Nonetheless, the wider debate takes place within the context of human rights and equality legislation, concerning who is eligible to give consent on behalf of a vulnerable adult on a vast range of issues, including whether invasive medical treatment is to be allowed; whether a secure bed is allowable to protect a person who might unintentionally fall and injure herself;[12] whether he or she may have care of any children born; what clothes a person should acknowledge. In any case, it is important to remember that the issue of consent is not simply one of who is eligible to give on behalf of another but also

---

12   This is a long-standing matter of contention between me and government authorities in respect of my daughter's safety.

whether the other understands the research question for which consent is being acquired. With due attention to these complexities, in their two-year project involving people with high support needs (2006, pp.227–2),[13] some of whom had the ability to communicate verbally, while others had limited, if any, such ability, Swinton and Mowat preferred to obtain first-hand, rather than vicarious consent: 'consent had to be demonstrated both verbally and non-verbally by the participant…in order for true consent to be given, it must be discussed within specific conditions: a calm environment, adequate time, openness and honesty' (pp.141–2). If, however, the explicit expression of such consent is set as a precondition of carrying out research into the experience of people with profound intellectual disabilities, questions inevitably arise concerning whether such persons have the capacity, first, to understand that, and for what, their consent is being sought and, second, to formulate and express consent in a way that can reasonably be interpreted as such.

Understanding the questions

It seems obvious, but nonetheless important, to acknowledge that acquiring responses to the qualitative researcher's questions is preceded by the necessity of the formulation by the researcher of verbal questions in the first place. Despite their assertion that it is appropriate for consent to be given on behalf of people with learning disabilities who are unable to give it for themselves, Walmsley and Johnson (2003, p.64) argue that for research capable of being assessed as genuinely inclusive '[t]he research questions, process and reports must be accessible to people with learning disabilities'. It must be debatable to what extent people whose intellectual disabilities are such as to limit their capacity for language might reasonably be assumed to be capable of understanding questions regarding their spiritual experience or spirituality in the first place. Indeed, it is possible that being questioned about their spiritual experience might well challenge human beings who are not understood to have particular intellectual deficits. This may, of course, depend greatly on the definition of spirituality provided, which, as Narayanasamay (1996, p.204) affirms, is evasive and difficult to ascertain.[14]

---

13 The participants' high support needs are described in terms commensurate with intellectual disabilities defined in my own work here as profound and complex.

14 See also Cobb, M., Puchlaski, C. and Rumbold, B. (eds) (2012) *Oxford Textbook on Spirituality in Health Care*. New York, NY: Oxford University Press.

Whose words are heard?

Finding an effective mechanism for ensuring that stories that are told about people with profound intellectual disabilities by others are actually the stories that they would choose to tell about themselves seems not only problematic but inherently impossible. The Swinton, Mowat and Baines (2011) project, 'Whose Story Am I?', demonstrates the tensions here, for the object of the research is specifically to allow the participants to enter conversations that will reveal counter-narratives to the stories told about them by others and by society as a whole. One part of the research focusses on the life story of Brian, a 36-year-old man who has no capacity for language nor any formal means of communication. The researchers spent 'a couple of hours talking about Brian with his mother and others involved in Brian's care' (p.7). In the light of the authors' attachment to Harré's positioning theory,[15] Brian's mother, having a special position in relation to Brian, is crucial to the telling of Brian's story. She clearly found the process of talking about her son beneficial: 'Since I can't talk to him, talking about him is good. He's a good person' (p.7). While society's story of Brian is, the researchers claim (p.8), a negative one (though arguably not exclusively so), his mother's is one that provides a much-needed counter-narrative which reflects 'the goodness of Brian's life' (p.8). The conclusion drawn from Brian's mother's perspective is that Brian is a good person – he is a good person, because his mother believes him to be a good person. This is Brian's new or reconstructed narrative, which the qualitative research has uncovered. It is evident that in the process of talking about her son, Brian's mother discovers something significant about her relationship with him and what he means to her. Her words, however, are fundamentally about just that – they are comments arising from the opportunity Brian's mother has had to tell a story about Brian and about *her relationship with him*. Brian's mother's description of Brian as a 'good person' is not less valuable for being a statement of how she perceives and feels about her son, yet it should not be mistaken for Brian's statement about himself. If, as Bailey and Tilley argue (2002, p.78), the 'goal of qualitative researchers is to provide ways of understanding experience from the perspective of those who live it', whose experience are Swinton *et al.* describing? Who is really participating in the theological conversation here? Is it really Brian, or is it his mother? Is this Brian's new narrative about himself? Surely, we do

---

15   Swinton cites Harré, R. and van Langenhove, L. (1999) *Positioning Theory.* Oxford: Blackwell.

not know what Brian feels or believes or would like to say about himself for he cannot tell us.

Provision of alternatives to language

This inherent impediment to the use of qualitative research in relation to people who do not use linguistically based means of communicating their experience was acknowledged, albeit fleetingly, by Swinton and Mowat in their project referred to above (2002),[16] when emphasis was placed on the need to offer alternative methods of response to those whose disabilities prevented them from being able to offer linguistically based, self-expressive responses. While the enterprise had at its centre the use of spoken or written language, there was nonetheless a genuine desire to include those who lacked the capacity to articulate their experience by verbal means. The researchers' motivation was authentic and explicit; they affirmed that 'to understand the experience of a historically marginalized group such as people with learning disabilities, it is necessary to utilize a method which will empower and genuinely allow their voice to be heard above the voice of the researcher' (2006, p.56). People whose voice was at best difficult to hear and at worst completely inaudible were included as participants 'regardless of their level of understanding' and thus creative approaches were adopted; participants described as having 'high support needs' were offered alternative means of self-expression in the form of 'pictures, symbols, colouring-pens and the use of an interpreter of non-verbal communication' (p.238). Given these acknowledged obstacles to communication, however, it might be asked whether the creative opportunities for participation that were offered represented, at least for some, less a statement of method than of aspiration on the part of the researchers. To what extent might it be possible for those who have no capacity to articulate their experience, whether through words or alternative tools such as those described here, to be genuine participants in a project of this kind, able to communicate on the subject of their spiritual lives?

It is by no means contended here that there are no effective means of communication with people with profound intellectual disabilities, as both those in close familial relationships and professionals involved in their support will affirm. It is, however, the case that any such communication with and from this discrete group of people is inevitably more basic than that which would be required to elicit from them

---

16   Recorded in Swinton and Mowat 2006.

direct information concerning their spiritual experience from which theological assumptions can be drawn. While expression of emotional responses to others, as well as to circumstances and environments, and articulation of basic needs might, for some, be possible, the key issue for the theological and wider use of qualitative research into the inner experience of such persons is that the kind of data being sought from them requires a level of understanding and capacity for self-expression that cannot be expected.

Nonetheless, such aspirations can readily be understood in light of the fact that the theory that people who do not use language to communicate can inevitably or always be encouraged or enabled to express themselves in other ways seems firmly ingrained in mainstream thinking in relation to the growing interest in advocacy for people with learning disabilities. Scott and Larcher, for example, insist that in this context 'communication is possible even in the most extreme situations' (2002, p.172), the emphasis being placed on an advocate to establish a channel of communication. Again, no evidence for such an assertion is (or could) be offered, since it is impossible to know what is not being communicated. Hulme's parallel statement 'if it's important, you'll find a way to tell me, and I'll find a way to understand' (1983, p.7), appears breathtakingly naïve. It would doubtless be refuted by many who live in the real world of caring for people with profound intellectual disabilities (and others for whom communicating is intolerably difficult) who daily contend with the difficulties of, for example, being unable to identify the specific cause of what they assume to be expressions of discomfort or unhappiness.[17] Speaking from personal experience, Morris affirms this point: 'I have witnessed, for example, the frustration, the vulnerability, of a person who does not have any language when they cannot tell you that something is wrong or that they are in pain' (2013, p.241). Arguably more in tune with the reality of the lives of people with profound intellectual disabilities, Walmsley and Johnson concede that among limits to inclusivity in qualitative research in this area:

> the most striking is the absence of voices of those people who do not speak, sign or otherwise convey their views in a way which others can

---

17   This reality was radically demonstrated within my own family when Rebecca was rushed for life-saving surgery after the inadvertent discovery that her bowel had been twisting for months to the extent that a significant part of it needed to be removed. Until the day of the operation when she ceased to eat and drink normally, she had offered no indication of what must have been excruciating pain in the weeks leading up to it.

readily understand. Whilst imaginative and heroic efforts have been made to access the inner worlds of people with profound disabilities, there is little evidence that they can be enabled to represent themselves directly, rather than through the eyes of those who are close to them, or empathetic researchers. (2003, p.184)

Participant validation

Once the data in any qualitative research project has been elicited, an assessment process is set in motion to ensure the validity of the outcomes. For this process to be successful, Corbin and Strauss (2008, p.301) insist that the researcher must be in a position to make an affirmative response to the question, 'can participants see themselves in the story… Does it "ring true" to them?' Of course, research participants who have significant capacity for linguistic expression *can* clearly meet this criterion, but in order to be confident of the reliability of the overall outcomes, it is essential to ask how participants who *cannot* offer the kind of responses expected can validate what has purportedly emerged during it. Corbin and Strauss again explain that research analysts 'construct something that they call knowledge' from the material collected from 'research participants who are trying to explain and make sense out of their experiences and or lives, both to the researcher and themselves' (p.10).[18] Is such a quest possible of attainment when the subjects are incapable of providing such potentially complex explanations?

Ironically, some of the benefits highlighted by Swinton and Mowat of employing qualitative research methods in the context of profound intellectual disability might equally be perceived as specific obstacles to accepting their argument. They assert that among the key criteria by which the credibility of the results of qualitative research might be judged is that it offers 'rich, thick descriptions' (2006, p.122) such that the reality which they are attempting to convey can be recognized by other researchers, even though they have only read about it rather than having been involved in eliciting it. If, as Swinton and Mowat argue (p.122), 'the idea of credibility is fundamental to the trustworthiness of a research project', how is such credibility to be assured when the participants cannot speak for themselves to offer their own responses or to confirm the responses offered by others on their behalf? Lincoln and Guba further insist that, 'credibility is crucial and…cannot be established without recourse to the data sources themselves' (1985, p.213).

---

18   Particularly cited as Corbin's view.

In other words, credibility in qualitative research is dependent, among other things, on the nature of the source material and the ability of those whose experience it articulates to validate its authenticity. Sandelowski concurs: '[a] qualitative study is credible when it presents such faithful descriptions of a human experience that the people having that experience would immediately recognize interpretations from those descriptions as their own' (2008, p.30). Whether use is made of the input of others, in research into the spiritual experience of people with profound intellectual disabilities the experience that is presented as having been investigated is *theirs*. How can they recognize it as their own when they lack the ability to contribute to its articulation? In the wake of the impact of Charlton's *Nothing About Us Without Us*,[19] movement towards inclusive research with people with learning disabilities is much to be welcomed. Qualitative research practice, however, must avoid the possibility that, in attempting to include people with profound intellectual disabilities as research participants, the exact opposite of what is intended is achieved: what *is* about them, while purporting *not* to be without them, is precisely that.

Resisting compromise

As some within the wider field of the social sciences argue that the criteria for reliability in research outcomes ought to become less taxing if this is necessary to promote the empowerment of oppressed groups who are the objects/subjects of the research, Silverman warns of the dangers of trends towards allowing the focus of the research to shift from what is reflective of the reality uncovered to the potentially wider benefits of the outcomes of the research (2011, p.220).[20] He insists (p.219) that 'downplaying the cumulative weight of evidence from social science research...lowers our standing in the community'. If theologians working in the field of disability studies are to preserve the integrity of their use of qualitative research methods, perhaps it is time to confront the uncomfortable but crucial question of whether this is an appropriate methodology of uncovering insights into the spiritual experience of those who neither understand nor express themselves through words.

---

19   Charlton, J. (2000) *Nothing About Us Without Us: Disability Oppression and Empowerment.* Berkeley, CA: University of California Press.

20   Silverman is paraphrasing the view of Stanley and Wise in Stanley, L. and Wise, S. (1983) *Breaking Out: Feminist Consciousness and Feminist Research.* London: Routledge.

Observer–interpreters

As well as offering opportunities for non-verbal communication, a supplementary method of gaining information is recommended in work in this area – that of employing an 'observer–interpreter' whose task it is to give attention to the research subjects' behaviour in order to draw conclusions concerning what was being communicated through it (Swinton and Mowat 2006, pp.240–1). Yet, in this context, difficulties persist: what happens if there is no observable behaviour to interpret? Even if particular behaviour is observed, there may be a lack of clarity with respect to criteria for establishing how anyone is qualified to translate what may or may not be significant gestures into reliable and valuable information. As the discussion below will highlight, behaviours are often interpreted in radically different ways in relation to the spiritual or ecclesial engagement of people with profound intellectual disabilities. How often must the behaviour be recognized for the interpretation to stand up to scrutiny? What of those for whom this solution is genuinely not an option? The implication of Swinton's and Mowat's claim to complete inclusivity seems to be that such people do not exist. The question of whether people so cognitively and linguistically challenged are really participants in the kind of research Swinton and Mowat are proposing is unavoidable. If we fail to respect the 'heterogeneity…within the broad group labelled people with learning disabilities' (Walmsley and Johnson 2003, p.184), and if the difference between people whose intellectual disabilities *do not* preclude both cognitive understanding of the questions posed and genuine self-expression in response to them and those whose intellectual deficits *do* is not acknowledged, how can the integrity of the research be established? Once again, in qualitative research, as in disability studies in general, 'impairment does matter'.[21]

The complexities of identifying participants

Despite the tensions involved in the use of interpreters for those whose intellectual disabilities are most acute, it is deemed by Swinton and Mowat to be congruous with the practice of such qualitative research that is essentially participatory, meaning that it occurs within 'a framework in which people move from being the *objects* of research to *subjects* and *co-researchers*' (emphasis added). The participatory nature of the research is intended to address some of the 'hidden power

---

21   See above.

dynamics within the research process and in the relationship between the researcher and those who are being researched' (2006, p.228). Yet, perhaps in a tacit acknowledgement of the unsustainability of the theory that everyone can express themselves in one way or another, they argue that the participatory aspect extends not only to the subjects of the research but to those who enjoy significant relationships with them. It might indeed appear reasonable to assume that if the aim is to uncover information concerning the experience of those who do not use words to communicate, then those who live most closely with such persons, enjoying relationships with them which are intimate and meaningful, are uniquely qualified to speak on their behalf. Yet such assumptions must be carefully considered; 'in whose voice and perspective the story is told' is, claim Holley and Colyar (2009, p.683), a key question for this form of research. Again, Denzin and Lincoln stress that 'qualitative researchers are concerned with "the individuals'" point of view' (2000, p.10). How is it possible to ascertain the point of view of people who cannot articulate it? Moreover, it is difficult to resist the argument that information about the spiritual experience of people with complex intellectual disabilities, which is accessed solely through their advocates who may or may not hold to a concept of spiritual experience or to one particular personal understanding of it, will be significantly filtered by the experience of those who speak for them. Such information must also be subject to the contingencies inherent in the difficulty of obtaining and confirming purported responses to complex questions, particularly when those questions relate to abstract concepts like spiritual experience and spirituality, value, meaning, connectedness, hope, transcendence and the existence of God and identity (Swinton and Mowat 2006, p.238).

Thus, while it seems appropriate to ask the interpreters/advocates about *their own* spiritual experience directly in relation to those persons with intellectual disabilities with whom they are in relationship, we might ask whether it is legitimate to determine that such information can comprehensively or accurately represent the spiritual experience of persons who entirely lack the capacity to directly express what is happening. Where the quest is for 'first-hand'[22] information, it is important to ask how the accuracy of the interpretations offered might be assessed. The crucial difference which must not be overlooked is between interpreting or speaking *for* someone about something you are certain they would say for themselves if they had the ability to do so and

---

22   See above.

speaking *about* someone without any degree of certitude of what they would say if they could speak for themselves. Not only the *quality* but the *category* of information attained in these varying contexts is hugely affected by each. In the former instance, the potential exists for authentic knowledge pertaining to the experience of those who have *not* spoken to be accessed on the basis of the data gathered; in the latter, the data recorded can only generate knowledge about the experience of the persons who *have* spoken. As Bailey and Tilley point out, 'the goal of qualitative researchers is to provide ways of understanding experience from the perspective of those who live it' (2002, p.577). If the aim is to gather information about the spiritual experience of people with profound intellectual disabilities, those who speak *about* them must, at best, be understood as 'indirect' participants in the research. If they are genuinely deemed to be actual participants, then the research must focus on *their experience,* not that of those about whom they speak.

Predisposition of 'indirect'/observer participants

A number of further factors become relevant here, including the issue of seeking responses to questions about the spiritual experience of people with profound intellectual disabilities from people who are, by virtue of the nature of the relationship, naturally predisposed to offering direct empirical evidence of their spiritual lives. Of course, as has been acknowledged at an earlier point, the same factor pertains to non-empirically based theological reflection in this area being undertaken by a person who is equally emotionally connected with such persons. Such subjectivity does not necessarily refute the validity of the research findings but, given that the role of these people is to specifically articulate the experience of those with whom they are in relationship, rather than simply their own experience, additional caution must be applied and genuine awareness of the dangers identified. If it is the case that 'the researcher must walk a fine line between getting into the hearts and minds of respondents while at the same time keeping enough distance to be able to think clearly and analytically about what is being said or done' (Corbin and Strauss 2008, pp.80–1), how much greater is the danger of excess subjectivity when the research material to be analysed is obtained from those who, for the most personal of reasons, must grapple with such tensions at a much greater depth? Ochberg (2003, p.130) argues that the researchers' 'approach to interpretation is influenced by what [they] want to see'. How much more the observer–interpreter–participant?

Primary concerns

Two points arising out of the discussion above merit particular emphasis. First is the relationship between data gained through qualitative research methods with people with profound intellectual disabilities, the generation of new theological insight or transformative knowledge and the degree of academic and theological rigour which is the cornerstone of the legitimacy of the method. Practical theology's qualitative research methods are not only particularly designed to elicit knowledge of the participants' experience but to use this with a 'prophetic freedom [in which]…theological understanding is presumed to be emergent and dialectic rather than simply revealed and applied' (Swinton and Mowat 2006, p.82), thus generating an expansion of current theological knowledge which has the capacity to change practice. Given the potential significance of this claim to new knowledge, it is vital that there is a sound, defensible and academically robust method of uncovering the research data and bringing it into conversation with the faith tradition. I suggest that, however laudable the researchers' motivation, when qualitative research is used inappropriately with those who cannot speak for themselves, the theological knowledge which is the purported outcome is less than sustainable, and that in seeking to achieve valuable insight into the spiritual lives of people with profound intellectual disabilities, this failed methodology results in potentially unreliable and detrimental conclusions.

A further aspect of the 'Whose Story' project where some of the 'knowledge' attained by challenging and re-describing of the narratives told about people with profound intellectual disabilities is presented as being of potentially enormous theological significance, not only for those whose experience is being investigated but for the wider Church, demonstrates the point I am making here, in relation to Mary, for example, who is a Quaker. The researchers relate how, although Mary's usual disposition is to make non-verbal noises, when the meeting of the Quaker community falls into silence, Mary's customary noises stop, and she too becomes quiet. This, alongside Mary's mother's account of Mary's earlier emotional response to receiving a serious negative medical diagnosis, indicates that Mary 'is a deeply sensitive young woman who picks up on subtleties in communication, emotion and mood' (Swinton and Mowat 2011, p.14). Swinton presents the following theological conclusions from this aspect of Mary's story:

> [I]f that is the case, then Mary's spirituality is a corporate rather than personal concept and experience...spirituality is being formed and held by her participation in the community. Mary's spirituality is not something that she alone has. It is something she shares in; it is an experience that rises beyond her; an experience that happens in the space between members of the community: the space of meeting. She is dependent on the community for her spiritual experience.

Swinton *et al.* use Mary's 'startling counter-narrative to contemporary understandings' (p.14) to raise the question of how human beings know God; to counter perceptions that this is primarily a personal thing, which they attribute to a belief that to know God requires an ability to understand and proclaim the name of Jesus. They rightly point out that this would exclude people like Mary. Mary's counter-narrative thus redescribes a broader theological narrative: 'Spirituality is something *we* have together. I am spiritual *because we are.*' Furthermore, they ask 'is knowledge of God *really* individual or do we always and necessarily know God primarily and perhaps only in community?' (p.14; emphasis added). The biblical mandate Swinton selects for such a position is to be found in the Apostle Paul's words in 1 Corinthians 3.16 (NLT): 'Don't you realize that all of you together are the temple of God and that the Spirit of God lives in you?'

In terms of how Swinton *et al.* use this piece of qualitative research in relation to Mary to produce fresh theological understanding, it is perhaps these latter statements that raise the greatest concern. First, they are claiming that only by sharing in the mood of the meeting, evidenced by her silence, is Mary's spiritual experience formed. Mary has no spiritual life of her own – she is dependent on a faith community for her spiritual experience. I am not contesting that Mary's silence might well reflect the reality of her experience. The argument here is simply that this interpretation is presented by Swinton *et al.* as being sufficiently robust as to generate wide-ranging theological insights which might be disproportionate to the amount and proven authenticity of the knowledge emerging from Mary's behaviour and implied telling of her own story. Because of the possible range of other interpretations and of other behaviours of people who also have profound intellectual disabilities in similar circumstances, the question arises of what would be the interpretation of a person like Mary whose non-verbal sounds continued throughout the meeting? Would this be evidence that for *that* Mary all hope of spiritual experience is lost, since there is insufficient empirical data on which to interpret her as having recourse to the corporate spirituality she needs in order to have a spiritual experience? It is significant that other disability theologians (and parents) relate parallel stories in which people with profound intellectual disabilities do *not* keep the silence of a service of worship, yet their breaking of the silence is deemed to be evidence of participation in and contribution to the community's worship.[23] Indeed, it might well be the case that some individuals are quiet on some occasions and not on others,[24] thus exposing the dangers of advocating important theological conclusions on the basis of anecdotal evidence in an area in which those whose experience is being described are wholly unable to confirm or deny what is presented.

Hypothetically, if the community folds and Mary no longer has access to it, does she also lose her access to a spiritual life? If Mary can only know and experience God as her community does, and as she is able to participate in her community in ways that are construed by people with greater intellectual capacity than she to demonstrate such participation, then Mary's experience of God must be derived from the people around her. This raises further questions. Does the depth of Mary's spiritual experience correlate to the depth of her community's? Indeed, if Mary's spirituality is precisely commensurate with that of the community, because the spirituality exists in the space between its members and is perhaps *only* a corporate entity, then is the community's directly commensurate with Mary's? If this is a communal spiritual experience, why should Mary be the follower and not the leader; the recipient and not the source? Should we assume that what we understand or experience is what Mary does not; or indeed that Mary does not experience more than we do? What is this narrative communicating about the wholeness and value of Mary' humanity? It is interesting that Swinton argues from Jesus' self-identification with the poor and marginalized in Matthew 25.31–46 that we can expect to particularly encounter Jesus in Mary. Why, then, is Mary dependent on the community for her spirituality? While 1 Corinthians 3.16 and other similar texts[25] indubitably explain that God is experienced among the members of the body of Christ, and the believing community is identified as an organic unit in which each member has an indispensable contribution to offer, should this

---

23   See, for example, Young, F. (2014) *Arthur's Call: A Journey of Faith in the Face of Severe Learning Disability.* London: SPCK, p.153.

24   This has been evident in participation in services of the Eucharist during my several visits to the original L'Arche community in Trosly-Breuil, France.

25   See 1 Corinthians 12.12–30; Romans 12.5.

be read in isolation from other significant biblical material that affirms the personal nature of the indwelling presence of God in the individual believer? Indeed, is the insistence in the same texts that each member of the body been assigned a particular gift to contribute to the whole not evidence that God is present and at work in each as an individual?

Exclusively individualistic perceptions of the divine–human relationship should rightly be challenged as Swinton *et al.* do here, but should the individual, personal, one-to-one encounter be entirely refuted? In Galatians 2.20, for example, Paul also states: 'It is no longer I who live but Christ who lives in me.' The biblical narrative makes clear that God is concerned with humanity as a whole, with communities of people and with human beings as individuals. As Barth insists in his discussion of the relationship and tension between the communal spiritual life of the community of faith and that of the individual member:

> [I]n all the common life…[the individual] is still himself. He is uniquely this man and no other. He cannot be repeated or represented He is incomparable. He is this in his relationship with God and also in his relationship with his fellows. He is this soul of this body, existing in the span of this time of his. (1961, p.754)[26]

The potential for a direct relationship between God and an individual person is a core theme of Scripture. There is nothing to suggest that I can 'remain in Christ' (John 15.7) on behalf of another person, or indeed, as would otherwise logically be the case, that my being cut off from Christ (John 15.6) (whatever that might mean) should mean that others in my community must be similarly treated. The ancient spiritual disciplines of solitude and community emphasize the importance of experiencing God both alone and together.[27] Is it theologically justifiable to argue that we might know God *only* as a communal experience? Can this be inferred from the interpretation of Mary's story? Is this description of the theological narrative in danger of going too far? Perhaps the impetus to achieve this conclusion is understandable if it emerges out of the underlying theological tensions inherent in doctrines of salvation in which human response to the offer of grace is presented as essential (to be explored below). As Swinton *et al.* go on to argue, 'God comes to us in friendship and accommodates to our needs quite apart from anything that we have to offer' (2011, p.15). Perhaps it should be added that God

---

26   The subject is helpfully explored in Shea, 'What does it mean to be saved?'
27   See, for example, Bonhoeffer, D. (1954) *Life Together.* New York, NY: Harper and Row.

can come to us in friendship quite apart from anything that we offer to one another.

It is clear that some of the impetus for this kind of research is founded on a need to defend the value of people with intellectual disabilities. I wonder, however, whether the efforts to hear the theological voices of those who cannot speak in a conversation about their spiritual lives betrays something more of an unnecessarily defensive stance on the part of disability theology that is evident in other aspects of the arena. Is qualitative research really capable of revealing and articulating the lived experience of individuals who have profound intellectual disabilities? Should theologians whose aim is to gain insight into their experience of God be looking elsewhere? There is no argument here for what Ward (2008, p.48) rightly criticizes as 'the assumption that it is necessary to adopt a distanced and supposedly "objective" perspective to think theologically'. Rather, it is the claim to be 'inside' the experience on which theological reflection is taking place that is contested. The issue of the identification of the 'voice' of people with complex intellectual disabilities is pivotal; is it ever genuinely possible to hear those particular voices specifically articulate *their own* spiritual lives, regardless of how creative the methods of self-expression we offer them might be? How can we know that what we think we are hearing is what they might actually want us to hear, should they want us to hear anything at all? Silverman's criteria for assessing research quality includes the ability to provide an adequate answer to the question: 'How far can our data, methods and findings be based on a self-critical approach or, put more crudely, counter the cynic who comments, "Sez you?"' (2005, p.229). His somewhat unusual expression of this point does not negate its legitimacy and importance for disability theology's use of qualitative research methods. If the theological reflection and meaning-making emerging from such methods is to be respected and persuasive, these issues must be addressed.

Second, and perhaps more importantly for our discussion, is the fact that underpinning this debate are more fundamental questions arising from the fact that such research is taking place. Might there be some unintentional reluctance to acknowledge persons whose intellectual disabilities are so comprehensive as to prevent them from expressing their spiritual experience through methods accessible to the rest of humanity? If so, from where does such reluctance emerge? Is it possible that there is a subconscious fear that, as some outside the field of disability theology (to be specifically highlighted below) argue, such persons are not fully capable of a genuine relationship with God – a proposition that is adamantly and rightly contested by those carrying out the qualitative research described above – so that, in order to be comfortable about asserting their capacity for spiritual life, we should assume that it can be identified and explored through cognitive and linguistically based methods?

My argument is that the lack of language-based articulacy which has been deemed to be hugely significant to achieving perceptions of the spiritual experience of people with profound intellectual disabilities is not an obstacle that requires to be surmounted by creative approaches in relation to alternative communication tools and observational and interpretive expertise. Rather it is the springboard for another conversation, potentially leading to different questions and wider theological insights. It is precisely *because* of the fact that people with profound intellectual disabilities do not use words to articulate their perception of their lived experience, nor do they have the cognitive abilities to process linguistic explanations of, or assent to, certain logical or theological propositions, that the discussion that follows is worth pursuing. The inadequacy of linguistically based methods aimed at extrapolating first-hand accounts of the experience of people with profound intellectual disabilities directs the focus to other and, within the Christian faith tradition, more reliable sources.

3

ISSUES OF THEOLOGICAL LANGUAGES

Moving on from the discussion of what I argue is a less than effective pathway along which to explore whether, or more appropriately, *how* people with profound intellectual disabilities might enjoy a spiritual experience of God, I want to suggest that we take a different route and that such insight can be found on a journey through the rich theological sources of the Christian tradition. It is along this alternative pathway that we will find solid ground for the case that the cognitive deficits of persons with profound intellectual disabilities do not prejudice their capacities or opportunities for being either recipients or conduits of a revelation of God, or, perhaps more adequately expressed, that God is not incapacitated by reason of their cognitive deficits from communicating and disclosing himself to and through them.

Revelation and the 'problem' of words

It is central to the issues under consideration, as I have already acknowledged, that the inability to operate within a complex linguistic framework intrinsically presents enormous, if not insurmountable, challenges to people with profound intellectual disabilities in terms of accessing an understanding of the world around them. Morris specifically highlights the consequences of these challenges in light of traditional approaches to understanding a human being's potential relationship with God and their influence on how people with profound intellectual disabilities are perceived:

> [W]hat is assumed...in practice, however much we might wish to redefine what faith is, is that in order to be saved, a person will normally have language and the intellectual capacities to learn a set of beliefs and make choices and decisions about them; what is assumed is able-bodied normativity. (2013, pp.236–7)

In such a context it might appear that the theological difficulties with which they are confronted are, at best, serious and, at worst, devastating.

One of the primary underpinning dilemmas for people with profound intellectual disabilities is that, in common with other religious faith systems, the Christian faith is intrinsically and hugely reliant on verbal language for its mediation and for the education of its adherents. At the source of this faith is a sacred text which the Christian tradition teaches contains fundamental information concerning the existence and nature of the Divine Being who is the faith's origin and centre.[1] It is acknowledged here that the Bible provides multiple evidence of divine revelation, accomplished directly or indirectly by a diversity of non-verbal means, most importantly the incarnation of Christ, but also including dreams and visions, natural and supernatural phenomenon, the created order and human experience.[2] Numerous aspects of the created world are also potential places where God might be personally encountered, including, for example, art, music and literature. All of these are important, although they are not the focus of this work and the group of people whose spiritual experience we are discussing. It is worth noting that in any case they are equally unlikely to have cognitive access to the divine disclosure facilitated through these entities as they are to the verbal revelation.

Nonetheless, the Bible self-identifies as the prime location of God's verbal revelation and continually presents itself as providing the reference points by which human beings can navigate the God-directed life of faith. It is, in mainstream Christian thought (albeit not in a unanimously agreed, equally weighted sense) the Word of God, in which are contained the words of God, which affirm the primacy and absolute necessity of grasping and obeying the words and Word of God. Psalm 119, for example, comprehensively demonstrates the significance of God's verbal communication to the life of faith (both Christian and, of course, Hebraic). Here God and his expressed Word are almost synonymous; the Psalmist expresses his love for God and for his Word

---

1   Of course, it is the case that people with profound and complex intellectual disabilities are not the only persons affected by the emphasis on 'words' in the Christian tradition of revelation, as Morris makes clear in his work with the deaf community. He does not perceive the absence of words to be a deficit in deaf theology, as this researcher does not for people with profound and complex intellectual disabilities, although for different reasons (2008, p.157).

2   For example: Genesis 2.24–5, Isaiah 6.1–6 (dreams and visions); Genesis 9.12 (rainbow); Exodus 3.2 (burning bush); 1 Kings 18.38 (fire); and Romans 1.19–20. This is poignantly illustrated in Elizabeth Barrett Browning's famous poem, *Aurora Leigh*: 'Earth is crammed with heaven and every burning bush afire with God, but only those who see take off their shoes.'

in equal measures (77); a longing for God is a longing for his Word (57–9). This Word is to be sought after and listened to (78), enjoyed and trusted (86), loved (127) and obeyed to the letter (34). It brings salvation (93), life (130), light (105), joy (111), comfort (50), protection (92), understanding (104), hope (49), guidance (37) and truth (43).

Furthermore, the centrality of the spoken word at or around the introductory point to the Christian faith, as well as in obedient Christian living, is clearly presented within the text. The Apostle Paul, for example, states that 'faith comes by hearing the message and the message is heard through the word about Christ' (Romans 10.17). Christ himself continually emphasizes to his followers the imperative of acting in accordance with his Father's verbally expressed commands, just as he, the self-identified Son of God, does in fulfilling the mission for which he came to earth (John 15.10, for example). Thus, as Sparks writes (2008, p.230), 'Christians receive the Bible as divine discourse, as God's authoritative words inscribed through human writers to human readers'. While Morris would agree that 'the role and significance [of the Bible] is increasingly perceived by many ordinary Christians as the benchmark for how to live and what to believe' (2006, p.166), he attributes this development largely to the rise in literacy in the West and resists any assumption that those with little or no access to the text might be perceived as 'less Christian' (p.167). It nonetheless remains the case that discussions of the spiritual experience of people with profound intellectual disabilities often have to contend with those who are committed to the absolute necessity of engagement with the text. Swinton highlights the same point in asking the question: 'How do we offer the Word to those who have no words?' (1997, p.22).

In relation to access to the gospel, Jensen, for example, unequivocally states (2002, p.36) that the 'achievement of the gospel is that people come to know God through informative and hortatory words about him. Whatever else the gospel is, it is verbal, an announcement by way of speech.' This verbal announcement which was 'to function as an instrument of salvation' is 'a word of God who speaks, creates, judges and saves'. He insists that 'the word of God means language' (2002, pp.46–8). Interestingly, Jensen concedes (2002, p.47) that his argument that the gospel, or in his terms 'the prime revelation of God', is a 'verbal occurrence' is an idea with which we may or may not feel at ease. One might ask why he should find it necessary to make such an observation. It might be an awareness of any potential Christological controversies that such an assertion might invoke; there is no evidence to suggest that he recognizes the inherent and extreme difficulties such a perspective places in the way of the availability of relationship with or salvation by God to those for whom words are difficult, confusing or utterly devoid of meaning. Whatever the reason for his concession, he recognizes Barth's contrasting position that the gospel revelation consists not primarily in words but in the person, Jesus Christ: 'According to Holy Scripture, God's revelation takes place in the fact that God's word became a man and that this man has become God's Word. The incarnation of the eternal Word, Jesus Christ is God's revelation' (p.1). Nonetheless, Jensen's is only one example of those who assert the absolute necessity of words for revelation and this remains a fundamental principle in contemporary Christian theology. Swain writes that while '"communication", theologically understood, involves more than the simple exchange of words... Nevertheless, communication, theologically understood, is never less than an exchange of words' (2011, p.8). This viewpoint will be further explored in what follows.

At this point, however, it is again stressed that any suggestion that, without apprehension of the words, no fruitful revelation or communication by God is possible, is a matter of enormous importance for our discussion. If intellectual reflection on language-based sources were to be an indispensable part of how a human being might meaningfully encounter God, then for people with profound intellectual disabilities there would be little hope for such encounters. Yet, as Morris again makes clear (2013, pp.136–7), this is the situation with which they are confronted, since 'the mechanism by which salvation is realized according to this tradition excludes, in practice, the person with dementia, mental illness, or profound learning disability from even the possibility of participation in the future kingdom of heaven'.

Revelation and God's speech

In this context, it is pertinent that there is considerable wider theological and philosophical debate as to the place of 'words' in divine revelation. In *Divine Discourse,* Wolterstorff (1995, p.18), focussing on discourse through words, asks questions of whether, how and why God might speak.[3] His interest is in interpretive methods of reading the text to see what God might be saying, in the context of philosophical understandings

---

3   Interestingly, he articulates his fundamental question in the familiar context of what it means to end a public reading of the Bible with the words, 'this is the Word of the Lord'.

of the human use of language. His work implicitly highlights the issue for people with profound intellectual disabilities, since he is clear that among adherents of the 'religions of the book' (by which he means Judaism, Islam and Christianity) 'most of their convictions about God are...formed in them by explication of sacred Scripture and meditation on the results thereof' (p.14). Yet, while he acknowledges that 'it has been widely thought that divine speech is reducible to divine revelation' (pp.9–10), he argues that they are in fact 'distinct phenomena' (p.13) and that 'revelation occurs when ignorance is dispelled – or something is done which would dispel ignorance if attention and interpretive skills were adequate' (p.23). Schneider too highlights the distinctiveness between God's speech and human language:

> [W]ords...are the intelligible physical sounds emitted by the vocal apparatus of a rational creature... Language, in other words, is a human phenomenon rooted in our corporeality as well as in our discourse mode of intellection and as such cannot be literally predicated of pure spirit. (1991, pp.27–9)

Thus, it is argued, God's 'speech' is a metaphor, not a literal description of a divine activity – to which Barth would perhaps reply, 'Church proclamation is talk, speech. So is Holy Scripture. God's Word means that God speaks. Speaking is not a "symbol"' (2009 [1955], p.132). Following contemporary philosophies of language, however, Wolterstorff affirms the idea that real communication of information comes through 'speech acts' (1995, pp.37, 75) and not speech alone. In his discussion of the topic, Briggs agrees (2008, p.76), citing the first act recorded in Scripture as one such 'speech act': 'Then God said: 'Let there be light' and there was light' (Genesis 1.3). The speaking of words does not in itself encompass the full extent of what was taking place in this act of creation. Moreover, true revelation consists in what Wolterstorff terms 'propositional or manifestational revelation', which is always an intentional activity on the part of the revealer. This is 'knowledge-transmitting revelation or true-belief-transmitting revelation' (1995, p.29; emphasis added) for which speech alone is inadequate; an additional act must occur for which only God can be responsible. Bray similarly describes the 'orthodox Protestant' position on the nature of Scripture in which 'the inner witness of the Holy Spirit is all important, because it is he who speaks through the text to their hearts and who applies the text to their lives' (1992, p.22). It is Wolterstorff's view (1995, p.35) that the intention of God in performing what he calls these 'illocutionary acts...is not to inform us of what we don't know but to take on duties *toward* us and require things *of* us; trust and obedience are the appropriate responses'.[4] Such divine acts may or may not be performed by verbal means and he insists that as the modes of discourse available to human beings are numerous (p.37), those available to God are more so (pp.37–57).

Both these elements of Wolterstorff's thought are highly pertinent to our discussion. First, his emphasis on the existence of the infinite number of modes at God's disposal to effect communication with human beings offers a potential response to any argument that inability to access the verbal revelation in Scripture might preclude anyone from experiencing a meaningful encounter with God. While there will inevitably be limitations to how and what human beings communicate in such a way as to be understood by other human beings, God, on the other hand, is subject to no such constraints. Consequently, there is no one with whom he cannot communicate and nothing he cannot express should he choose to do so. In this regard, however, I do not accept Wolterstorff's argument that 'revelation occurs when...something is done which would dispel ignorance if attention and interpretive skills were adequate' (p.23), and the latter part of his statement seems somewhat at odds with his assertion of the innumerability of God's modes of communication. The logic of the proposition that the occurrence of genuine revelation is dependent on levels of attention and the adequacy of interpretive skills is that God's capacity to reveal himself would be curtailed by the ability of the one to whom the revelation is being directed.

Second, Wolterstorff's argument that the 'responsibility' for facilitating self-disclosure rests entirely with God (a key element of his discussion of the place of words in divine revelation[5]) is equally significant here, although his perspective is not without its opponents. The issue of contention pertains to whether it is possible for obligations to adhere to God in relation to carrying out the acts he has determined to accomplish. In Alston's words, for God 'there is no foothold for the "ought"' (1989, p.108). Quinn critiques the philosophical logic underpinning Wolterstorff's argument that God chooses to take on obligations towards human beings – an argument Wolterstorff seeks to demonstrate largely

---

4   The prescribed responses of trust and obedience are also problematic for people with profound and complex intellectual disabilities, but only if one is seeking for verbal or other identifiable expression of them. This will be discussed later in my work.

5   Wolterstorff 1995, Chapter 6.

by use of human examples of character-based actions. Quinn, like Alston, insists that we cannot attribute to God the status of being obligated to do anything (2001, pp.259–69). Quinn's position is convincing on the extent to which the logic of Wolterstorff's examples can rightly be challenged, but a flaw in the supporting evidence does not necessarily negate the truth of the conclusion. Wolterstorff refutes the argument that it is impossible for God to assign himself obligations towards human beings – a proposition formulated on a number of pillars, the central one being the philosophical and theological argument that one can only be required to do something which is morally good if one has the freedom not to do it, and since God cannot *but* do what is morally good, he can attract no obligation to do so. Woltersdorff contests the claim that the sole criterion for obligation to exist is the possibility of deviation from its fulfilment (1995, pp.108–9). The element of 'requiredness' can, he argues (p.111), be re-construed in understanding the obligations which attach to God as 'character-required... The fact that certain actions are character-required of God with respect to God's loving character...is simply an aspect of the internal structure of that character-formation which is *being a loving person.*' This is an important idea that I will go on to develop, contextualizing it in relation to people with profound intellectual disabilities and arguing that God's inclusion of people who do not have capacity to access the verbal revelation is something that emerges from his own being and character. It is acknowledged that Wolterstorff's theory comprises the reciprocal requirement of a trusting obedient response to God's self-disclosure, yet we might ask why, while choosing to communicate with human beings, he would make requirements of some of them, in this context, people with profound intellectual disabilities, which they could not overtly meet.

My intention is not to negate fundamental understandings of the importance of the verbal communication of what God desires for human beings to know of him, but to further explore the nature and to some extent the content of the revelation of God, proposing that there *is* a way in which spiritual experience which is generally perceived to be encountered within a largely cognitively and linguistically based faith framework can be accessed by people who lack the cognitive and linguistic skills to operate intentionally within it. The fundamental question here is whether the intellectual deficits of any human being can be so great as to deny him or her access to knowledge of God which, Scripture informs us, is God's expressed desire.[6] Adequately addressing this issue requires a reorientation of attention away from the deficits of people with complex intellectual disabilities, towards the God who is understood to be both the ultimate author and inspirer of the written text[7] and the origin of all human awareness of the spiritual and the divine.

Revelation and communication

Beyond the debate about the various means by which it is facilitated, as the foundation of all Christian theology, identification and comprehension of God's self-revelation has been the task and objective of believers and theologians across 2,000 years of Church history. As Headlam states (1934, p.7), 'the primary question in theology must be what the source of our knowledge of God is'. Here it is worth reiterating that Scripture in itself cannot comprise all there is to communicate nor is the communication its own end. Temple explains that 'what is offered to man's apprehension in any specific Revelation is not truth concerning God but God Himself' (2003, p.322). The underpinning theological proposition here is not that Scripture is God's revelation but that God reveals himself. Thus the quest for a valid apprehension of the nature of God's revelation is pervaded by the understanding that a revelation *of* God can only ever come *from* God. On this point, Jensen comments: 'revelation is a matter of God's drawing near to us…not of our seeking and finding God' (2002, p.48). Without his self-revelation, he is invisible and inaccessible.[8] Demarest (1992, p.13) agrees that any understanding or belief in relation to God 'can…only consist in what is revealed by God of Himself… Only God can make known God.' Moreover, any human awareness of the transcendent emerges from what Scripture intimates to be a God-designed feature of the human psyche which alerts human beings to the existence of the transcendent. 'He has set eternity in the human heart yet no one can

---

6   See, for example, 1 Timothy 2.3–4: 'This is good and pleases God our Saviour who wants all people to be saved and come to a knowledge of the truth.'

7   Acknowledgement is made here of the huge disparity of views on many issues relating to the nature of the text, the level and operation of divine inspiration within its creation, its relationship with its human authors, and the degree to which their human influence should be accounted for in the way in which the text is received. Some of these controversies will be alluded to later in this chapter.

8   John 1.18; 1 Timothy 6.15–16.

fathom what God has done from beginning to end' (Ecclesiastes 3.11).[9] In this light it might be deduced that God has sufficiently revealed himself in order that the God-imbued, innate human potential for an awareness of him is capable of being realized by every human being.

Crucially in this context, whether one frames it in terms of an obligation in Wolterstorff's terms or simply a way of being predicated on the loving character of God, it seems clear that the self-disclosure of God is, in its nature as well as its content, a God-designed bridge which spans the otherwise unbridgeable gap between the infinite God and a finite humanity which, without this act, remains helpless to construct such a bridge and, moreover, to conceive of the need for one. Swain adopts a Trinitarian perspective in this context, highlighting the inherent place of communication within the Godhead (*ad intra*): '[t]he eternal life of the Father, Son and Holy Spirit is a life of perfect communication and communion [which] exists before us, apart from us and without any need of us' (2011, p.5). Yet, he argues, Scripture explains that this aspect of God's being, coupled with his desire (though not his need) 'for something beyond and outside of Himself' (p.5) overflows into a desire for communication beyond the Godhead towards those he has created (*ad extra.*) This desire, will and purpose are, he claims, embodied in word and sign and ultimately in Christ.

As this divine desire for communication with human beings is played out, however, the creation narrative and the fundamental biblical principle of finite humanity's incapacity to apprehend God in the fullness of who he is assume enormous significance. As the Apostle Paul explains, the ways and being of God are past finding out (Romans 11.33). Sparks affirms this understanding: '[t]here is simply no way to transfer God's infinite perception of reality into a finite human mind' (2008, p.243).[10] Within the same creation narrative, however, lies the doctrine of *imago Dei*, of which, as has already been noted, theological interpretations proliferate both within and beyond the parameters

---

9   The precise meaning of the Hebrew, here translated as eternity, is a matter of debate. Bartholomew offers the possibility that it could mean of the following: 'world', 'a sense of the past and future', 'a sense of duration', 'ignorance', 'distant time' and 'a consciousness of God'. Bartholomew, C. (2009) *Ecclesiastes: Baker Commentary on the Old Testament: Wisdom and Psalms.* Grand Rapids, MI: Baker Academic, p.166.

10   Owing to the comprehensive nature of his discussion of the theory of accommodation, Sparks' work provides an important but far from exclusive source for the enquiry that follows.

of disability theology.[11] The degree to which it is essential to acquire a conclusive understanding of the term remains an ongoing matter of debate. Clines, for example, argues (1968, p.53) that 'the importance of the doctrine is out of all proportion to the laconic treatment it receives in the Old Testament'. Berkouwer, on the other hand, insists that the 'image of God is...far less central in the Bible than it has been in the history of Christian thought' (1988 [1962], p.67).

In this developing debate, however, a recent move away from the complexities of *interpretation* to a consideration of the *significance* of *imago Dei*, exhibited in some of the most recent biblical scholarship, directs focus to a more fundamental perspective on the doctrine. At the conclusion of a highly comprehensive exegesis and analysis of historical and contemporary expositions of the concept, McKeown (2008, p.279) highlights as its most significant aspect the intrinsic implication that if human beings are created in the image of God, then God and human beings are in some sense 'on the same wave-length...compatible beings'. Accepting this, there must be a means (or a range of means) by which such communication can take place. The question in our context, then,

---

11   Alternative interpretations of *imago Dei* have proliferated throughout the history of theological enquiry. Christological interpretations permeate the views of many theologians, even though they variously advocate additional understandings of the doctrine. Augustine emphasizes the existence of the human soul and its capacity or immortality in the Trinitarian aspects of mind, memory and will. The Reformers' emphasis is on capacities for morality and righteousness, although Calvin also cites anthropomorphic, theomorphic and corporeal biblical material as a basis for interpretation. Relational interpretations are espoused by Martin Buber and, later, Barth. Others assert the image as a conferral of a divine stamp on human beings as the recipients of divine authority with which they are endowed and on the basis of which they represent God in the stewardship of the created world; many of these stress the contextual implications of the Near Eastern culture into which the phrase was spoken. For a range of literature in which the range of interpretations is discussed, see Augustine, *De Trinitate*; *On Genesis Against the Manicheans*; Westcott, F. (1986) *Christus Consummator*. London; Torrance, T. (1957) *Calvin's Doctrine of Man*. Grand Rapids, MI: Eerdmans; Barth, K. (1958) 'The Creation of Man' in *Church Dogmatics, vol. 3.1*, trans. Edwards, J.W., Bussey, O. and Knight, H. Edinburgh: T&T Clark; Hall, D.J. (1986) *Imaging God: Dominion as Stewardship*. Grand Rapids, MI: Eerdmans; Bromiley, G. (1988) 'Image of God' in *International Standard Bible Encyclopaedia, Vol. 2*, ed. Bromiley, G. Grand Rapids, MI: Eerdmans (original work published in 1979); Hughes, P. E. (1989) *The True Image: The Origin and Destiny of Man in Christ*. Grand Rapids, MI: Eerdmans; Sarna, N.H. (1989) *Genesis: JPS Torch Commentary*. Jewish Publication Society; Bray, B.G. (1991) 'The significance of God's image in man.' *Tyndale Bulletin* 42:2, pp.192–225; Middleton, R. (2005) *The Liberating Image: The Imago Dei in Genesis 1*. Grand Rapids, MI: Brazos Press; Towner, W.S. (2005) 'Clones of God: Genesis 1.26–8 and the image of God in the Bible.' *Interpretation* 59, pp.241–56; Webb, S. (2006) 'In whose image?' *Books and Culture* 12:4, pp.10–11.

concerns how God enacts his own desire for self-disclosure to human beings, including people with profound intellectual disabilities. In what ways does he inhabit the cohesion between his being, his desire and his action in such a way as to offer the possibility of establishing a relationship of intimacy with human beings in a way that is accessible and appropriate to the fundamental yet variously embodied limitations of their finitude? The following discussion will explore one important aspect of the answer to this question.

Revelation by accommodation

Christian (and Jewish)[12] theology's answer to this question has, to a significant extent, been formulated in terms of the theory of accommodation.[13] Van Bemmelin provides a helpful definition of the theory (1998, p.221): 'God, in His Self-revelation to humanity, accommodates Himself to the mental and spiritual capacity of human beings so that they can come to know Him, learn to trust Him and ultimately love Him.' Benin too describes accommodation or condescension (using the terms interchangeably) as 'divinity adapting itself and making itself comprehensible to humanity in human terms. It is the adaptation and the adjustment of the transcendent to the mundane' (1993, p.1). The theory has been formulated, promoted and accepted throughout Church history by a remarkably diverse cross-section of theological scholarship. As Benin further comments (p.93): 'the breeze of accommodation…blows…through the nooks and crannies of almost countless works, and an examination of each work would fill volumes'. While his proviso that 'there is a certain danger in trying to describe the history of an idea and capture its myriad applications in seemingly countless different literatures and times' (p.209) is acknowledged, nonetheless, the theory of accommodation remains a prominent player in the hermeneutic theatre.[14] The following necessarily selective discussion of some of its manifestations and complexities will

---

12　Theories of accommodation proliferate in historical Jewish theology. One of its most prominent exponents, writing in the twelfth century CE is Maimonides (1135–1204) See Maimonides, M. (1963) *The Guide of the Perplexed, Vol. 1*, trans. Pines, S. Chicago, IL: University of Chicago Press; Benin, S. (1984) 'The "Cunning of God" and Divine Accommodation.' *Journal of the History of Ideas* 45:2, pp.179–91.

13　Accommodation is variously referred to in theological scholarship as 'theory', 'idea', 'concept' and 'doctrine'.

14　As the recent work of Frances Young indicates: Young, F. (2013) *God's Presence: Current Issues in Theology*. New York, NY: Cambridge University Press.

demonstrate its relevance for perspectives on the spiritual experience of people with profound intellectual disabilities.

Accommodation: interpretive roots

From the outset, it is important to note that although instances of its use relating to specific theological questions and controversies serve to encapsulate aspects of its meaning and purpose, this theory was not originally postulated as a response to any single or self-contained theological issue. Rather, it has emerged as a more general response to the challenges of biblical interpretation and the historical and ongoing difficulties inherent in appropriating the ancient text within a contemporary context. Thus Benin refers to accommodation as 'an exegetical device' (1993, p.1). Funkenstein, in tracing the 'exegetical career' (1986, p.213) of the theory, locates its origins in a Jewish and a legal, rather than a Christian and an exegetical, context. Its medieval manifestation in the form of the Latin phrase *Scriptura humane loquitor*, 'Scripture speaks the language of man',[15] is, he points out, a translation of the Jewish phrase *dibra tora kileshon bne 'adam*, literally, 'Torah spoke like the language of [the sons of] man'. Benin notes (1984, p.180) that the Latin version is best rendered into English with Wolfson's phrase (1961, p.3): 'theology...stoops to speak the language of ordinary men'. The transition of the principle of accommodation from legal to exegetical usage, he argues, took place during the medieval period (Funkenstein 1986, p.214). Conversely, Van Bemmelin identifies the origins of the term within the rhetorical tradition of the ancient Romans who:

> used the word [accommodation]...in rhetoric to express the idea that an orator would adapt himself to his audience in his choice of words, gestures and emotions so that he could move their hearts and persuade their minds in whatever direction he wanted. (1998, p.221)

It is clear that a considerable proportion of the spectrum of debate concerning the existence and nature of accommodation is premised on a general (although, for some, reluctant) inability to ignore both the fact and degree of diversity of perspectives within Scripture and the dissonance between Scripture's worldview and that of the contemporary reader. Additionally, the balance between divine inspiration and the

---

15   Funkenstein cites as an example of the usage of the phrase the work of Thomas Aquinas in *Summa Theologica*.

human authors' limitations and capacity for error, and, to a lesser extent, differences between what Scripture seems to convey and objective scientific fact[16] have also been important aspects of the discussion of the theory. What follows is a brief overview of the forms in which these specific issues have been addressed by use of the theory of accommodation.

Intra-biblical diversity or discrepancy

On the first issue, when Sparks poses the important question as to how we know that accommodation has occurred, he specifically evidences (2008, p.230) points where Scripture is perceived to be self-contradictory, presenting 'diverse viewpoints on the self-same matter, respecting…matters of history, linguistics, ethics, theology and religious practice'. At such points, he argues (p.240), instances of accommodation are revealed and it is this that makes it 'an indispensable aspect of interpretation'. To fail to account for accommodation in the text, then, is arguably to make a theological error. Although encompassing aspects of New Testament teaching, for example with regard to contradictions between John's Gospel and the Synoptics, the most commonly perceived manifestation of the challenge of diversity or inconsistency relates to the differences between the obligations imposed by God in the Old and New Testaments. The issue of the Old Testament prohibition of the consumption of pig flesh,[17] which is specifically revoked in Acts 10, when Peter is called to eat precisely that which had until that point been declared unclean, offers a prime example of the dilemma purported to emanate from intra-biblical diversity. This text will assume further significance later in this work from a different, but related, perspective.

This use of the theory of God's accommodative action has a lengthy provenance in theological scholarship, as evidenced by a succession of scholars, beginning with the Church Fathers, including, for example, Justin Martyr (c.103–165)[18] and Origen (c.184–253). Young comments (2013, p.27) that 'the fathers recognized that God accommodated the divine word to the human level not only in the incarnation, but also in

---

16 Recent modes of interpretation have attempted to present a way of reading the text and understanding the origins of the text which mean that the divergence in scientific explanations in Scripture and in science are not so problematic as would *prima facie* appear to be the case. See Wolterstorff 1995, pp.228–9.

17 See, for example, Deuteronomy 14.7: 'The pig is also unclean; although it has a divided hoof, it does not chew the cud. You are not to eat their meat or touch their carcasses.'

18 Justin's argument that the 'task of accommodation was to compose an apologia for Christian non-observance of Torah' is most comprehensively recorded in his *Dialogue with Trypho*, cited in Benin 1993, p.2.

the human language of the Scriptures, which necessarily used types and symbols to speak of what transcends everything in the created order'. In the fourth century, the theme was strongly reiterated by Gregory of Nyssa (c.330–395) and John Chrysostom (c.347–407), among others. Pertinent aspects of their perspectives will be noted below. Yet it should be highlighted here that some contemporary scholars, like Swain, do not specifically characterize the issue of biblical interpretation in which the theory of accommodation arises as a dilemma, and are content to allow for a discrepancy between the Old and New Testament obligations God places on his people. From the perspective of 'progressive revelation', he contends that what was required of the people of God in the Old Testament was simply a precursor to and appropriate picture of what would be fulfilled in the New Testament. 'We do not leave one behind when we embrace the other but find the old integrated into the new' (2011, pp.23–4).

Whether defined in Swain's terms or in the more negative formulation presented by Sparks, general agreement exists that God's accommodative, self-revelatory action is ongoing and often changes both in form and content to meet the requirements of specific people, living in specific contexts, within the framework of his cosmological and eschatological plan to bring all things to perfection (Romans 8.19–21). As Ramm comments, 'revelation must have an anthropomorphic character' (1870, p.99), and if this character is person, time and context-specific, it might reasonably be expected that the people who have profound intellectual disabilities might be accommodated by God in a way that precisely befits their particular situation.

Problems of worldview

The second interpretive challenge in which the theory of accommodation has taken shape relates to Scripture's worldview which to scholars and believers at various points in the history of Christian thought has been at odds with their experience of the world around them. One aspect of this issue is articulated by Sparks (2008, p.230): 'ancient authors used literary genres quite different from our own to audiences living in contexts and facing concerns that were sometimes considerably different from ours'. In her earlier work, Young (2013, p.19) cautions against over-emphasizing the importance of cultural diversity: 'the Bible does not just refer to particular events, or people or things of the past. It refers to other realities which it takes to be realities: God, covenant, atonement, worship... Can these be dismissed as belonging to that culture?' Later, however, she affirms Sparks' position that accommodation is a tool for the necessary exegesis consequent upon 'the limited realm of human understanding, with its risks, potential for distortion in transmission, inevitable particularity within a particular culture and time' (p.27). One prominent manifestation of divergent experiences is located in the discrepancies between biblical explanations of aspects of scientific and historical realities and those offered by objectively established knowledge uncovered throughout post-biblical history, in relation to, for example, the creation narrative and Copernicus' heliocentric theory.[19] So controversial was the latter's perspective on the shape of the earth that many of his contemporaries, both Catholic and Reformers (Luther among them), expressed vociferous opposition to his ideas.[20] Those who castigated Copernicus for his views were committed to a literal interpretation of Joshua 10.12, where God is reported to grant Joshua's request to make the sun stand still, thus, it was understood, proving that it was the sun which was ordinarily revolving and not the earth. Copernicus' supporters used, as did those who rejected a literal reading of the creation narrative, the theory of accommodation to contend for an allegorical interpretation of the recorded event. For such proponents of the theory of accommodation, Funkenstein explains, the Scriptures 'do not contradict science but neither do they contain all of it' (1986, p.216). He notes (p.219) that Jewish as well as Christian exegetes postulate this 'doctrine of permissible allegorization [which acknowledges that] language is, by its nature ambiguous and analogical'.

Calvin's perspective on the matter of scientific anomalies within the text, a view which is apparently more open than that of his Reformer contemporaries, articulates an important accommodative position in which explanations are tailored to fit the intellectual or educational background of their audience:

> [n]or did Moses wish to withdraw us from this pursuit by omitting such things as are peculiar to the art; but because he was ordained a teacher of the unlearned and ignorant as well as the learned, he could not fulfil his office unless he descended to this more elementary method of instruction. (1948, pp.86–7)

---

19 The debate is commonly referred to as the 'Copernicus Revolution' – a sign of the enormity and rarity of the challenge it presented to the geocentric beliefs of ancient Israel.

20 See for example, Luther, M. *Tischreden*, 1.419, English quotation from White, A.D. (1920) *A History of the Warfare of Science with Theology in Christendom, Vol. 1*. New York, NY: Appleton, p.126. Cited in Sparks 2008, p.232.

Significantly for the focus of our discussion, Calvin makes the point that the absence of specific information in the text does not preclude the existence of such information; nor does it invalidate its pursuit, since the human author of the texts in which this scientific 'information' was recorded was relaying only such revelation as could be apprehended or was needed by those to whom the information was addressed. Perhaps it is the case that the search for empirical evidence of the spiritual experience of people with profound intellectual disabilities is in part predicated upon the absence of direct biblical content on this specific subject. In the face of this absence, the weight of other material in the text which stresses the centrality of intentional engagement with the propositions, ideas and instructions conveyed in its words has potential to stimulate a desire to uncover alternative sources of information. Yet, while there is no specific reference in Scripture to whether and how those who cannot engage with the sacred text can nonetheless enjoy a relational experience of God, the biblical content itself offers an abundance of information from which insight into that which is not explicitly outlined can be deduced. Thus the content of the linguistic revelation which cannot be apprehended by *some* provides knowledge which *others* have sufficient capacity to process, so that an understanding of the position of the former in relation to the God who is the source of the revelation can be established.

Human authorship

Further discussions and theories of accommodation emerge with regard to the limitations of the human authors of the text. Augustine's (354–430 CE) comment in *Homilies* on John's teaching on the incarnation serves as a key example:

> John spoke of the matter not as it is but even he, only as he was able…it was a man that spoke of God. Inspired indeed by God, but still a man. Because he was a man he said something; if he had not been inspired he would have said nothing. But because he was a man inspired, he spoke not the whole, but what a man could, he spoke.

Augustine's perception on the limitations of such divinely inspired human insight is consonant with what some modern theologians (and philosophers) would describe as practical realism – an understanding that '"perfect" human knowledge is an illusion which mistakenly confuses good and useful knowledge with perfect, God-like knowledge' (Sparks 2008, p.43). On the wider issue of divine accommodation to the limitations of the human authors and readers of the text, and God's incapacity for error, Sparks (p.256) emphatically insists that 'the voices of accommodationists from the first century to the present are on this point unanimous…accommodation does not introduce errors into Scripture; it is instead a theological explanation for the presence of human errors in Scripture'. Differences of opinion on the complexities of this issue, including the existence of error and the extent to which and how account should be taken of human fallibility in the text, proliferate (and cannot be explored within the confines of this book).[21] The most pertinent principle in our context is that which underpins any use of the theory of accommodation: that although and because human beings (even divinely inspired human beings) cannot know God as he is, he condescends to reveal to them what he wants them to know of himself.[22]

Accommodation: motifs of the divine disposition

The origins of the theory of accommodation, found primarily in hermeneutical discussions, provide important insights that support the contention that God chooses to tailor his revelation to fit the needs of those to whom he is revealing himself. An examination of the theory does not, however, merely offer evidence for the possibility that God would do such a thing; it also illuminates aspects of the disposition of God towards human beings that underpin the fact, form and extent of his accommodative action.

Accommodation: a picture of divine flexibility

In one of the principal texts cited to substantiate the idea of accommodation as progressive revelation, Ezekiel 20, God declaims the unfaithfulness of his people following their escape from Egypt and how they turned aside from his specific instructions on whose fulfilment his continued favour was to be contingent. Conversely, however, for the most part, the regulations which God ordained in this period were not portrayed as obligations whose burdensome nature would be punitive in relation to the disobedience of the people of Israel, but as opportunities to find renewed relationship and life, notwithstanding their misconduct:

---

21 For an interesting synopsis of the issues involved in the modes of interpretation of errantists and errantists, see Wolterstorff 1995, pp.227–9; also Young 1990, Chapter 1: 'The Quest for Authenticity.'

22 The incompleteness of the knowledge of God provides a foundation for apophatic mysticism to be acknowledged later in this work.

'I gave them my decrees and made known to them my laws, by which, the person who obeys them shall live. Moreover also I gave them my Sabbaths, as a sign between us, so they would know that I the Lord made them holy' (11–12). The fact that this text stresses the 'goodness' of God's laws, makes it perhaps more remarkable that, a little later in this narrative, God speaks what might be perceived as the extraordinary words, 'I gave them other statutes that were not good and laws through which they could not live; I defiled them through their gifts – the sacrifice of every firstborn – that I might fill them with horror so that they would know that I am the Lord' (24–5). In a dramatic instance of his accommodated revelation, God's response to his people's disobedience involves giving them commands and obligations which would *not* lead to life. Bowen (2010, p.117) describes these commands as God's 'shock therapy to move Israel out of their persistent rebelliousness'. By drastically confounding and disturbing his people in order that they might in the end be enabled to see who he is, God demonstrates the importance he attaches to a life-changing revelation of himself in the human context. In contrast to the thrust of its earlier part, 'that God gave "not good" laws suggests that God's reputation is not, after all, the over-riding concern of this chapter' (p.117).

This issue parallels a wider debate concerning the difficulty of accepting that God would require of his people what were conceived to be distasteful practices, akin to those of neighbouring idolatrous nations whose forms of religious observance the Israelites were all too often prone to adopt. In response, and with unequivocal use of a theory of accommodation which provides explanation in both allegorical and literal senses, Aquinas writes:

> [T]he ceremonies of the old law had two causes; one literal, in that they were directed to divine worship; the other, figurative as directed to the prefiguring of Christ. The sacrificial ceremonies withdrew men from offering sacrifices to idols… They were instituted so that the people in their eagerness to offer sacrifice might do so to God rather than to idols. (*Summa Theologica I*, IIae, pp.102–3)

In the context of our discussion, such a picture of the extent to which God will accommodate himself to human ways and waywardness in time and context supports the idea that he will allow no obstacle to persist in preventing the apprehension of his revelation by human beings. For people with profound intellectual disabilities, then, an inability to engage cognitively with the words of the gospel, which Jensen and others hold to be indispensable, cannot be construed as an obstacle. The diversity and particularity of God's modes of accommodation generates confidence in their capacity to encounter God, or rather his capacity and determination to encounter them, undermining the urgency of a search for empirical evidence of whether, where, when and how these encounters occur.

The general understanding of accommodation as a device for continual adaptation of the divine revelation to meet the demands of a particular time, circumstance and culture to facilitate a divine–human relationship was also used to legitimize the considerable degree of diversity within the practices of the Church (Funkenstein 1986, p.225).[23] Such variances further demonstrate the flexibility within the spectrum of God's approach to his communication with humanity, for which Strabo (paraphrased by Funkenstein) argues, 'God Himself has set an example' (p.225). Does this continuous flexibility, when held alongside the aspects of the revelation which stress God's love for and desire for salvific encounter with all of humanity, offer a vision for God's revelatory intervention in the lives of those for whom engagement with a word-based revelation is not accessible? If, as Funkenstein argues, 'religion has progressed in accord with the refinement of human capacity' (p.217), why would such progression not extend to a level that encompasses people who have profound intellectual disabilities? Tertullian's earlier argument that not only is the accommodated revelation progressive but the capacity of its recipients also, in that 'human mediocrity was incapable of accepting everything at once' (1.4, 1209), supports Funkenstein's view. Must such progression be understood only in a chronological and linear sense? Might it not also operate within the context of the broad spectrum of human intellectual capacity? This idea that the relationship between accommodation and progressive revelation takes account of levels of knowledge and education re-emerges in a consideration of divine condescension.

Accommodation: a means of divine condescension

Calvin's work has offered a significant contribution to the debate concerning the importance of the accommodation theory. Battles explains (1998, p.21) that '[f]or Calvin, the understanding of God's accommodation to the limits and needs of the human condition was a central feature of the interpretation of Scripture and of the entire range

---

23   The author cites the work of Walafrid Strabo to substantiate this position.

of his theological work'. He contextualizes Calvin's position (aligning it with that of Van Bemmelin) within the tradition of classical rhetoric in which 'the verb *accommodare* is widely found in the Latin rhetoricians in the same sense of fitting, adapting, adjusting language, of building a speech-bridge between the matter of discourse and the intended audience' (1998, p.22).

Calvin's position is helpfully epitomized in the following unequivocal statement in which he refers specifically to God's response to the deficiencies of human comprehension:

> For who is so devoid of intellect as not to understand that God, in so speaking, lisps with us as nurses are wont to do with little children? Such modes of expression do not so much express what kind of a being God is as accommodate the knowledge of him to our feebleness. In so doing He must, of course, stoop far below His proper height. (1844, pp.263–4)

This is perhaps the central metaphor of the theory of accommodation and is common to many of the arguments of its proponents: it describes the way in which God can be understood as stooping to the level of human beings in the way in which an adult stoops to the level of a child. The underlying principle here is pivotal to the fresh perspective presented in this work, namely that it is legitimate to understand that divine revelation is often, if not always, attuned to the capacities of its particular recipients to apprehend it. In the case of Moses' hearers of scientifically unsustainable explanations, these are people whom Calvin would describe as having limited education and understanding; in our context, they are people with profound intellectual disabilities.

Calvin's perspective is pre-dated by much earlier theological voices. Chrysostom, for example, as well as highlighting the anthropomorphic language of the Bible as God's accommodation to human limitations (to which further reference will be made below), establishes the principle that God condescends to weaker natures, by illustrating how he does so in relation to all created beings, whether angelic or human (Benin 1993, p.68). In relation to the prophet's extraordinary vision described in Isaiah 6.1–2 in which the seraphim must cover their faces in the unendurable presence of God, Chrysostom comments that '*C'est pour Dieu, se fait d'apparaître et de se montrer non pas tel qu'il est, mais tel qu'il peut* être *vu par celui qui est capable de cette vision, en proportionnant*

l'aspect qu'il se présente de lui-même à la *faiblesse de ceux qui le regardent.'*[24]
Benin, in consonance with Chrysostom, describes similar imagery as
'proportional revelation…if one hears a prophet claim to have seen
God, this does not mean the divine essence but a manifestation achieved
through divine condescension' (1993, p.68). This, Sparks argues (2008,
p.239), is the 'true nature of accommodation: accommodation provides
greater access to the divine truth by depicting some things as other than
they are'. It is perhaps worth emphasizing that the greater access afforded
by accommodation is greater only in the sense of exceeding what could
have been accessed had divine condescension not been necessary. Thus
human beings are, for the most part, permitted by the linguistically based
accommodation of Scripture to see more of God than they naturally could,
by seeing less of him than there actually is to see, as the full revelation would
render him entirely inapprehensible by or blindingly incapacitating not only
to the human eye but to the entirety of the human person. In Isaiah's record
of his vision, it is the language that paints the picture, but even the picture
is far removed from the reality. Words are clearly not the only source of
revelation, and those for whom words are not relevant should not be
deemed incapable of accessing an experience of God that might perhaps
be even more immediately presented than that which is depicted in
words. This idea is developed below.

Accommodation: an expression of goodness and desire

Origen's response to the contextual interpretive issues highlighted earlier
sets the use of accommodative biblical language firmly within the positive
parameters of the desire and benevolence of God in disclosing himself to
human beings, despite their inability to apprehend him as he is.

> Just as when we are talking to very small children we do not assume
> as the object of our instruction any strong understanding in them,
> but say what we have to say accommodating (*harmosamenas*) to the
> small understanding of those whom we have before us…so the Word
> of God seems to have disposed the things that were written, adapting
> the suitable parts of his message to the capacity of its hearers and their
> ultimate profit. (Origen V. XIV)

---

24 'It is for God to appear and reveal Himself, not as he is, but in the way he can be seen
by one who is incapable of seeing him. In this way, God reveals Himself in proportion
to the weakness of those who behold Him.' St Jean Chrysotome *Sur l'incomprehensibilité
de Dieu* (Homélies I-V) (SCh 28 bis), 2nd ed. A.M, Malingrey (Paris: Les Editions du
Cerf, 1970) III, 3 722/200 (my translation).

Gregory of Nyssa describes the 'ultimate profit' to which Origen alludes in terms of an apprehension of the love of God.

> We account for God's willingness to admit men to communion with Himself by His love towards mankind. But since that which is by nature finite cannot rise above its prescribed limits or lay hold upon the Superior Nature of the Most High, on this account, He, bringing His power, so full of love for humanity down to the level of human weakness, [*hemeteron asthenes*]. (Gregorii Nysseni *Opera*, *Vol. 3.1*, pp.1048–9)

In this sense, accommodation is presented both as a *tool* for revelation and a depiction of the extent of God's loving desire for self-disclosure and relationship. If this understanding reflects a tenable explanation of what is occurring when accommodation is identifiable within the text, then it seems legitimate to ask whether God's accommodative activity of self-disclosure must be confined within the text. Might God, out of the reservoirs of the same love that motivated his accommodative communication found within the biblical text, be assumed to continue to engage in such accommodative action in ways that are proportionate to the capacity of other potential recipients of his revelation? If this were to be the case, we might ask in what ways and to what extent he might do so? Is there any evidence from which to conclude that at some point on this continuum or spectrum of human capacity the adaptation process has, will or must come to an end?

Gregory's perspective is further expanded when he presents the view that the metaphor for understanding God's accommodative action should not only encompass the use of simpler language than might be the case but be extended to include the idea of God not using comprehensible language at all:

> [S]o the Divine power…though exalted far above our nature and inaccessible to all approach, like a tender mother who joins in the inarticulate utterances of her babe, gives to our human nature what it is capable of receiving and thus in the various manifestations of God to man he both adapts Himself to man and speaks in human language and assumes wrath and pity and such-like emotions so that through feelings corresponding to our own infantile life, might be led as by the hand, and lay hold of the Divine nature by means of words which His foresight has given. (Gregory of Nyssa, *NPNF* 2, 5:292)

So his metaphor depicts God communicating by non-linguistic means, like the mother of a newborn infant, stooping below or, perhaps more appropriately expressed, *beyond* the level of verbal expression. She channels her deepest emotion to her baby in such a form that the infant will be capable of grasping what she is communicating, namely her love for her child. Not only does she lower the level or depart from the natural vehicle of her own speech; she takes up the baby's own mode of self-expression; she adopts the precise 'non-verbal' sounds and gestures which are the infant's sole options for expressing him/herself. There is nothing ambiguous about what is occurring in this encounter; anyone witnessing the scene will understand what is passing between mother and baby – a non-linguistic, but no less comprehensible, immediate or intimate, communication of love.

While Gregory's explanation might be criticized as an extreme interpretation of aspects of God's self-disclosure, it can be defended in the light of clear evidence in the biblical text of the parenthood of God both as reality and metaphor. In the former instances, the language is not metaphorically anthropomorphic but descriptive of the actuality of relationship. Trinitarian Christian belief avers that God, in His co-eternity, co-equality and co-essence, is Father, Son and Spirit.[25] Clearly, the action of parenting and the status of parenthood is intrinsic to God's being, and, through Christ, by his Spirit, this organic and most intimate relationship is extended to those who receive the grace which allows it to be appropriated (John 1.14). So the Apostle Paul writes of human persons being 'adopted' into the family of God (Romans 8.16–17). In addition, the biblical text specifically uses the mother–infant relationship as a simile to illustrate the depth of emotional connection between God and his people: 'Can a mother forget the baby at her breast and have no compassion on the child she has borne? Though she may forget, I will not forget you!' (Isaiah 49.15).

Fundamentally, the significance here of such a depiction of God's accommodative self-disclosure lies primarily in the idea that what might be described as God's chosen 'accommodative range' – the degree to which he will adapt his ways of being and communicating – is not limited to what can be accomplished by the simplification or 'watering-down' of complex theological concepts. God does not simply 'take the edge off' the more complex aspects of his being in order to

---

25   A broad range of sources on the doctrine are summarized in Sanders, F., 'The Trinity' in Webster *et al.* 2007, pp.35–53.

disclose himself to those he has made and with whom he would be in relationship. Rather, he does what needs to be done and, moreover, what is instinctively to be done, in order to reveal himself and his love. The descriptive and metaphorical evidence of God's parenting activity across the biblical text substantiates the idea that God's accommodating action might not only involve communicating by means of less complicated verbal language than might be the case if a parent were speaking to an adult rather than a child. It might also involve communicating without recognizable words at all, to those for whom words have no power to convey meaning. Moreover, such revelation, given without the use of verbal expression might even seem, like a mother's babbling with her infant, to be somehow more immediate and unconfined than anything words can embrace, however powerfully they are utilized. Gregory's explanation of God's range of accommodation suggests that God will use whatever form of communication is necessary to bridge the gap between himself and any human being's ability to apprehend him.

Accommodation: communication in anthropomorphism

Additional support for my argument emerges in the historical debates which focus on the use of the theory of accommodation to explain the significant degree of anthropomorphic and corporeal depictions of God[26] contained within the Hebrew Bible. The theory is here used to reconcile the seeming incongruity of God's self-description in anthropomorphic language with one of the core messages of the text – the intrinsic difference in the essence and being of God from that of the human beings he created. Fairburn (1859, p.107) emphasizes that the Church Fathers explained 'Scripture…as accommodating itself to men's infirmities or habits when it speaks of God as possessing human parts and passions'. Furthermore, accommodation offers a response to the specific problem raised by the cultural context in which the text was written. In this context, an anthropomorphic depiction of God seemed, in a largely pagan culture, to demean the status of a divine being.[27] Norris comments that this use of anthropomorphism was consistent with the first of Gregory of Nazianzus' hermeneutical principles, namely that:

---

26   These are numerous and recurrent, particularly throughout the Old Testament canon. See Numbers 11.23, 'the arm of the Lord'; Isaiah 37.17, 'open your eyes, Lord, and see'; Psalm 34.17, 'the Lord's ears are attentive to my cry'.

27   For a concise discussion on this point, see Middleton 2005.

[s]ome things that do not occur in reality are mentioned in the Holy Writ... God has neither human emotions nor acts in human ways even though Scripture says he does. He has no body in any normal sense. Such things are apparently ascribed to him but they do not exist. (Wickham and Williams 1991, p.204)

Seisenberger (1911, p.446) insists that 'it is a well-considered design that the Holy Scripture speaks of God as of a being resembling man, and ascribes to him a face, eyes, ears... This is done out of consideration for man's power of comprehension.' There is, Norris comments, 'a human *need* for mental pictures, for bodily analogies' (1991, p.204). If God provides the mental pictures because they are necessary for human beings to apprehend him, might he equally make adequate and appropriate provision for the needs of those for whom the comprehension of analogies is not accessible?

Accommodation: the fundamental aim of communication

Further on the use of language, Benin comments (1993, p.94) that for Augustine, 'communication is the key'. Augustine's focus on both written and spoken aspects of the divine revelation is particularly interesting in this context for, in his perspective on accommodation, communication, both in its means and content, is not confined to words. God has, he explains 'played with our infantile character by providing parables and similes – such as fire and smoke and the cloudy pillar, as by visible words' (1961, p.98). Undoubtedly, words are, for him, both the greatest communicative tools and the greatest signs by which revelation was accomplished, yet they remain only tools and signs. Particular words in themselves are not the beginning and end of any communicated revelation; they are to be understood as more than their immediate meaning might convey; they are signs to realities beyond themselves and they stimulate or emerge in response to a quest for such realities (Markus 1957, pp.69–70). According to Benin, Augustine's position was that 'human teachers teach through words but Christ the "Interior Teacher" dwelling in our minds, provides both the appropriate vocabulary and the reality behind the words' (2003, p.95). This play on words makes use of the word 'vocabulary' in a metaphorical rather than a literal sense, providing a vibrant elucidation of the argument that, for people with profound intellectual disabilities, their inability to process verbal language is entirely irrelevant to a capacity for divinely constituted spiritual experience. Why would there not be a 'vocabulary' of communication between them and the 'Interior Teacher' which does not consist in human language? Arnold reminds his readers (1989, pp.128–9) that 'the very means by which we receive our knowledge, which is language and the observation of the senses, are themselves so imperfect that they could not possibly convey to the mind other than imperfect notions of the truth' – perhaps also the knowledge of how God might convey such truth.

Revelation and accommodation in Christ

It is impossible to explore any concept of biblical revelation without acknowledgement of the foundational premise of Christian theology that God's ultimate revelation was not accomplished in human words but in the divine Word λόγος (*logos*), God's incarnate presence among human beings (John 1.1, 14). In its fullest expression, the Word of God as revealed to human beings is not a 'word' in its common sense at all, but a human being, flesh and blood, tangible and vulnerable (albeit one whose divinity was not diminished by the humanity in which he participated).[28] Benin (1993, p.65) summarizes the prominent perspective on the incarnation among theologians who emphasize the theory of accommodation as 'the extreme example of accommodation and condescension'. A comprehensive discussion of the subject is far beyond the limits of this work and what follows is a brief attempt to highlight some of the particular issues which pertain to the general subject under investigation – that of the relationship between revelation and verbal language.

As Young highlights (2013, p.71), 'Christian theology affirmed that God had accommodated the divine self to the limitations of human language and our creaturely existence, both in Scripture and in the incarnation'. Indeed, she expresses the view that 'the complete incarnation of one who was totally transcendent was the crown of accommodation' (p.395). Before embarking on an exploration of what it means for God to be revealed in the Person of Jesus Christ, it is appropriate to acknowledge Barth's statement (2009, p.113) that 'this "God with us" [that] has happened…is incapable of any exegesis or of even the slightest addition or subtraction'. The subject of the exploration which follows remains a profound mystery (Colossians 1.26). The

---

28   So Barth argues that 'genuine Deity includes in itself genuine humanity' (1967, p.50, first published 1960).

foundational principle of Christological thought, however, is that Christ is not simply an additional revelation but the ultimate revelation of God; the revelation which (or, more appropriately, who) supersedes all that has come before (Hebrews 1.1–3). Young succinctly summarizes Barth's position: 'the true "subject" of theology and of Scripture is the incarnate Lord, and only in so far as Scripture and theology communicate that Person through narratives about him is it persuasive or "authoritative"' (1990a, p.170). Similarly, for Rahner, as Carr comments (1973, p.367), 'the single mystery of divine self-communication is given in the doctrine of Christ'. Also asserting the revelatory uniqueness of Christ, Ritschl argues that 'Christ founds his religion with the claim that he brings the perfect revelation of God, so that beyond what he brings no further revelation is necessary' (1990, p.289). Baillie makes the same point: 'It is in Christ that we see God. We see Him veiled and humiliated, but it is nevertheless God that we see' (1939, p.196).

Perhaps the most significant statement of Christ's divinity and revelatory essence is John 1.1–3: 'In the beginning was the Word, and the Word was with God and the Word was God.' While the most common translation of the λόγος is 'word', it is a much more complex and a multi-dimensional term than a basic usage of this term conveys, with inherent connotations of 'mind', 'idea', 'thought', 'rational plan'. It was not an exclusively Hebraic idea but was commonly found in other religious traditions and, significantly, given the New Testament context, in Greek philosophy where it 'denoted something like the world-soul… the rational principle of the universe' (Morris 1992, p.115). As such, the term would be widely recognized by its first hearers and understood as signifying something very important.

While, as Morris highlights (pp.115–17), some commentators have understood John's thinking here to have emerged out of the context of a Hellenistic understanding of the term, it is the term's Jewish background that has been most significant for its comprehension among many biblical scholars. Referring to what is most commonly conceived as the parallel passage to John 1.1–3, Morris comments (p.118) that 'the Word [in John 1.1–3] irresistibly turns our attention to the repeated "and God said"' of the opening chapter of the Bible. The Word is God's creative Word (Genesis 1.3).' Bernard too is uncompromisingly aligned with the Hebraic perspective on the term, asserting (1948, p.1) that it:

> finds its origin in the Jewish teaching about the Word of God rather than in the philosophy of Greek Gnosticism…it is the Hebrew doctrine

of the Divine Word going forth (λόγος προφόρικος) rather than the Greek doctrine of Divine reason (λόγος ἐνδιάθετος).

This position is supported by the fact that Hebraic references to the 'Word of God' inevitably connote concepts of the divine wisdom and the law (again prevalent in Psalm 119) both as spoken words and as entities which stand in close relationship to God, as well as the understanding of the Word as 'an effective agent for accomplishing of the divine will' (Morris 1992, p.115). McHugh, while acknowledging Greek and other influences on John's articulation of the earthly appearance of the *logos,* reiterates the correlation between 'Word of God' in Christ and the 'Word of God' of the Old Testament where the 'sense of John 1.14 is that all that had previously been true of the Word and Wisdom of God in the Old Testament is from a particular moment in time, the moment of the incarnation, embodied in Jesus of Nazareth, Jesus the Christ' (2009, p.95).

Other contemporary scholars such as Endberg-Pedersen make an argument for an expanded reading of the text. While accepting that 'the concept of λόγος...is often, and rightly, connected with the figure of "wisdom" in Hellenistic Jewish literature' (2012, p.30), he nonetheless promotes a case for identifying the origins of John's use of the term in Stoic thought in which λόγος and πνεῦμα (*pneuma*) are 'two sides of the same thing'. He proposes that the λόγος present at and instrumental in creation came to be present in the person Jesus at his baptism when the πνεῦμα descended on him.

> The *logos* was present together with God at the beginning of time and the whole cosmos and everything in it were created by the *pneumatic* (and the cognitive *logos*) when this physical force gave structure to the world... The *logos* also became flesh when it came to be present as *pneuma* in...the human being Jesus. (p.35)

Thus the man Jesus becomes the *logos* of God by the indwelling of the Spirit of God. This way of reading John's Gospel through the lens of the double-sided entity which is *logos* and *pneuma* is pertinent to an understanding of how the incarnate God comes to be present not just *to* but *within* human persons – something which will be further explored below.

While a definitive conclusion to the debate as to which perspective had the greatest influence on John's description of Jesus in the Prologue to his Gospel seems elusive, William Temple's concise articulation (1947, p.4) of the Hebraic and Greek understandings and roots of *logos*, which we might assume were both at play in the author's mind, provides a helpful summary:

> [The *logos*], alike for Jew and Gentile represents the ruling fact of the universe, and represents that fact as the self-expression of God. The Jew will remember that 'by the Word of the Lord were the heavens made'; the Greek will think of the rational principle of which all natural laws are particular expressions. (p.4)

Morris' conclusion on the issue is that, 'for [John], the Word was not a principle. But a living Being and the source of life; not a personification but a person and that Person divine' (1992, p.123). Brunner adopts a similar position: 'The fact that He Himself takes the place of the spoken word is precisely the category which distinguishes the Old Testament revelation – the revelation through speech – from the New Testament revelation, the revelation in Christ' (1950, p.27). Thus it is clear that the 'Word' in the Old as well as the New Testament is both a word and much more than a word, and that the *logos* of the New Testament is a Person, the Person of Christ, the Second Person of the Godhead. Nonetheless, as has been alluded to above, the use of the incarnation to support ideas of revelation without verbal communication based on the *logos* passage in John 1 is strongly contested by some scholars of whose Jensen's is a representative voice. 'The revelation is not the proper nouns "Jesus Christ", but the proposition, "Jesus is Christ, the Lord." The divine word comes to us in, and not apart from, the words of this gospel' (2002, p.49). It might be asked whether Jensen is confusing the content of revelation – that Jesus Christ is Lord, albeit this is perhaps a somewhat limited account of its content – with the revelation itself which or who is Christ. If what God 'said' through human authors is an accommodation of who he is, then in the coming of Christ we actually have who he is. The concept of the revelation of God as a proposition rather than a Person is far from convincing.

What is clear is that this revelation in Christ challenges 'all abstract presuppositions about God's nature, both ancient and modern. To know God we begin not with general definitions of the "divine", but with the particular Person, Jesus of Nazareth' (Campbell 1995, p.396). Godet insists (1969, p.290) that John 'wished to describe Jesus Christ as the *absolute revelation* of God to the world, to bring back all divine revelations to Him as their living centre, and to proclaim the matchless grandeur of his appearance in the midst of humanity'. Yet Jesus Christ, the *logos* of God, not only respected but continued to utter the words of God (John 14.10), thus precluding any possibility that God's self-disclosure in Christ negates or undermines either the spoken words of the Old Testament or the spoken words of the New. On the contrary, Jesus declared his purpose to be that of fulfilling the Law, not abolishing it (Matthew 5.17), and yet it was in his personal engagement with humanity in its own place and within its own limitations that this fulfilment of the Law was achieved. God's engagement with humanity is not distant or propositional but present and relational. The *logos* of God and all that the Person of Christ does to bridge the gap between God and human beings both reveals the depth of God's desire to engage in relationship with them and demonstrates that, in the enacting of this desire, he is not only far from constricted by linguistic methods but that such methods alone are entirely inadequate to the task. On the contrary, the language which communicates so much of what is known of God is merely a communicative tool used to point to the reality which is God himself.

Implications for people with profound intellectual disabilities

While the argument here has been presented through the interpretation of words, the nature and content of what has been explored is such that it offers grounds for conceiving of the possibility of non-verbally founded experience of God for people who have no use for words at all. Again, it is important to re-emphasize that if such a proposition is valid, its validity does not rest on a need to dispense with words in order to experience God. It offers an *additional* and not a *contradictory* perspective which pertains specifically to people with profound intellectual disabilities as people whom we must conclude God loves and desires to be in relationship with, but who cannot be made alert to that relational encounter with him by some of the means through which others can. Carson succinctly articulates the fundamental argument being made here: 'If the transcendent personal God is to communicate with us, his finite and sinful creatures, he must in some measure *accommodate* Himself to and condescend to our capacity to receive that revelation' (1986, p.26). It is my view that people with profound intellectual disabilities are inevitably included within this 'us'.

Acknowledging the complexities of the *logos* concept, the reality that the greatest act of accommodation is not verbal but relational, not a proposition but a person, confirms a basis for the understanding that access to words is not the defining aspect of any person's potential to be reached by and experience God. This chapter has highlighted some important components of the theological argument that experience of God is accessible to those who have no cognitive capacities for linguistically based comprehension. The immense significance of words within the grand scheme of God's self-disclosing action has been acknowledged, and a range of material emanating from a biblical theology of God's self-revelation has been explored, from which have emerged significant principles underpinning the argument that God acts to facilitate encounters with people with profound intellectual disabilities. The fundamental aim of accommodation is relational communication between God and human beings. Words are not the exclusive means by which this communication occurs. Words are merely signs and pointers to a reality which is behind and transcends the means of its expression – the person Jesus Christ who is the greatest accommodation to humanity's inability to apprehend God.

The breadth of human incapacity

What, then, might be the appropriate 'vocabulary' for persons who do not apprehend verbal communication? Whatever it is, it cannot be beyond the capacity of God. For Calvin, as Battles (1998, p.35) comments, human capacity was the key concept in the discussion of accommodation. It is, in part, the theory of accommodation that informs us that human capacity is not the determinant issue in the divine–human relationship. Those who argue for the indispensability of words, and the intelligence to understand and respond to them, are in danger of underestimating the depths of universal human incapacity when it comes to understanding God. Battles is adamant on this point:

> We try to measure God's immeasurableness by our small measure. But it is God who knows the incalculable difference in measure between His infinity and our finiteness, and accordingly accommodates the one to the other in the way in which he reveals Himself to us. (p.35)

Ultimately, it is not human incapacity in any form that matters, but God's infinite capacity to accommodate his revelation to it. At its centre, the Christian revelation of God is a matter of mystery, crafted and implemented by the supernatural power and activity of its divine author, and what lies within this mystery and how and what is communicated in it cannot be fully accommodated to human understanding. Again commenting on the Nazianzian view, Norris underlines this point (1991, p.112): '[i]ntellectual activities may lead us part of the way; they may even point to God's existence, but God's essence is beyond our powers of expression. Enfleshed human beings do not have the capacity to grasp God's nature except in faithful acceptance of the mystery.' It would, then, be inappropriate to attempt to restrict the depth of this mystery in a way that supports a view that the revelation might be inaccessible to some of those created human beings, simply as a consequence of their lack of linguistic ability. As Sparks (2008, p.253) warns, 'We are wise to hesitate before we say what God can and cannot do.'

Returning to Swain's comment (2011, p.8) that 'communication, theologically understood is never less than an exchange of words', the counter-question that might be posed is whether a non-verbal encounter with God should inevitably be perceived as *less than* words. Does the absence of words inherently mean a lesser degree of revelation than that which might be achieved by linguistic means? Cannot God be encountered personally, either before or apart from their utterance? The substantial theological scholarship which perceives verbal expression and cognitive appropriation of truth to be essential for apprehending God creates tensions in relation to the view that, for some, words or the lack of them do not have the last word. The following chapter will further investigate some of these tensions while attempting to expand the parameters of such constraining theological horizons in the context of people with profound intellectual disabilities.

4

THEOLOGICAL OBJECTIONS AND POSSIBILITIES

Emerging from the wider theory of God's accommodation to humanity, we have uncovered a fresh way of thinking about the spiritual experience of people with profound intellectual disabilities, founded on the premise that the self-disclosure of God to such persons is no less conceivable than is his self-disclosure to any human being, albeit that the means by which this is achieved might appear markedly different, or, in fact, might not be apparent at all to other human beings, and its occurrence need not be empirically identifiable. If God's encounter with people who do not have profound intellectual disabilities is entirely dependent on his condescension to their capacity to apprehend him, then his ongoing condescension to people who do is nothing more than an aspect or further unfolding of his accommodative action.

In further developing this understanding, it is essential that we critique potential frameworks within which the depth of God's condescension might be understood, especially in light of the inability of people with profound intellectual disabilities to engage with traditional sources of revelation. At the outset, however, it must be emphasized that there is no intention here to contest widely accepted tenets of the Christian faith. The purpose of what follows is not to create a theological courtroom where opposing parties assume an adversarial stance in order to reach adjudication as to which version of two contradictory narratives is accurate. Instead, a contextualized perspective specific to the particular issue of the spirituality of people with profound intellectual disabilities is put forward. Nonetheless, while this perspective does not involve a contradiction of wider established doctrinal understandings, it has potential to add to the body of theological knowledge by offering additional insights emerging from the discrete area of a theology of profound intellectual disability.

Theological tensions

The ideas and perspectives presented in my work are entirely predicated on the Christian theology of the God who creates, loves and pursues relationships with human beings. Yet, throughout this faith tradition, the ultimate cost of such pursuance is continually and unambiguously identified as the sacrificial death of Christ, necessitated by the condition of human sinfulness. Any argument that intentional intellectual human response to this radical divine intervention is *not* a necessary aspect of appropriation of the reconciliation it offers has potential to raise theological questions concerning the role of the human being in the reception of the offer of divine grace. The soteriological perspective which emphasizes dual divine and human agency in the process of salvation and thus promotes the necessity of specific subjective human action in response to God's pre-emptive grace is a significant one. Indeed, this is one aspect of the wider debate regarding human agency which permeates much of the anthropological perspectives advanced by recent disability theology and, as has been highlighted in the preceding discussion of Haslam's work, is a matter of some continuing concern.

In the soteriological context, what is understood by some to present a difficulty for people with profound intellectual disabilities is articulated by Migliore:

> Christian life is based on the grace of God in Jesus Christ to whom we are united by the power of the Spirit. On the objective side, new life in Christ is rooted in God's transforming work of justification, sanctification, and vocation. On its subjective side, Christian life is the free appropriation of God's grace in faith, in faith, hope and love. (2004, p.235)

For many systematic theologians in the Reformed tradition, acquisition of the knowledge of the gospel message and thus of a correct way of thinking about God paves the way for the resolution of the moral and relational incompatibility of the holy, infinite God and the sinful, finite human being. In this sense, the mind is of central importance. Grudem (1994, p.709), for example, asserts: 'Of course it is necessary that we have some knowledge of who God is and what He has done, for "how are they to believe in him of whom they have not heard?"' Baillie argues that:

> [the spiritual life] finds its only beginnings in the revelation to our finite minds of One whose transcendent perfection constitutes upon

our lives a claim so sovereign that the least attempt to deny it awakens in us a sense of sin and shame; and thus is initiated the sequence, ever extending itself as the revelation of the divine nature becomes deeper and fuller, of confession, repentance, forgiveness, reconciliation and the new life of fellowship. *There is no other spiritual sequence than this.* (1939, p.119)

This is a key aspect of the soteriological debate. Grudem (1994, p.670) explains that the Reformers' *ordo salutis*, the proclamation and hearing of the gospel, followed by an intentional personal response of faith and repentance begin the process of what actually occurs at the point when a human being comes into an initial saving and transforming relationship with God. In Martin Luther's thought, the concept of *apprehendere*, which signifies the reception by the human being of the saving faith offered by God, significantly involves an intellectual process. 'For Luther...*apprehendo* means intellectual apprehension, understanding and comprehension...whereby the object of the knowledge becomes the property of the knowing subject' (Vainio 2012, p.141). Coming to know Christ, Barth insists (1962, p.39), occurs through a faith response by which 'God grants [to the human being] grace to *think* correctly about Him...and comes within his system as the object of his thinking'. Grudem echoes this position, insisting that intellectual assent to the tenets of the faith, though not representing the entirety of the process of personally appropriating the salvific action of God, is nonetheless an essential component. What he perceives as the necessary element of repentance involves:

> a heartfelt sorrow for sin, a renouncement of it and a sincere commitment to forsake it and walk in obedience to Christ... [This is], like faith, an intellectual *understanding* (that sin is wrong), and emotional *approval* of the teachings of Scripture regarding sin and a *personal decision to turn from it*. (1994, pp.711–13; emphasis added)

Commenting on what they perceive to be the pivotal importance of the intellect, specifically in relation to the participation of people with profound intellectual disabilities in a relationship with God, Peter and Mary Birchenall (1986, p.150) insist that 'people with a profound mental handicap possess a limited ability to reason at the complex level, and are therefore not able to...develop any sort of faith'.

Potential theological parallels

One potential strategy for addressing some of the theological issues briefly articulated above might be to look for comparable situations to that in which people with profound intellectual disabilities find themselves.[1] Perhaps the most obvious parallel source of insight lies in theological perspectives on the status of infants. Neither they nor people with profound intellectual disabilities can access linguistic communication; neither can process complex theological ideas; neither can make cognitive responses to postulations of truth. The subject of the soteriological status of infants and of children deemed to have not yet attained the intellectual maturity to positively or negatively respond to the offer of grace in Christ, often referred to as the age of understanding, or of accountability or discretion,[2] has been one of intense historical controversy and division both across and within denominational boundaries. This contentiousness is particularly evident in the debate within and between Catholic and Protestant theologies concerning the concept of original sin, the innocence or, in the view of some, sinfulness, of infants,[3] in addition to issues of the role of sacrament, baptism, predestination and divine election. It is inherently impossible to begin to do justice to the depth of theological perspectives in this complex area,[4] but the following brief discussion of selective opinions on the issue represents an acknowledgement of the breadth of the diversity of voices across a broad spectrum of theological positions, and highlights some which are particularly pertinent to this subject.

Among the earliest prominent contributions to the argument, Augustine's position is interesting for its apparent ambiguity. Stortz (2001, p.84) explains that while he insists that baptism of infants is a precursor to their right standing before God, and that 'in [God's] sight

---

1   The position of those who never hear anything of the Christian gospel message might be further proffered as such an example, but the differences between this situation and that of people who lack the cognitive skills to demonstrate an understanding of what might be readily available to them, as well as the body of theological debate on the subject, preclude its exploration here.

2   Two points are noted here: first, there is no specific biblical source for this term, although the Old Testament indicates that an age of moral responsibility to the Law was recognized at around the age of 12 years; second, the concept nonetheless occupies a prominent place in theologies of infants as the following discussion will demonstrate.

3   An explication of the origins and nature of these differing views can be found in Bunge, M. (2006) 'The child, religion, and the academy: developing robust theological and religious understandings of children and childhood.' *The Journal of Religion* 86:4, pp.549–79.

4   A comprehensive exploration of this subject is provided in Bunge 2001.

no one is clean of sin, not even the infant whose life is but one day upon earth', yet this sin is 'unworthy of punishment: without language the infant could not understand [God's] rebuke'. On the Reformist viewpoint, Watt (2002, p.442) notes that Calvin believed that baptism was the sign of purgation but not the actual means of justification and that 'children who died without baptism *could* be saved, provided that they were heirs to the kingdom of God'– an implicit statement of his position on divine election. As Spitz highlights, for Luther 'the difference between original sin and actual sin is not very consequential because the Scriptures do not distinguish these terms' (2001, p.89). Luther's fundamental identification of baptism as the point of the removal of guilt and of the Lord's Supper as the sacraments which constitute what McGrath (1993, p.159) highlights as the *two* as opposed to the pre-Reformation *seven* means of grace emphasizes the pivotal role of baptism in Reformist thinking (Spitz 2001 pp.82, 89).

Importantly, however, in his discussion of the soteriological status of (baptized) infants, Luther is adamant that the question of whether they possess or exhibit an intentional faith response to divine grace is irrelevant. In his letter to Philip Melanchthon of 1522 he insists that:

> the fact that children cannot believe on their own does not disturb me at all. For how will 'these prophets' prove that children do not believe? Perhaps by the fact that children do not speak and express their faith. Fine! On that basis [we have to ask] how many hours [of the day] even we are Christians, in view of the fact that we sleep and do other things? Can't God in the same way keep faith in small children during the whole time of their infancy, as if it were a continuous sleep?[5] (1963, pp.367–8)

Despite Luther's focus on intellectual activity at the point of later intentional commitment to the grace imbued at baptism, the broader significance of the theological concepts which he terms *fides aliena,* meaning, as Krodel comments (p.336) that 'faith originates in God, outside the individual' and *fides infusa* (p.338), connoting the actual effects of God in the human being (Vainio 2012, p.141), if applied and developed beyond Luther's theology of baptism, serves as a potentially important aspect of an understanding of the spiritual experience of

---

5   The 'prophets' are identified as the Zwickau prophets whose views were cited by Melanchthon in the letter to which this was Luther's persons, no longer extant. See Krodel, *Letters,* 364, fn. 28.

people with profound intellectual disabilities. If faith is a divine gift which precedes any overt response to revelation, people with profound intellectual disabilities subject to such grace will not be disqualified by their inability to demonstrate any response to it.

For an initial Methodist understanding, Heitzenrater (in Bunge 2001, p.294) explains that Wesley's perspective is not always clear, but he does interpret the suffering of children as a consequence of their participation in sin: 'children...are not innocent before God. They suffer; therefore, they deserve to suffer' (1831, p.318). Puritan writer Jonathan Edwards expresses perhaps one of the most extreme positions on the inconceivability of divine leniency towards newborn infants in light of what he believes to be their original sinfulness, insisting that it is 'exceeding just...that God should take the soul of a newborn infant and cast it into eternal torments' (1994, p.169).

While such views deny any possibility that infants exist in an initial state of innocence, others (to varying degrees) believe that their ignorance of sin, either original or actual, and consequently of moral obligation, accords them a special status before God, and that a gracious, just and loving God could not reject them on the basis of their immaturity. Aquinas, for example, despite his sacramental theology, believed that God does not consign infants to hell, although if unbaptized they are sent to limbo (Bunge 2001, p.16). As far as modern Catholic theology is concerned, the sacrament of baptism as the means of grace remains the over-arching principle, although in his discussion of recent trends Whitmore comments that recent theological engagement with the subject of infants and children has been largely limited to issues of procreation and education (1997, pp.161–85). In this context, Hinsdale stresses the importance of Karl Rahner's theology of childhood, although she admits that he wrote relatively little on the subject and what he did write has been markedly under-explored (2014, pp.1–2). Considered by some to be the most influential Catholic theologian of the twentieth century, Rahner's significance in developing Catholic theology and challenging Neo-Scholasticism is unarguable. Kilby (2007, p.xv) asserts that 'Rahner was born into one kind of Catholic Church, and he dies in a rather different one, and he himself, his own writing and lecturing, had a good deal to do with the change.' His perspective on the dangers of Neo-Scholasticism formed a hugely significant contribution to a period of theological renewal in Catholic theology which reached a climax with the Second Vatican Council (1962–1965) (Hinsdale 2014, p.1). Both his theology of childhood and his wider human anthropology are of potential relevance to our discussion, although the acknowledged dense and complex nature of his metaphysical theology means that what follows here (and below) will be a selective and specifically focussed discussion of some pertinent aspects of it.

In relation to the specific issue of the fate of infants who die prior to the age of understanding, Rahner did not dispute Catholic theology on the sinfulness of every human person from the youngest age, averring that a child is 'already and inevitably the origin of that person to whom guilt, death, suffering and all the forces of bitterness belong as conditions of his very existence'. Nonetheless, he argued that 'all this remains within the compass of God, of His greater grace and his greater compassion' (Rahner 1971, p.40). There is undoubtedly a degree of ambiguity with respect to what he actually means here and in related articulations of his theological stance – his insistence on the importance of baptism as the means of entry into the Church and the life of God, intrinsic to his Jesuit heritage, and his reluctance to address the subject of the unbaptized child, for example. Yet, within this position, Rahner maintains that, in their origins, children are 'encompassed by God's love through the pledge of that grace, which, in God's will to save all humankind, comes in all cases and to everyone from God in Christ Jesus' (1982, p.39), and, as Vorgrimler comments (1986, p.23), the 'everyone' here is an exceedingly important aspect of this thought. While, as Hinsdale points out (2014, p.19), he believes that it is awareness of sin and guilt that leads to awareness of grace and redemption to which a human person must submit, the question of how such awareness and submission takes place is open-ended. In the same sense, particularly for those who cannot acknowledge awareness and acceptance of grace in any way that might be interpreted as such by other human beings – specifically here, people with profound intellectual disabilities – we should perhaps be particularly cautious in setting criteria (as Birchenall and Birchenall seek to do) by which such grace can be apprehended and such acceptance can be measured.

Ostensibly, the most positive aspect of a theological alignment of people with profound intellectual disabilities with infants lies somewhere within the range of arguments which to some degree embrace the proposition that children who have not developed sufficient understanding to intentionally either accept or reject the offer of divine grace are exempt from any potential rejection by God. Bunge draws attention to the position of Menno Simons, for example (2001, p.17), whose insistence on the supremacy of prevenient grace, which operates alongside the innocent state of infants, means for him that there is a difference between inherited sin and actual sinning, and that 'until the age of discretion children remain "innocent" through the grace of Christ'. While not by any means their primary focus when discussing children and childhood, Schleiermacher's and Barth's perspectives, though differentiated by the basis on which they reach their conclusions, portray a similar view on the matter. The former, as Devries (in Bunge 2001, p.334) highlights, perceives children as 'naturally innocent, not encumbered with the supposed inheritance of original sin'. Barth's position is predicated on the understanding that grace precedes and does not wait for the response of faith. Thus he affirms the position of children who have not reached the age of discretion:

> Even though they cannot know it, or take up any attitude towards it, He has come into the world for them too, and is also their Lord and Deliverer… Before they can hear, they are already recipients of the word of God's *coup d'état* which is spoken of in His history. The grace of God which appeared in Him, even before they can respond thereto with gratitude or ingratitude, has already embraced them with high objective reality as *gratia praeveniens.* (1969, p.181)

While Barth's argument here seems particularly pertinent to people with profound intellectual disabilities, there are, nonetheless, some hugely important restrictions on the depth of spiritual experience he envisages. While we might accept that they, like infants, might live in the light of objective, prevenient grace, this is, he argues, a 'first of chapter' of their history that should not be confused with a second, their free movement of faith and obedience in response to God in Christ (pp.181–2). He, with Migliore, expounds a 'twofold objective and subjective fulfilment of revelation' (2009, p.1), so that even if grace precedes faith or grace inherently involves the donation of such faith as is required to begin the process of relationship with God, something more remains to take place in order for this relationship to flourish.

Ultimately, any perspective on the status of those who cannot offer what is perceived to be a recognizable, intellectual or verbal assent to the precepts of faith (whatever one believes their content to be) becomes a matter of personal conviction based on interpretation of Scripture and the faith tradition. Again, it must be emphasized that the perspective articulated here is a contextual argument taking place in the discrete area of people with profound intellectual disabilities and there is no contention that overt response to the grace of God is, in any general sense, meaningless. My position, however, implicitly embraces an understanding that people with profound intellectual disabilities cannot be beyond the parameters of God's love, grace and capacity to encounter, in a continual and relational manner, merely on the basis of their cognitive deficits. Fundamentally, there are no parameters to be exceeded. Thus, as in the previous chapter on the theory of accommodation, the discussion here strongly affirms Swinton's contention (2010, p.144) that 'the assumption that our relationship with God is in any way dependant on the presence or absence of human capabilities is a theological mistake'. A profound intellectual disability is not the decisive factor in whether or not a person might experience God. The logical consequences of a contrary view is that the onus for facilitating such an experience rests upon the human person, and that there exists a limitation on God's ability to reach them as a direct consequence of their cognitive disabilities. Such an understanding leads into the trap of what Tillich (1978, pp.92–100) refers to as 'self-salvation', the perhaps inadvertent but nonetheless erroneous idea that the achievement of salvation is the responsibility of human beings, evidenced by a variety of manifestations of attempts they make to respond appropriately to God's grace. In relation to such evidence, Luther, in his letter to Melanchthon (1963, p.370), asks: 'Who can see faith?' In agreement with Tillich, Gillibrand rightly argues that in relation to humanity's ability to 'correctly' engage with God so as to achieve salvation:

> the capacity remains with God, the incapacity with humanity. Thus rather than seeing disability as belonging to a certain group within humanity, it belongs to all. The problem is when we see grace as overcoming human disability, and of bringing salvation and healing to some. This problem occurs within the classic schema when revelation, the capacity of God to save us, becomes distorted into self-salvation. (2010, p.70)

My contention here is that it is indeed in the perspectives challenged by Gillibrand, and not in the level of a person's cognitive ability, that the real problem is to be found. In order for people with profound intellectual disabilities to experience God, there is no need for a particular 'overcoming' to occur; the pivotal factor in the creation of such an experience is essentially the same accommodative action as that which facilitates God's self-disclosure to any human being.

Theological shortcomings

Adopting such positive theologies which have been applied to cognitively immature infants where prevenient grace is the dominant principle presents a defensible case that people with profound intellectual disabilities might find a place of eternal safety under the same theological umbrella. On such bases, it might be assumed that since they do not understand things about God, he will not hold against them any assumed lack of personal faith commitment to the gospel. Alternatively, as Weiss Block comments (2002, p.51), although it is not a position with which she is in agreement, a person with an intellectual disability *can* be viewed as 'a holy innocent, without sin, incapable of any wrongdoing, saved by reason of their disability'. Whether or not this is an accurate depiction of their soteriological status, however, for an understanding of the potential of people with profound intellectual disabilities to enjoy a personal experience of God, neither perspective is adequate. While some might be satisfied by a successful conclusion to a search for theological evidence of their eternal security, care must be taken with regard to any assumption that their spiritual experience can be entirely defined by their soteriological status.

There is a hugely important danger that merely paralleling people who have profound intellectual disabilities with infants who die before attaining 'the age of understanding' has potential to diminish a perception of their spiritual experience. Applying the principle represented in Luther's 'continuous sleep' metaphor to people with profound intellectual disabilities creates an excessively passive perspective on their potential for an ongoing, life-giving relationship with God. If Barth's view is correct, they seem forever excluded from a 'second chapter' of their spiritual history of God, contingent upon 'their free movement of faith and obedience in response to God in Christ' (1969, pp.181–2). An alignment with the prevenient grace position on pre-age-of-discretion infants might appear to offer them a 'get-out-of-jail-free card' which affords them safety in the life to come, but it does not overtly attend to the possibility that they might enjoy a meaningful experience of God in the here and now; that they might have a spiritual life of their own. The argument that this is all that can be envisaged for people with profound intellectual disabilities is again exemplified by Birchenall whose position on this is adamant and disquieting in equal measure:

> Severely mentally handicapped people are denied the very substance of a rational productive existence... Such an existence gives no real

opportunity for inner spiritual growth, or the nourishment of the human spirit, both of which are important when coming to terms with the meaning of Christianity. It gives no real opportunity to experience the joy of seeking a lifetime relationship with the Almighty, because concepts involved are complicated and require a level of awareness which the profoundly mentally handicapped do not have. (Birchenall in Swinton 2010, p.14)

His comments provoke a number of questions. First, it is important to ask how he can be certain that this is the case. Might the joy of a lifetime relationship with God come from *God seeking them*? Is such an experience inevitably contingent upon an ability to be conversant with complicated concepts? What level of capacity to cope with complications does a person have to attain and how is this to be discerned? How high does a person's IQ need to be and who decides?

Despite apparent parallels with infants in terms of their intellectual development, people with profound intellectual disabilities are not children, although they are often treated as such in society and faith communities alike. Weiss Block (2002, p.50) correctly criticizes perceptions of a personal with a disability as 'an eternal child'. They do not live in a state of experiential suspension; they do not necessarily immediately or very soon after birth pass through their temporal existence into their eternal one, as do children who die at a very young age. Many grow up and become adults, albeit that their cognitive development does not conform to the trajectory of those whose intellectual abilities assume a higher place on the IQ spectrum. If, as my work argues, it is accepted that people with profound intellectual disabilities are in some way – which we may not be able to identify from without – capable of an experience of God or, more pertinently, that God is capable of and willing to afford them such, then it must also be accepted that this is not necessarily a static experience. On the contrary, it might have a fluidity, an unfolding that makes it continually alive in their experience, rather than merely precipitating the donation of a visa which will gain them entry to the heavenly realms but lacking any meaning or substance for the present reality of their lives. Rather than confining perspectives of their experience to a safe passage to the world to come, can it instead be envisaged that they might experience an ongoing divine encounter which Von Balthasar (1994, pp.373–83) expounds in terms of an ever-intensifying relationship with God which, he insists, is inherent in any authentic experience of salvation?

Indeed, Rahner's theological thinking on the nature of childhood has the potential to dispel any false divisions between encountering

God in infancy and encountering him in adulthood. In elevating the status of a child to more than a 'pre-adult' – something he identifies as an erroneous historical aspect of Catholic thought – he condemns the fact that a human being's existence and experience of God are often understood in a linear sense by which one lives one's life in phases. Such an understanding, he argues, owes more to the perspectives of modernity than to an authentic interpretation of the scriptural tradition, and he insists that 'we do not move away from childhood in any definitive sense, but rather move toward the eternity of this childhood, to its definitive and enduring validity in God's sight' (1971, pp.35–6). Thus the goal toward which we advance (eternal life) is not something added on to this life. It is a gathering up of the totality of one's life. Temporal existence is not brought along behind oneself, but is made present to oneself (Hinsdale 2014, p.16). A human being in childhood may have experienced less of the temporal existence than an adult, but his or her grasp of non-temporal existence is just as legitimate and in fact is commended by Christ as a quality that befits all those who participate in the kingdom life (Matthew 18.13). In the context of people with profound intellectual disabilities, such an understanding calls into question any assumptions that those who cannot engage cognitively with the precepts of faith might live a life of spiritual dormancy, inhibited by means of their intellectual deficits from experiencing God in an ongoing way. Furthermore, the concept of grace and the self-communication of God to the reception of which all human beings are predisposed, articulated throughout Rahner's work, is that these are not static but ongoing experiences and thus should be expected to be of such a nature as to remain a constant reality in the lives of those who have profound intellectual disabilities, just as in those who do not (Rahner 1961, pp.297–318). In this context, Swinton's rhetorical question (2010, p.144) is pertinent and legitimate: 'What would rule out the possibility that "the Almighty" might seek a lifetime relationship with the profoundly disabled person quite apart from that person's ability to intellectualize and/or articulate that relationship?'

Further on the relevance of an ability to use language, Reimer and Furrow's fascinating qualitative research project into the relational consciousness of Christian children, which forms part of an enormous body of work in this area,[6] might appear to shed light on the discussion.

---

6   Among the most prolific of contemporary commentators are David Hay and Rebecca Nye. See Hay, D. and Nye, R. (1996) 'Investigating children's spirituality: the need for a fruitful hypothesis.' *International Journal of Children's Spirituality*, pp.6–16; (2006) *The Spirit of the Child*. London: Jessica Kingsley Publishers.

(Their work is cited despite the reluctance to parallel people with profound intellectual disabilities expressed above, on the basis that it is the question of language rather than age that is emphasized in their comments.) While their research leads them to understand the role of language in their subjects' sense of 'self' and its relationship to spiritual awareness and formation to be hugely significant, nonetheless they conclude (2001, p.19) that 'spirituality is syncretistically present in the child prior to his ability to verbally explain it'. An assumption that their observations are accurate, however, does not eradicate the methodological issue which Swinton's comment highlights explored above: that of whether there is really any need for, or effective means of, attempting to hear from people with profound intellectual disabilities what they cannot articulate. Do such attempts actually betray a degree of underlying theological nervousness with respect to the relationship between God and people with profound intellectual disabilities? Furthermore, if what Swinton refers to as the 'lifetime relationship with the profoundly disabled person' which God facilitates is inherently possible, on the sole basis of God's ability and desire to facilitate it, in what sense is it the case that this relationship must, as he and others argue, be mediated by the loving attention of other people?

Despite the challenges of Barth's insistence on the objective and subjective aspects of the divine–human relationship for those who cannot offer what is humanly identifiable as a subjective response to God's offer of grace, he emphasizes the dangers of making unwarranted assumptions or displaying over-confidence in attempts to comprehensively define or describe an individual's encounter with such grace. Owing to their importance for this research, his comments on the subject are set out at some length below.

> It would be fruitless to…[consider] what conditions must be fulfilled in God and in ourselves to enable this revelation to encounter us – in order subsequently to look around and see whether revelation actually encounters us in accordance with these conditions. Even in the most searching consideration and determination of such conditions…there lurks a fallacy. In such considerations we put ourselves…midway between God and man, with a twofold assumption, the claim to know what God can and must do, to know what is necessary and appropriate to us men so that revelation between Him and us can become an event. This illusion and assumption will certainly betray itself when the second element, our claim to know our own needs and possibilities, is secretly put forward as the measure of and the compass of the first, our claim to

know the divine possibilities and necessities. In such circumstances, it is inevitable that even the most conscientious theology will prescribe for God what His revelation must be and how it is to be handled, if He is to count upon our recognition of it as such. But the revelation of God cannot be circumvented in this way. (Barth 1956, p.3)

The kind of linguistically and cognitively based theological judgmentalism represented by Birchenall is importantly undermined by such a warning.

5

ARGUMENTS FROM SCRIPTURE

It is undisputed that theology's attachment to language, of whatever form, as a means of accessing the revelation of God is entirely legitimate. Even the description of any means of non-linguistically based revelation which alerts us to its existence is in itself expressed linguistically. Yet it is equally important to recognize that words do not simply *describe* God's accommodation but are *intrinsically an aspect* of it, and thus are not in themselves the revelation. Barth insists (1956, p.1) that when seeking to understand the divine–human encounter, 'we have to deal, in the first place, with the incarnation of the Word, with Jesus Christ as God's revelation for us, and after that with the outpouring of the Spirit as God's revelation in us'. Having already acknowledged the revelatory significance of the incarnation, particularly in Chapter 3 above, we now turn to consider the second of Barth's foci – the work of the Spirit. The aim is to further substantiate the case that God pursues and establishes encounters and relationships with individual human persons in ways that are often unpredictable and sometimes without the pre-occurrence of linguistically based interaction.

The ministry and action of the Spirit: a very brief introduction

The coming of the Spirit, as Jesus promised (John 15.26; 16.13, 15; Acts 1.5), and his ministry made possible added a fresh and transformative dimension to the human apprehension of God. Revelation of God by accommodative means is, in the work of the Spirit, brought to fulfilment in the immediacy and internalization of the experience of God. The Spirit's descent upon and indwelling of human beings achieved the inner human reception of the very presence and power of God which is the source of the Christian's ability to live faithfully and become transformed into the likeness of Christ. The significance of the Spirit's unfolding ministry in the world and the Church cannot be overstated. As the subject of this book is the spiritual experience of people with profound intellectual disabilities, and not the Church as a whole, however, aspects of the Spirit's personal engagement with human beings as the facilitator of the revelation and reception of God's grace will be the emphasis of this chapter.

In a discussion of how we might understand the possibility that this Spirit-endowed inner experience of the life of God might be received and enjoyed by people with profound intellectual disabilities, biblical explanations and narrative instances of the Spirit's ministry are potentially of enormous significance. Paradoxically, where some might perceive an inability to construct an overt response to the verbal proclamation of the gospel to be an obstacle to their reception of the Spirit, there are some intriguing biblical perspectives on the nature of the Spirit's mode of encounter with human beings which, it is argued here, significantly mitigate the weight of such negative perceptions. The focus here will be biblical motifs of the unpredictability of the Spirit's activity, particularly in the context of the experience of the Spirit which occurs *before*, rather than *after*, a verbal proclamation of the gospel.

On the actual nature of the Spirit's engagement with human beings, Welker points out the irresistible impact of both corporate and individual aspects of this ministry: 'the Spirit is always associated with deep experiences, experiences of awesome power…[which] can "overcome" individual persons, can "rest" upon a single bearer of the Spirit, and it can be "poured out" upon many human beings' (2007, p.236). The most obvious biblical illustration of the latter occurrence is the story of Pentecost (Acts 2.1–40), where the coming of the Spirit upon human beings preceded the proclamation of the gospel in Peter's subsequent explanation of what had occurred. It is unsurprising that the event was announced by 'a sound like the blowing of a mighty wind from heaven' (v.2), given Jesus' own teaching: '[t]he wind blows where it wishes, and you hear the sound of it, but cannot tell where it comes from and where it goes. So is everyone who is born of the Spirit' (John 3.8). The emphasis of Jesus' parabolic teaching here (Lindars 1972, p.154), and of Luke's use of the same simile of the wind, particularly highlighted by Witherington (1998, p.132), to describe what the Pentecost event was like, is on the unpredictability, mystery, irresistibility and unmanageability of the Spirit's work. As Keddie explains, 'the Spirit works according to his hidden power and secret will…it is a sovereign act of God's grace… not an act of human will' (2001, p.132). Pink comments that the wind is inherently irregular; it does not always blow with equal force. Thus, in the experience of some, the Spirit's action is 'powerful…radical… [and] revolutionary' (1975, p.118). Such a perspective is supported by the history of what are known as 'revivals' of which testimony is offered of the radical, overwhelming visitation of the Spirit in human gatherings, at particular times and in particular locations, with ensuing inner transformation. This evidence of the unpredictability and strength of the Spirit's intervention is strongly reminiscent of the experience at Pentecost. Yet, on the other hand, and perhaps with particular pertinence to the subject of our discussion, Pink (1975, p.118) stresses that, in marked contrast to such obvious manifestations, 'with others, the Spirit works so gently, His work is imperceptible to onlookers'.

While further explication of the Pentecost event would have been one possible direction for the focus of the current discussion, given the vast volume of material available on the subject, we will approach an exploration of the pre-emptive activity of the Spirit from a different and less obvious angle, with the aim of uncovering fresh insights which might further underpin the argument of this thesis. This will comprise a narrative exegesis of what might be considered a parallel event (Witherington 1998, p.134), albeit on a much smaller scale, in which there is evidence of the coming of the Spirit upon individual human persons prior to a verbal explanation of the source and meaning of the event. The following study of this extraordinary occurrence recorded in Acts 10 is presented to support the case that since the Spirit, like the wind which blows where it will, can and does supersede or pre-empt linguistic explanation of the gospel, even in the context of those who have capacity to engage with its verbal proclamation, the same Spirit might be experienced by people who can *never* access any subsequent explanation.

Acts 10–11: a narrative of the miraculous intervention of the Spirit

The broad significance for the Christian Church of the events recorded in Acts 10 and the subsequent report of them in Acts 11.1–17 can scarcely be overestimated. Hargreaves (1990, p.100), for example, makes the bold claim that 'thousands of years ago someone somewhere invented the wheel and since that time the way human beings live has been different. Peter's eating a meal with Cornelius was like that.' This remarkable narrative relays an extraordinary sequence of events which was to turn the burgeoning Jewish Christian community's understanding of God and his interaction with human beings on its head. Among aspects of its wider significance, the story has a significant role in the debate concerning the theory of accommodation; as noted above, commentators have used the transformation from Deuteronomy 14 to Acts 10 as a vivid example of divine condescension in action.

The historical credibility of the events

Luke's appreciation of the significance of the encounter between Cornelius and Peter is unambiguous, since he recounts or refers to it on three separate occasions in Acts 10–15, and, despite debates concerning the factual and interpretive elements of Luke's narrative, there is general agreement among commentators on the centrality of this record in terms of its catalytic effect on the spread of the gospel of Jesus Christ beyond Judaism into the Gentile world. The intense detail, in contrast with other significant events, in Acts 8, for example, and the unlikelihood that Luke would have 'invented something so momentous and departing from normal patterns of contemporaneous ecclesiology' (Dunn 1996, p.134) support the credibility of Luke's account.

The significance of the supernatural

There are two pivotal moments in this narrative. The first is when Peter abandons his objections to sharing table fellowship with a Gentile such as Cornelius (10.48) – according to Leviticus 20.24–6, for example, the separation of Jews as a people set apart by God was most significantly symbolized by this prohibition on partaking of the same food as Gentiles. The second occurs when the Spirit descends on the assembled Gentile audience (10.44). Both of these bear witness to the placing of the seal on God's inclusion of those who were previously outsiders to his redeemed community, and thus this narrative is first and foremost to be understood as one which has the most profound implications for the future of the Christian Church. As a human-to-human encounter, it is very personal; as a divine–human encounter it is momentous and over-powering. Willimon (1988, p.94) comments that, '[i]n the story, Cornelius (like Peter) is an almost passive actor in a drama being directed at every turn in the plot by someone greater than Cornelius or Peter'. These *directors* are heavenly beings who enter the natural human experience to bring about cultural, religious and personal transformation by the supernatural tools of visions, dreams and angelic visitations which force the human beings involved beyond the place of what seems rational and (in Peter's case) religiously acceptable. As Barrett comments, '[f]rom first to last in this story it is God who takes the initiative' (1994, p.529).

The story begins with an extraordinary occurrence as Cornelius, an officer of the Roman centurion based in Caesarea, is visited by an angel (10.3). The 'otherness' of the heavenly realm makes itself tangible within the ordinariness of one man's life, of which Cornelius gave a detailed report: the time at which the visitation occurred; the angel's addressing him by name; the message that God 'remembered him' and that his acts of piety have 'come up as a memorial offering before God' (10.4) – evidence of his attraction to Judaism and to Jewish piety (Dunn 1996, p.133). The latter phrase has significant resonances throughout the biblical canon. The Greek here, ανέβησαν (*anebesan*), connotes the ascending of an offering as a sacrifice and correlates to the Hebrew word for sacrifice.[1] On this point, Bruce (1990, p.261) notes that Cornelius had 'every qualification short of circumcision which could satisfy Jewish requirements'. Considerable debate surrounds the weight of Cornelius' piety in terms of its potential for rendering 'Cornelius acceptable to God or accepted' (Dunn 1996, p.142). While scholars agree that either interpretation may be supported by a reading of the Greek, Dunn (p.225) argues that the core truth is that 'fearing God' and 'working righteousness' are 'what membership of the covenant involves'. As the story reaches its climax, however, it becomes clear that, for Cornelius, a radically different and new experience of God is to be essential.

The following day, Peter who is at prayer on the roof of the house of his host, Simon the Tanner, falls into a trance at a time coinciding precisely with Cornelius' men's approach to Joppa. It is noteworthy that God reveals his will to Peter and Cornelius in contrasting ways, although we are not given a reason for the variance. This diversity in form of revelation and the fact that both occurred without any human contribution again highlight something of the range of God's chosen means of self-disclosure. Dunn (1996, p.131) comments that 'the double testimony of divine approval given by the complementary visions puts the issue beyond doubt'.

The unsettling of theological preconditions

During the trance, Peter receives a vision which Spencer identifies as the point at which 'the heavens open up to expand the mission of the church' (2004, p.118). He is commanded to eat from a range of animals,

---

1   See Leviticus 2.2, where the memorial relates to the part of the meal offering which was burnt, thus ascending to God in a sweet aroma.

all of which are outside the bounds of what he, according to his current understanding, could lawfully consume (10.10–13).[2] As Bruce (1990, p.218) comments, 'this was all wrong, as Peter's ancestral conscience told him'. In Ezekiel 4.13–14, it was God's anger against his people that called them to eat defiled food. Thus Peter's understandable response is 'Surely not, Lord!' (10.14). Again, Dunn insists (1996, p.138) that it would be a mistake to underestimate the 'importance of the dietary laws to Peter and the new distinctive but still Jewish movement'. Yet God confirms this inconceivable command (10.15) in a statement of seeming self-contradiction, when set against the background of the Jewish tradition and belief system: 'Do not call anything impure that God has made clean.' Where, in Ezekiel 4, the departure from the food laws was a sign of God's retribution, Peter's call here was to become a symbol of his impartial grace. This new revelation is requiring Peter to set aside what he considers to be fundamental to the way in which God operates and to reformulate his understanding of his own identity. Moreover, the submission required of Peter here is not merely to eating what he understands to be unclean food, but to the unpredictable and sometimes shocking consequences of the sovereignty of God who is dismantling Peter's scripturally well-founded beliefs about how a faithful member of God's chosen people should behave. He is being led by this same God beyond his previously validated understanding to a place of utter surprise and even abhorrence.

The pertinent aspect of Peter's experience at this point for a discussion of the spiritual experience of people with profound intellectual disabilities lies in the possibility that contemporary and historical Christians have become so attached to carefully constructed theological understandings that little space is left to be surprised by and open to what God chooses to reveal and to whom and how. Could the spiritual experience of people who cannot access this revelation through accepted cognitive processes be an issue in which settled interpretations of the conditions for human beings' spiritual relationship with God might face a divinely instituted challenge?

Peter's vision is not only of a sheet full of forbidden food but also of a truth of which he may have lost sight or perhaps had never comprehended at all – that God is infinitely greater than a human being's apprehension of him.[3] Because he is infinite in his being, the human

---

2   Leviticus 11 provides the comprehensive list of prohibited animal consumption.
3   Isaiah 55.8.

attainment of knowledge of God is an inexhaustible pursuit. Morris' comment (2008, p.74) on Anselm's classical definition of theology as 'faith seeking understanding' is apposite: 'the act of revelation is always accompanied by concealment'. Peter is learning that, after all, what matters is not the 'rules' but the intentions of the God who instituted them to serve as a revelation of a deeper truth and ultimately of himself. The rules constitute part of God's self-revelatory, accommodative action; by establishing and later superseding them,[4] as God is doing here, their original purpose is more profoundly demonstrated – the truth that God is over all, beyond all, and yet, by his grace, offers the possibility of intimate relationship to all human beings. Again, such a revelation counters what Post (2010, p.27) describes as the 'hypercognitive' position on the process of entering and maintaining a spiritual life which infers that there are physiological, psychological and intellect-based rules which might preclude an encounter between God and people with profound intellectual disabilities. It is worth noting that the continuation of such cognitively based approaches to soteriology is typically exemplified in current controversies, anecdotally, yet frequently, reported by parents of children who have profound intellectual disabilities, in relation to access to the sacraments.[5]

As Peter, 'thoroughly perplexed' (Larkin 1995, p.158) by what has taken place, struggles to understand what seems incomprehensible, Cornelius' men arrive at the gate of the house in which Peter is staying just as the Spirit announces their arrival and significance to him (10.17). At this stage, it remains inconceivable to Peter that he is about to witness the out-pouring of the Spirit upon persons who are, by all of Peter's previous understandings, beyond the range of God's embrace. Nonetheless, accepting their explanation, he and others from Joppa travel to Cornelius' house (10.23–4). On their arrival at his home, Cornelius can scarcely contain his exhilaration (10.25), while Peter explains to the large number of people who have gathered to receive him that his presence there is a departure from his customary religious practice (10.27–9). Because God has emphatically shown him that what

---

4   There is considerable debate as to whether God is here abolishing this aspect of the law or merely overriding it. Witherington (1998, p.358), for example, argues that Luke does not specifically say that food laws were abolished *per se*.

5   As a parent and as a teacher on this subject in both formal academic and informal contexts, I have been approached by a number of parents who are confronted by such challenges. This issue is identified by others working in this field: see Webb-Mitchell, B. (1993) *God Plays Piano Too: The Spiritual Lives of Disabled Children*. New York, NY: Crossroad, p.17, and Swinton in Reinders 2010, p.142.

is *now* forbidden is considering anything impure or unclean which God has declared to be clean, Peter is compelled to take what is an enormous intellectual, emotional, cultural and religious leap.

Cornelius recounts his side of the drama, articulating his profound sense that the whole assembly is gathered in the presence of God in order to listen to everything the Lord has commanded Peter to tell them (10.30–3). The idea that God would presence himself in the home of a Gentile is, for someone of Peter's religious heritage and belief, incomprehensible, yet Peter contests nothing of Cornelius' interpretation of the current situation and, commencing to speak in response to Cornelius' explanation, is evidently beginning to understand more clearly both what God through Christ is doing in the world and also for whose benefit. Suddenly (10.34), Peter grasps the reality of the often overlooked truth embedded in the Old Testament: there really is no partiality with God (see, for example, Deuteronomy 10.17; 2 Chronicles 19.7; Ephesians 6.9; Romans 2.11; Colossians 3.11, 25) and that 'there is neither Jew nor Greek; male nor female; slave nor free – all are one in Jesus Christ' (1 Corinthians 12.13). Similarly, it is argued here that there is space in this new inclusive community for people with profound intellectual disabilities, albeit that others might be unable to identify their access route. Remarkably for Peter, it is a Gentile, an outsider to the covenant people of God, who is the catalyst of this transformative revelation which will determine the entire course of his ministry from this point onwards.

What comes first?

In response to this new awakening, Peter begins to recount the narrative of the life of Jesus. The questions of how far Peter managed to proceed with his speech and what response was or was not made by his audience to what they were hearing, prior to the dramatic interruption of the Spirit is of particular relevance in the context of a discussion of the spiritual experience of people who have profound intellectual disabilities, in relation to broader soteriological perspectives articulated by systematic theologians of whether hearing, cognitively understanding and identifiably responding in faith and repentance to a comprehensive explanation of the salvation story is essential to bringing about a meaningful encounter between God and a human being. As an example, Baillie's view (1939, p.119) is worth quoting again: 'confession, repentance, forgiveness, reconciliation and the new life of fellowship. *There is no other spiritual sequence than this.'*

In the Acts 10 narrative, biblical scholars also continue to vigorously debate the possibility that the intervention of the Spirit occurred separately from and in advance of a process of hearing and understanding the gospel, repentance, confession, faith and conversion being concluded. Undoubtedly, Luke chooses to emphasize the fact that Peter's speech was interrupted by the obvious intervention of the Spirit. Had there been nothing noteworthy to highlight, we might presume he would not have mentioned it. Indeed, with some degree of scepticism, Dibelius (1956, p.97) expresses doubts as to whether the sermon in its recorded form actually took place at all, alleging that the level of detail given is a construct of Luke rather an entirely factual account of what Peter actually said. He highlights the inappropriateness of such a long speech at this point and the absence in the body of the text of any record of a particular reference to the issue in hand – the question of Gentile evangelization. Spencer (2004, p.126) agrees that Peter's lengthy sermon is 'slightly out of step with God's agenda – what is needed is not extended interpretive speech but prompt decisive action'.

On the other side of the interpretive argument, Foakes-Jackson insists that Peter's speech is 'peculiarly appropriate to the occasion' (see Bruce 1990, p.212), and Dodd describes it as fitting the 'form of *kerygma* used by the primitive church in its earliest approaches to a wider preaching' (1936, p.56). Despite highlighting the fact that Peter makes only a brief reference to Jesus' death, a fundamental premise of the salvific message, Larkin (1995, p.165) also emphasizes the expansive content in the rest of the speech. Dunn (1996, p.132) stresses the importance of the speech for Peter, as well as for his Gentile audience:

> It is important to note that the first part in the process is the conversion of Peter himself…this is every bit as much a conversion as in Saul's case – a conversion from traditional and deeply rooted convictions which had completely governed his life until that moment… It took the further event of the Spirit's coming upon Cornelius in such an unexpected, unprecedented way…to complete Peter's conversion.

Nonetheless, despite subsequent attempts on the part of some commentators to partly or completely 'air-brush' this sequence of events from Luke's account of the encounter, his testimony is clear: Peter does not reach the end of his story, nor is there an expression of assent to its content on behalf of Cornelius and his household, before the Spirit intervenes to come upon all who are listening (10.44–7). In his subsequent explanation of his action at the Council of Jerusalem, Peter specifically emphasizes this point: 'As I began to speak, the Spirit came on them as He had come on us at the beginning' (11.15).

It is interesting to note that among the commentators who write emphatically about the comprehensive nature and completeness of Peter's speech in Chapter 10, some omit any comment on Peter's own testimony in 11.15 – see, for example, Larkin (1995, pp.171–2). Those who resist an interpretation of 10.44 which reflects the *prima facie* factual record of the events, clearly favour a more conservative and, arguably, a safer theological perspective. With reference to the timing and nature of the Spirit's interruption, Larkin's view again serves to exemplify the underlying theological assumptions which influence such restrictive readings of the text: 'salvation blessings come to those who hear, receive, believe and hold fast to the Word… So the Spirit falls on them' (1995, p.166). Furthermore, Dunn, seemingly flying in the face of Peter's own explanation of his actions, insists (1996, p.145) that Peter's sermon had, in fact, concluded prior to the Spirit falling on those who heard it and that the sermon was 'heard with assent in the one proclaimed'. He does note, however, that the order of these events is in at least one respect exceptional in that the usual sequence of baptism followed by the Spirit's coming was reversed – perhaps an acknowledgement of the degree of ambiguity concerning the occurrence. Barrett, somewhat paradoxically, confirms that 'according to 11.15, the events took place as Peter began to speak', yet goes on to say that Peter had said so much that by the time the Spirit fell 'there was nothing else for Peter to say' (1994, pp.528–9).

On the other side of the debate, Bruce' exegesis of the record (1990, p.264) is representative of that of other scholars who insist without any ambivalence that Peter's own version of the events in Acts 11 confirms the account of Acts 10 – that he had not finished speaking when the Spirit came on his hearers. He makes the direct comparison between the order of events here and that evident on the Day of Pentecost (1990, p.230): 'reception of the Spirit comes first. There is no explicit mention of faith in the immediate context' (although he argues that it is nonetheless implied). Chase (1902, p.79) is even more emphatic in stressing the monumental significance of what is happening here, in that Peter had not yet finished his address when 'the Pentecost of the Gentile world' took place. Witherington (1998, p.259) strongly concurs:

[s]cholars have often pondered what is said here and what is said in 11.15 where Peter says that he had *begun* to speak when the Spirit fell on Cornelius and company. There is, however, no great mystery. As Luke makes clear, Peter was interrupted by God's Spirit falling on the audience. From Peter's point of view he had only just begun to speak when this happened.

For Marshall and Petersen, this is a deeply significant factor in the narrative as they unhesitatingly state (1998, p.404) that 'God dramatically confirms Peter's deductions by sending His Spirit on the centurion and his companions before Peter has finished speaking.' Moreover, Witherington does not find the order of events surprising at all, citing further examples in Acts 17.22, 22.22, 23.7 and 26.4. Specifically referring to the Cornelius narrative, he comments (1998, p.359) that '[o]ne of the regular features of these narratives about conversions is that God takes charge of the situation, even interrupting an apostle, to bring someone new into the fold'.

If such an interpretation of Luke's account is sustainable, the possibility arises that, in a specific context of God's choosing, 'normative' theological understandings of the prescribed process leading to conversion might be overridden by his sovereign and unfathomable activity. The evidence within this narrative of the prior activity of God, its infinitude in manifestation and unpredictability, supports the case that he might enter the experience of people with profound intellectual disabilities in ways that are outside of what are perceived as (our) accepted theological norms. In establishing relationships with them, cognitive deficit cannot be beyond God's power to overcome, even if the ways in which this is achieved are not readily understood by human beings. Perceptions that inability to cognitively grasp and make humanly identifiable intentional responses to the verbal proclamation of the gospel should preclude people with profound intellectual disabilities from enjoying a meaningful relationship with God are exposed as dubious at best.

Accepting the incontrovertible

It is clear now that, for Peter, no lingering doubt remains. The entire uncircumcised audience is displaying irrefutable signs of being empowered and inhabited by the Spirit of God; signs resonant with those witnessed and experienced by Peter and the other disciples at Pentecost; signs which they recognize to be the unmistakable hallmarks of God's saving presence within.[6] God comes upon them and seals their belonging to him; his presence in them is undeniable.[7] Thus the question of Cornelius' acceptance or acceptability concludes here as the 'primacy of the Spirit is seen as the mark of God's acceptance' (Gooding 1990, p.145). Peter has been confronted by what Bruce (1990, p.230) strikingly refers to as a 'divine *fait accompli*'. The Spirit has broken through every previous exclusionary barrier in what Spencer refers to as 'a forceful, undeniable fashion' (2004, p.126).

Peter's rhetorical question, 'can anyone keep these people from being baptized?' (10.47), as Witherington stresses, indicates his inability to oppose the God-driven reality unfolding before him: '[h]aving received the substance of what the sign of water baptism points to, having received the change agent, the very Spirit of God, it seemed inappropriate to withhold the sign that they were part of the body of believers' (1998, p.360). If God is present within these people, the historical, religious obstacles that preclude such an event are swept away. What religious understanding or accepted process can stand in opposition to God's presence?[8] Later, when called to Jerusalem to explain what was perceived to be an unjustifiable decision to baptize those who are understood to be outside of God's covenant, Peter reiterates the pointlessness of resistance to God's obvious activity: 'So, if God gave them the same gift as He gave us who believed in Jesus Christ, who was I to think that I could stand in God's way?' (11.17). The believers in Jerusalem also found this to be an unanswerable question.

The overall significance of the narrative for Peter and the Church

The fact that this narrative is the longest in the Book of Acts is a strong indicator of its importance. Its significance is, of course, largely centred on the opening of the apostles' minds to the ministry of spreading the

---

6   Dunn retains his emphasis on the wider significance of the events: 'This is the moment when new religions or sects are born – when what has hitherto been taken for granted as a fundamental and defining principle is called in question and the question is heard as the voice of God' (1996, p.138).

7   It is noted that this reading of the text is specifically refuted by David Gooding who asserts that 'the gift of the Holy Spirit demonstrated that God had accepted these repentant and believing Gentiles exactly as He had repentant and believing Jews' (1990, p.124).

8   Perhaps this explains some of the motivation for practical theologians' use of qualitative research methods with people with profound and complex intellectual disabilities – empirical evidence is one means of attaining assurance that the Spirit is present.

gospel to the Gentile world. Yet, as Willimon comments (1988, p.94), this record is contained within a book which 'is the church's attempt to understand its experience of God, an experience which can be quite confusing when it leads us towards people whom we had not expected to meet'. Peter might reasonably have believed that he had reached the end of his experience of the supernatural interventions which had the capacity to turn his thinking and his life on its head. Jesus had come; he had lived, taught, died, risen, appeared in his resurrected form and ascended to heaven. The Spirit had already come in power at Pentecost as a sign and seal of all that had been promised, although he would have realized that, even at that point, the coming of the Spirit (Acts 2.1–2) preceded Peter's expounding of the story of Jesus. Nonetheless, he might justifiably have assumed that the gospel revelation was now complete, and through the ongoing dissemination of the message, many thousands were being saved. Yet, here again, God interrupts Peter's settled agenda with a fresh revelation.

Furthermore, God is revealing his presence not merely *with* but *in* those who lack many, if not all, of the prerequisites for what Peter believes to be crucial to an experience of God. God shows himself to be present in a way that contradicts God's conditions for being present; in a place where, in Peter's terms, God simply cannot be; and in individuals who have no previously established right or capacity to be the location of his indwelling Spirit. God has transparently stepped outside of what Peter conceives of as his prescribed sphere of activity and appears, perhaps more than ever, beyond Peter's understanding. God reveals himself little by little but never completely. Peter no longer has any unassailable position from which to quote the 'rules' but is compelled to witness God's presence in a place and in people of God's own choosing.

The significance of this narrative for people with profound intellectual disabilities

Peter's encounter with Cornelius communicates the fundamental precepts that God is all-embracing and impartial; that his self-revelation is untameable and unpredictable, and that if he is the beginning of all of human beings' interaction with him, an experience *of* God can precede and always supersedes a belief *about* God. This is, above all, a conversion story – perhaps as much for Peter as for Cornelius. Willimon (1988, pp.103–4) sums up the essential common character of this and similar Lukan narratives:

God is the chief actor in all Lukan accounts of conversion. Even the smallest details are attributed to the working of God. Conversion is not the result of skilful leadership or persuasive preaching or biblical interpretation. In many accounts, the mysterious hand of God directs everything. Even our much beloved notions of 'free will' and 'personal choice' and decision appear to play little role in conversion in Acts. Conversion is a surprising, unexpected act of divine grace.

These remarkable events demonstrate how little certainty can be achieved with respect to the range and mechanisms of God's gracious approaches to individual human beings. Here is a warning of the dangers of proscribing how God must act to initiate relationships with them and a demonstration that 'conversion is a by-product of the gospel, the result of one's encounter with the power of the Spirit, not the gospel (Willimon 1988, pp.103–4). Gaventa (1986, pp.151–2) insists that Luke has 'no interest with the utilitarian question of *how* people become converted, or how the church ought to evangelize'. This and similar accounts of conversion in Luke and Acts are, as Willimon emphasizes, 'stories about God's actions, not the church's programs' (1988, p.105). Might it be the case that rational, intellectually reliant human beings, who understand the ways of God through a system of beliefs given to them by God, are in danger of confining their grasp of him and what he does to a sphere which is, to their minds, acceptable, predictable and comprehensible? Is there a danger of assuming a false certainty in relation to where, how and in whom God can be expected to be present? Is it possible that tightly held formulae for what God might do in an individual, how he might do it, and how we might recognize it, is to some extent humanly, rather than divinely, determinative?

Alongside adopting a rigorous exegetical approach to the text here, I strongly affirm Young's view that 'the biblical narratives, treated imaginatively…can become luminous of the reality beyond human expression' (1990a, p.165). The narrative of the Spirit's activity in the encounter between Peter and Cornelius demonstrates that soundly based constructs of how God's engagement with human beings and their responses to him come to take place should not be so rigid as to preclude from our imaginations the possibility that he might choose to act in a way that is surprising. Is it always the case that hearing and understanding the story is a precursor to receiving the One who created it? The evidence of Acts 10 is that the action of the Spirit on the lives of individuals who *do* have the capacity to engage verbally and conceptually with the basis of this action can precede its explanation. On this basis, the action of the Spirit on those who do not have the same capacity cannot be precluded. Thus in the narrative of Peter and Cornelius we find one piece of the interpretive prism through which we might perceive that God can and does act in ways that bring about spiritual experience within the lives of people with profound intellectual disabilities.

6

THE MYSTICAL EXPERIENCE OF GOD

The argument at the heart of this book is that an inability on the part of people with profound intellectual disabilities to demonstrate empirically robust and humanly identifiable information concerning their experience of God is no indication that such a spiritual experience is not accessible to them. As the preceding discussion demonstrates, however, it is not the case that there is nothing that can be discovered about whether and how they might experience a relationship with God. There are alternative pathways through the wider riches of the Christian tradition along which there is much worth exploring. This chapter highlights an additional source of investigation – the Christian mystical tradition, in which first-hand testimony of experiential encounters with God and the interpretation of such evidence offer significant insight into this subject.

At the outset of this discussion, it is acknowledged that, as Charry comments, '[o]f all the sources of Christian theology, experience is the most awkward and ambiguous' (2007, p.413). Yet its ambiguity does not undermine its value as a locus of theological insight, and Charry is correct in asserting that it is, in some measure, its destabilizing potential that renders it important. In keeping with this position, in the following discussion, one aspect of the experiential sources articulated throughout the history of the Christian Church – specifically that termed 'mystical perception' – will be explored. This will not be presented as the definitive lens through which the spiritual experience of people with profound intellectual disabilities might be envisaged, nor as the only usage of the subject of mysticism in contemporary disability theology, although it approaches the subject from a different angle than has previously been presented.

It is important to emphasize here that the aim is not to 'prove' irrefutably that a particular form of Christian mystical experience exists, nor, as the following discussion will acknowledge to be a common theme of more recent contributors to the debate on the subject, is the intention to use the content of purported mystical experience for generating epistemic and doxastic understandings. Furthermore, there is no implicit denial of the potential of people with profound intellectual disabilities to encounter God in the world around them and in reciprocal relationships of love which can hugely influence their lived experience. Rather it is to present the case that if, within the context of Christian theology and the faith tradition, it is possible that this is one mode of God's self-disclosure – one means by which human beings come to experience him directly – then it provides a way of envisaging how they might be participants in an inner experience of God beyond cognitively and linguistically mediated encounters. Within the theological and biblical framework already discussed, a direct encounter between people with profound intellectual disabilities is an inevitable outworking of who God is and what he can and does do. What follows is a presentation of one way of thinking about how it might occur, which might have the effect of 'destabilizing' prescriptive views on their ability or inability to experience a spiritual life.

The challenges of definition

The general phenomenon of mystical experience (the concept is by no means confined to Christianity) is the object of centuries of description, analysis and debate, albeit under various terminological guises. McIntosh (1998, p.11) suggests that the term 'mysticism' 'is something of an academic invention; earlier eras referred to the most intimate and transforming encounter with God as "contemplation"'. Wigner comments: '[t]he word *mysticism* suffers the same fate as words like *religion, God,* or even *love*. It is tossed out in casual conversation, but when one is asked to define mysticism, one can easily be at a loss for words' (2007, p.331). I follow Rahner in opting not to offer a precise definition of the general subject.

> We do after all possess a vague empirical concept of Christian mysticism: the religious experiences of the saints, all that they experienced of closeness to God, of higher impulses, of visions, inspirations, of the consciousness of being under the special and personal guidance of the Holy Spirit, of ecstasies, etc…without our having to stop to ask…in what this proper element consists. (1967, pp.279–80)

Furthermore, although individual mystical experiences will be particularly significant to the ensuing discussion, it is acknowledged at the outset that this is but one aspect of mysticism.

What is obvious, however, is that at the heart of mysticism (and not merely in the semantic sense) there is a fundamental element of mystery. As such, the subject is to some degree antithetical to a rationalistic, critical mindset and poses a challenge to the ordinary vocabulary of human life. Wigner further explains that the difference between everyday sensory experience in the natural world and mystical experience 'creates difficulty in definition due to the bias of human language towards explanation of common experiences which are shared among all human beings. Resultantly, any experience outside of ordinary life events can be very difficult to describe' (Wigner 2007, p.332). Despite both the limitations of human language and the prevalence of the rationalistic mindset, however, reports of such seemingly inexplicable experiences are not uncommon and remain an object of fascination within science, psychology, parapsychology and popular culture,[1] although the majority of scientific investigation continues to favour a naturalistic interpretation of purportedly transcendent events (Wiebe 2004, p.81).

Insights from Rahner's anthropology and mystical theology

In this context, Rahner's anthropology, of which his theological position on children is a small part, his theological reflections on human experience in general, as well as on mysticism, provide intriguing perspectives. What follows is a very brief discussion of particularly pertinent elements of his thinking. He argues that:

> To be human is to be spirit, [that is] to live life while reaching endlessly for the absolute, in openness before God... Only that makes us human: that we are always on the way to God, whether or not we know it expressly, whether or not we will it. We are forever, the infinite openness of the finite for God. (1994, p.53)

Carr (1973, p.371) helpfully summarizes relevant aspects of Rahner's reflections on the significance of human experience as a theological source, adjudging this to be his 'most original thought':

> If man is essentially spirit, open to the self-communication of God through revelation, incarnations, and grace, then these moments of the single mystery of Christianity are at once – dialectically – anthropocentric and theocentric. Human experience, both as transcendental and as objective, conceptual reflection of that reality, finds its meaning

---

1   See, for example, the work of the Alister Hardy Religious Experience Research Centre, www.trinitysaintdavid.ac.uk/en/lrc/librariesandcentres/alister-hardy-religious-experience-research-centre.

and explanation in Christian revelation. Conversely, the truths of Christianity, especially the core truth of the self-communication of God, transform human experience.

Fundamentally, 'to Rahner, God's self-offer as holy mystery, revelation and love actually constitutes human identity. To be human in its most radical sense means to be the addressee of God's offer of self' (Egan 1997, p.xi). Imhof and Biallowons (1991, p.115) explain that it is Rahner's belief that:

> [p]eople…have an implicit but true knowledge of God perhaps not reflected upon and not verbalized – or better expressed: a genuine experience of God, which is ultimately rooted in their spiritual existence, in their transcendentality, in their personality, or whatever you want to name it.

Thus, as Egan comments, 'the human person is, to Rahner's way of thinking, *homo mysticus*, mystical man' (2013, p.43).

Admittedly, Rahner develops this theological anthropology in terms of human freedom to respond to this divine offer (1982, p.361), and, as Allik correctly points out (1987, p.21), he believed that 'the goal for the human person is the complete integration of self with the free decision for God'. If Rahner is correct, and if this is construed as an independent intellectual decision, it seems to be one of which people with profound intellectual disabilities are not capable. On the other hand, it is not possible to know whether and how the action of God might facilitate their reception of his offer in a way that cannot be humanly analysed or defined, as is the case with any potential response to his grace. Most importantly for this discussion, however, it is in our transcendent humanness that we possess the capacity for spirituality – perhaps a key explanation of what it means to be 'on God's wave-length' and it is this capacity which is kindled and kept alight by God's continuous gracious approach. Accordingly, Rahner's emphasis on the intrinsic human capacity for spiritual experience and the absolute spiritual nature of human beings, which must include those who have profound intellectual disabilities, is of potentially enormous significance in this context. Interestingly, Reimer and Furrow, as part of the outcomes of their qualitative research into the spirituality of children, affirm the view that 'spiritual experience and perception are not only socially derived, but are an outgrowth of individual participation in transcendence' (2001, p.18), which is ultimately not cognitively dependent, although development of cognition affords particular capacities for its expression. How can transcendent human beings who happen to have profound intellectual disabilities be pronounced lacking in such a fundamental aspect of the human condition?

Rahner was not without his opponents among both liberal and conservative wings of the Catholic Church, and it was to some extent his openness to integrating a revelation through experience of God with the more abstract theological teaching of the Catholic Church that led to the severe criticism he received from the right, who protested against his dominant influence on the Second Vatican Council (Vorgrimler 1986, p.121).[2] Yet Rahner could not accept a theology of precepts that did not embrace and embody the fundamental connection with the supernatural and supra-rational mysterious God which lies at the heart of Christianity. It was this place beyond words which was the location of the source of the meaning of his life:

> I could never feel the pain of longing, not even deliberately resign myself to being content with this world, had not my mind again and again soared out over its own limitations into the hushed reaches which are filled by You alone, the Silent Infinite. (1999, p.7)

Towards the end of his life, he spoke freely about the immediacy of God's presence (1982, p.374ff.): 'I have experienced God directly. I have experienced God…in the trinity of his approach to me… I have experienced God himself, not human words about him. This experience is not barred to anyone.'

Rahner understands the term 'mysticism' on a number of levels. He embraces a mysticism of everyday life by which God is found and experienced in the ordinary acts of living and being in the world (1983, p.81). He also recognizes a 'mysticism of the masses' (1979, pp.35–51), which describes the sometimes extraordinary experiences of contemporary charismatic movements, although he cautioned those involved to be self-critical in relation to how they interpret the occurrences. Finally, he places enormous value on the testimony of the classical mystics (1981, p.92), because from them one 'hears the views of the person who himself experiences most clearly and with the least distortion the relationship which exists between the human subject and the reality we call God'. This view of the significance of the sources of classical Christian mysticism

---

2   This comment by Georg May, a church lawyer, is cited as a statement typifying the position articulated in various pamphlets and brochures published by Rahner's critics.

provides the backdrop for the following discussion of how they might be interpreted and understood in the context of people with profound intellectual disabilities.

The theological content of mystical experience

A chequered history

A comprehensive survey of the history of Christian mysticism cannot be offered here, but it is important to acknowledge that post-biblical expressions occur as early as the Patristic period and continue to the present day – sources tracing these records are noted below. It is worth noting that while the Reformers in general were cautious of the possibility of mystical appearances, often because of what they perceived to be the dangers of spiritual impostors, Luther 'acknowledged a…form of revelation…that occurs when 'God speaks face to face and enlightens the heart with the rays of His Spirit' (1958, p.17). Wesley's journals also record a significant number of personal experiences of this kind (Wiebe 2004, p.108), and Charry particularly identifies the significance of experience in the lives of Robert Barclay and Jonathan Edwards (2007, pp.426–8).

From his fascinating empirical research in the area of mystical experiences among Western Christians, Wiebe (2004, p.111) comments on the contemporary ecclesial environment in which 'religious experience is not always accorded respect'. William James, renowned exponent of the importance of mysticism within the Christian faith tradition, in his seminal contribution to the subject, first delivered in the prestigious Aberdeen *Gifford Lectures* in 1901–12, laments the significant loss of attention to theistic mystical experience:

> In the Christian Church there have always been mystics. Although many have been viewed with suspicion, some have found favour in the eyes of the authorities… It is odd that Protestantism, especially evangelical Protestantism, should seemingly have abandoned everything methodical in this line. (1995, p.379)

James specifically offers four characteristics of a mystical experience (1995, pp.371–2): (1) it is ineffable; (2) it is noetic, in that it provides insight into depths of truth unplumbed by discursive intellect; (3) it has an essential element of transciency; and (4) it intrinsically involves passivity on the part of the subject. While recognizing the merits of rationalism in constructing an understanding of human existence, he, like Rahner, insists that:

> it is as if there were in human consciousness, a *sense of reality, a feeling of objective presence, a perception of what we may call 'something there'* more deep and more general than any of the 'special and particular 'senses' by which the current psychology supposes existent realities to be initially revealed. (1995, p.52; emphasis added)

James illustrates both the passivity and what might be termed 'beyond rational' (although not irrational) certainty intrinsic to the mystical experience described in the testimony of one of those he cites as exemplary cases of the phenomenon: 'I did not seek Him but felt the perfect unison of my spirit with His... Since that time, no discussion I have heard of the proofs of God's existence have been able to shake my faith' (1995, p.66). Mystical states, contends James (1995, p.414), 'break down the authority of the non-mystical or rationalist consciousness, based upon the understanding and senses alone. They show it to be only one kind of consciousness.' The case for such a view will provide the impetus for the discussion that follows, which will be advanced by reference to further prominent contemporary and historical material, both academic and testimonial.

Current ecclesiological and theological perspectives

Unsurprisingly, then, current arguments within the Church on issues of the existence and reliability of mystical experiences occupy well-trodden ground. Yet, despite the general academic ambivalence towards the subject referred to above, a notable degree of interest in historical mysticism has remained alive within theological scholarship.[3] A renewed focus on the contemplative tradition[4] has issued a challenge to recognize again the inherent reciprocity between the forming of theological

---

3   Significant recent contributions to the historical and contemporary significance of the subject include Chan, S. (1995) *Spiritual Theology.* Leicester: InterVarsity Press; Holt, B. (1997) *A Brief History of Christian Spirituality.* Oxford: Oxford University Press; Louth, A. (1981) *The Origins of the Christian Mystical Tradition.* Oxford: Oxford University Press; McGinn, B. (1991) *A History of Western Christian Mysticism, 3 Vols.* London: SCM; McGinn, B. and McGinn, P.F. (2003) *Early Christian Mystics.* New York, NY: Crossroad; Sheldrake, P. (1995) *Spirituality and History.* London: Darton, Longman and Todd; (2011) *Spirituality and Theology, Trinity and Truth.* London: Darton, Longman and Todd.

4   Of which the works of Thomas Keaton and Thomas Merton are perhaps the most prolific.

propositions and the spiritual experience in which the reality behind them takes shape. Indeed, so intimately interconnected are they that one cannot survive without the other. Merton warns that:

> we must not separate intellectual study of revealed truth and contemplative experience of that truth, as if they could never have anything to do with one another…the two belong together. Unless they are united, there is no fervour, no life and no spiritual value in theology, no substance, no meaning and no sure orientation in the contemplative life. (1972, pp.197–8)

Carson's critique of the emergent Church's theological positions and practices highlights its attempt to make connections with post-modern social trends which include a willingness to 'embrace the experiential delight in mysticism' (2005, p.37). For him, however, the fundamental issue that the Church must address in the transition from a modern to a post-modern social climate is its epistemology: how do we know what we know? He welcomes post-modern epistemology's exposure of and antidote to Enlightenment rationalist arrogance and its overestimation of the role of reason in human understanding, but he is among those who insist that some objective knowledge or truth *is* attainable, and he refutes (pp.103–5) the moral relativism which adheres to post-modern constructionist worldviews. As will become clear in what follows, it seems that theological epistemological discussions (and Carson's contribution is no exception) invariably emerge out of or lead into an exploration of the relationship between intellect and heart; truth and experience.

The contribution of William Alston
Rationale for the use of Alston's work

Among the most influential scholars in the discussion of the existence and significance of Christian mystical experience over the past 25 years is William Alston. His extensive contribution to this subject has stimulated much critique and response among other contemporary voices in the debate. His work has been selected as a pivotal, though not exclusive, resource for the current discussion for a number of reasons. First, his approach to the subject is both philosophical and theological in nature; second, it has built upon earlier relevant, well-respected contributions; third, it continues to stimulate widespread critical thinking in the area; and, finally, he begins from a Christian theistic standpoint, and thus his reflections on mystical experience are not primarily concerned to establish the existence of God – this is already a 'given', as it is in this discussion.

Alston's motivation

Alston's most-debated contribution to academic reflection on experiential mysticism is his 1991 work, *Perceiving God*. His declared intention in the book is epistemological (a common feature in the territory occupied by such debates): 'to defend the view that putative *direct awareness of God* can provide justification for certain kinds of *beliefs about God*' (1991, p.9). It should be emphasized again that the purpose of the current part of our discussion parallels that of Alston only indirectly, in that, although the relationship between mystical experience and theological belief is an important one and will be highlighted below, our objective is not primarily concerned with whether mystical perception provides epistemic justification for constructing beliefs about God. Instead, the focus here is on the *actual occurrence* of the mystical experience which Alston defines as 'mystical perception' (pp.9ff.) (the concept will be expounded below) and its potential for developing an understanding of the possibilities of direct, internal experience of God as an aspect of the lived experience of those who have available to them neither the cognitive nor linguistically based means of apprehending him in other ways, specifically, here, people with profound intellectual disabilities.

Indeed, Alston himself is at pains to affirm that although forming epistemological arguments is a ground for his philosophical reflection, it is not the objective of mystical perception *per se*. To emphasize this point, since it articulates an important springboard for understanding the purpose and context of the current part of our investigation, it is worth quoting him at length here.

> I certainly don't want to suggest…that [the epistemological value of mystical perception] is its only theoretical interest or that it is its main importance for the religious life. On the contrary, according to the Christian tradition the main significance of mystical perception is that it is an integral part of that personal relationship with God that is the fundamental aim and consummation of human life. Without God and me being aware of each other in a way that, on my side, is properly called 'perception', there could be no intimate relationship of love, devotion and dialogue that, according to Christianity, constitutes our highest good. (p.12)

Stimulated by, paralleling and contextualizing these general comments of Alston's, I explore below the possibility that God and people with complex and profound and intellectual disabilities might be 'aware of each other in a way that, on [the latter's] side, is properly called "perception"' and in this way experience that 'intimate relationship of love and devotion and dialogue that, according to Christianity, constitutes our highest good' (p.12).

The parameters of Alston's subject

Defining 'mystical perception'

It is fundamental to his subsequent argument that Alston should identify the specific type of perceptual model which provides the pivotal axis of his work in *Perceiving God* – what he terms 'mystical perception' or 'direct experiential awareness of God' (p.35), which takes shape in a mystical experience, although not in the commonly understood meaning of the term, as will become clear (p.11). Mystical perception is a very particular awareness of God in which he appears or becomes present directly to the subject (p.35) and which, importantly for our purposes, contrasts with 'thinking about God, calling up mental images, entertaining propositions, reasoning, engaging in overt or covert conversations, remembering' (p.14). Alston cites Francis de Sales' testimony as an exemplar of such an experience:

> [T]he soul…sucks in a manner insensibly the *delights of* His presence, *without any discourse…* She sees her spouse *present* to her with so sweet a view that reasonings would be unprofitable and superfluous… Not does the soul stand in the need of the *memory* for she has her lover *present*. Nor has she need of the imagination for why should we represent in an exterior or interior image Him of whose presence we are possessed of? (p.15)

A distinctive aspect of the kind of experience that is the focus of Alston and of our discussion is the directness or immediacy of this kind of non-cognitive divine presentation. While in some mystical experiences God's presence is mediated through awareness of something other than himself (Beardsworth 1977, p.13), in the more direct awareness of mystical perception the totality of the experience consists in God's 'immediate appearing'. Thus, it is fundamental to a direct awareness of God that it involves God himself being presented and not simply some experience or emotion which one believes to have come from God (Alston 1991, p.28). We might, perhaps, call this an effortless and, from a human perspective, non-precipitated awareness of God; the recipient is in no sense a contributor to the experience.

Alston describes this perception (p.16) in terms of 'the subject [being] passive...no powers of attention or reasoning, no activities of formulating propositions is involved'. Fr Roué's account (Poulain 1950, p.83) serves as an example: 'in the mystic union, which is a *direct apprehension* of God, God acts immediately upon the soul in order to communicate Himself to her; and it is God, *not an image of God,* not the illusion of God, that the soul receives.'[5] It is within this perspective of a mystical perception of God that our consideration of the spiritual experience of people with profound intellectual disabilities is conducted. In such an experience, might we envisage that what cannot be communicated to people with profound intellectual disabilities by cognitive and linguistic propositions might instead be disclosed by God's immediate and direct inner appearing?

Baillie on 'directness'

Alston's position on the direct awareness of God's presence echoes, to some extent, the much-respected earlier contribution of John Baillie, who understands that the apprehension of God by faith is 'a primary mode of awareness. Faith does not deduce from other realities that *are* present the existence of God who is *not* present but absent: rather it is an awareness of the Divine presence itself, however hidden behind the veils of sense' (p.88; emphasis added). On the other hand, however, he insists that our perception of God is always mediated through nature, history and society (p.89) and that 'the immediacy of God's Presence to our souls is a mediated immediacy... God reveals Himself to me only through those who have gone before, yet in so doing reveals Himself to me now' (pp.181–5). One might, however, ask how he can be certain on this point – how can we be sure that God does not also become immediately present beyond and without recourse to such sources? The fact that Baillie cannot claim to have had such an experience (and he is not alone in this situation, as James (1995, p.37) also attests) should not be taken as irrefutable evidence that it is theologically inconceivable or phenomenologically impossible. Furthermore, he does acknowledge elsewhere (1939, p.155) the possibility of a supra-sensory and immanent

---

5   Alston, in contrast with other commentators, does not conceive of a state of undifferentiated unity between the perceiver and the God she perceives.

experience of God: 'no other reality is nearer to us than [God]. The realities of sense are more obvious but His is the more intimate.'

Alston's source material

Anecdotal validity

Mirroring James' approach, Alston's source material is a selection of autobiographical accounts of what he refers to as mystical perception. He is undoubtedly and unapologetically arguing from experience. As he states at the outset (1991, p.12), 'our only access to the subject matter is through the reports of persons who take themselves to be experientially aware of God'. These narratives are primarily, though not exclusively, historical; some are from well-recognized sources while others are anonymous. The validity of anecdotal accounts for the generation of evidence that mystical experience exists is not universally accepted, as the later discussion of Alston's critics will demonstrate. McIntosh, however, affirms Alston's implicit assumption that such accounts retain enormous value:

> A mystical text is analogous to a scriptural text in its functioning; just as the biblical witness can be God's chosen 'site' for a new encounter between believers and the Incarnate Word, so a mystical text functions, non-canonically, of course, as another location for the Word's encounter with believers. (1998, p.130)

He contends that mystical texts are a part of the 'Christian community's participation in that "speech event" which constitutes the community – the Trinitarian speech of God in creation, the calling of Israel, the Incarnation, death and resurrection' (1998, p.137). It is in agreement with this perspective that such texts are included as an important source of consideration for this strand of the exploration of the spiritual experience of people with profound intellectual disabilities.

Tensions between experience and intellect

In the context of using such evidence to present his case, Alston specifically enjoins the debate concerning the relationship between abstract theology and affective experience, particularly emphasizing the indispensability of the latter: 'there is no substitute for being there' (1991, p.293). Yet it has been argued that, in relying on human accounts of mystical experience, he is in danger of elevating this above intellectual theological engagement. Alston's reference to what is known within the Catholic tradition as 'infused contemplation' serves to illustrate the point. This prayer has highly distinct characteristics as described by Fr Duplancy:

> (1) an inner perception...of a very special presence of God...[and] (2) a suspension, complete or only partial, of acts of the intellect, the memory, the imagination and the exterior senses which might prevent the will from possessing this ineffable presence in perfect peace. God does not become present to the object's awareness through anything apart from being present as Himself. (cited by Alston 1991, p.15)

As a further example of the kind of intellect-surpassing nature of the mystical experience to which Alston refers, Teresa of Avila's testimony is worth quoting:

> In short, she is utterly dead to the things of this world and lives solely in God... Her intellect would fain understand something of what is going on in her but has so little force now that it can act in no way whatsoever... How...can one have such certainty [when one cannot understand it]? These are secrets of God's omnipotence which it does not appertain to me to penetrate. (iii, p.481)

In the broader context of the debate, James' comments (1995, p.73) support the view that intellect cannot be elevated above the level of affective experience; in fact, he seems to argue that the reverse is the case:

> Our impulsive belief here is always what sets up the original body of truth...and our articulately verbalized philosophy is but its showy translation into formulas. The unreasoned and immediate assurance is the deep thing in us. The reasoned argument is but a surface exhibition. Instinct leads, intelligence does but follow.

Yet there is much rejection of the inference that mystical experience can be in any sense separated from cognitive processes. McIntosh, for example, argues that mysticism (here he uses the earlier term, contemplation) 'holds together two elements we often see as contrasted as though they were mutually exclusive, namely the affective or loving impulse and the intellectual or knowing impulse' (1998, p.11). Both components are intrinsic and essential. Contrasting mystical theology and dogmatic/systematic theology, Louth agrees that the former:

provides the context for direct apprehensions of God who has revealed Himself in Christ and dwells within through the Holy Spirit; while [the latter] attempts to incarnate those apprehensions in objectively precise terms which then, in their turn, inspire a mystical understanding of the God who has thus revealed Himself. (1981, p.10)

It would be a mistake, however, to interpret Alston's approach as promoting a battle between intellect and experience. It is his position also that mystical experience presupposes a context of beliefs and symbols within which it can be known as *religious experience*. In fact, he argues, it is in part the solidity of the theological framework or 'background beliefs' (to be discussed below) that offers validity to the possibility that the mystical experience is genuine (1991, pp.81–94). In arguing that one is not subordinate to the other, he would concur with Sheldrake (2011, p.3) that 'theology that is alive is always grounded in spiritual experience'. Rahner too insists on the fallacy of conceiving of intellectual engagement with the faith as in any sense detached from its experiential impact, insisting that 'there is such a thing as a mystical component to Christianity' (in Imhof and Biallowons 1986, p.182).

Interpreting the text

Even if the validity of autobiographical accounts of experiential transcendent encounters with God is accepted, the question remains, as it does with other such evidence, of how these accounts are to be processed in a way that respects but does not over-emphasize their capacity to contribute to the body of theological understanding. On this point, McIntosh, like Alston, insists on some recognizable, consistently theological content without which the mystical experience becomes an empty and insignificant journey into self-consciousness. He summarizes and affirms a number of tests which have to do with the potential for the text to speak into wider ecclesial life, as well as its impact on the life of the recorder and the reader, particularly the question of whether it is driving him or her towards the self-negating pattern of discipleship which was embodied in the life of Christ (1998, pp.143–5). Within this framework, McIntosh proposes a number of hermeneutical approaches to specific texts, highlighting the need for a blend of caution, openness and anticipation when discussing their import. He advocates (p.122) a 'consideration of the hermeneutical clues, the interpretive "directions", implicit in the *activity of mystical theology* itself', which he categorizes as the 'cataphatic–aphophatic' structure of reality as outlined in God's cosmological narrative (pp.122–3). The aphophatic element of the texts reminds us that 'what' is being experienced or perceived is not an object, another 'thing' in the body of things (but bigger and in some incomprehensible material respect, different); rather the perception is of the infinite and ineffable Divine Being. Consequently, we are reminded that the mystical perception of God in which the mystical experience takes shape is intrinsically extremely limited in terms of 'what' is being perceived of God – the understanding which also underpins the theory of accommodation discussed above.

People with profound intellectual disabilities

With respect to the focus of this book, the use of the kind of empirical evidence offered by Alston is particularly pertinent, but issues of interpretation, specifically in relation to the role of the intellect, are also highly significant. Texts that emphasize a suspension of acts of the intellect, memory and will as an essential aspect of this intimate experience of God seem to place people with profound and intellectual disabilities in an inherently advantageous position in relation to mystical perception. The implication of how the presence of God becomes more immediate in the absence of the distractions of intellectual self-consciousness seems to support the idea that they might encounter God in this way. Thus, on the one hand, it might be argued that in the reception of an experience of mystical perception, the 'intellectually disabled' and the 'intellectually able' find themselves on a level playing field. On the other, if a personal ability to apprehend and hold together both the intellectual and affective aspects, of which mysticism is the sum, is a prerequisite for any personal encounter with God, the possibility of spiritual experience for people with profound intellectual disabilities might be deemed unattainable. This issue is explored below.

Acknowledging the critics

It is essential to the academic and theological integrity of my work that a number of the arguments raised by Alston's many critics be acknowledged and engaged. Given the vast amount of literature that has both preceded and succeeded Alston's work, the issues raised below are necessarily limited, selected on the basis of their potential to develop a perspective on mystical perception for people with profound intellectual disabilities.

In relation to perhaps the most obvious objection to his position, Alston overtly acknowledges and challenges the rationalistic, philosophical and scientific scepticism in relation to his argument:

> Many people find it incredible, unintelligible, or incoherent that there could be something that counts as *presentation,* that contrasts with abstract thought in the way sense perception does, but is devoid of sensory content. So far as I can see, this simply evinces a lack of speculative imagination. (1991, p.17; emphasis added)

As his case unfolds, however, it is clear that a rationalistic aversion to the use of the imagination does not constitute the only ground of disagreement.

The role of the senses

First, it is noted that the possibility of mystical perception of God without recourse to the senses is far from universally accepted within the history of Christian theology. Gilson (1924, p.64) summarizes Aquinas' dissenting perspective which typifies that of those who do not admit of the possibility: 'the only road which can lead us to knowledge of the Creator must be cut through the things of the sense. The immediate access to the Cause being barred from us, it remains for us to divine it with the help of its effects.' Aquinas' overall position is implicitly, in one important respect, in tune with the fundamental significance of the theory of accommodation – that finite human beings do not have access to the fullness of the 'Cause' (God) but only to that which can be apprehended within the limitations of our humanity. Yet, while we readily understand that *complete* access to the fullness of God is barred from us, why should we presume that *immediate* access to what *can* be apprehended of him is similarly barred? Is the 'divination' of the Cause dependent on the capacity of those to whom the Cause is revealed? Or is the opposite the case? My argument is that, because no human being could ever know all that there is to know, and on the basis of what we do know, it is reasonable to expect that God is capable of and desires to meet those who cannot avail of his revelation in ways that are open to the intellectually able. That we cannot know how he might do so does not prove that he cannot. It is simply another of the things we cannot know. Alston rightly insists (1991, pp.21–2) that God is too big to 'be contained within the paltry confines of my experience'. He is also too big for his ways of encountering another human being to be contained within the paltry confines of what my (as an intellectually able person) experience of encountering him tells me he is able to do.

Alston's emphasis on background beliefs

Alston's advocacy of the existence of mystical perception – the direct presentation or appearing of God – requires him to address the issue of whether it represents an authentic encounter with 'God' himself. Therefore he adds the necessary condition that what is encountered in the perception of God is consistent with what is generally agreed to be true of God:

> Putative perceptions of God are not self-authenticating but instead are in principle subject to being shown to be correctly or inadequately based by certain considerations… But this is possible only if we have a stock of knowledge or justified belief concerning the matters in question, in this case concerning God, His nature, purposes and activities. (1991, p.295)

On this basis, Alston analyses the personal accounts provided by his examples, to find 'modes of divine appearance' which are consonant with background beliefs about God – in other words, that which is revealed to be true of God from other sources of the tradition. He is not alone in insisting that Christian mystical perception cannot stand alone as a detached phenomenon, as McIntosh's emphasis on the need for assessment of the acuity of the content of mystical experiences makes clear. Nonetheless, mystical perception is not to be perceived as merely an additive to already substantiated belief; rather it is to be understood as a contributor to the body of belief, with potential to create new places of divine encounter. It seems that Rahner would agree with this proposition since, as Carr comments (1973, p.376), he believed that 'experience could be a genuine source for theologizing, an equal partner in the dialogue with the objective word revelation'.

If Alston's hypothesis is correct, what does this mean for people with complex and profound intellectual disabilities, given their inability to cognitively access the background beliefs which it is claimed are necessary to making theological sense of and, more importantly, to establishing grounds for believing in a mystical perception of God? Perhaps this question might be answered by another: is it necessary that *the one who perceives* God is *also the one who can access* the background beliefs? If it is conceded that intellectual engagement with the theological precepts which underpin or are underpinned by mystical perception is a necessary element of authentic mystical experience, must this be present in every individual instance? If the theological framework or background beliefs for such experiences exist, might the experience take place, even for those individuals who do not grasp the structure that supports it? If we can identify in the Christian faith tradition such evidence as would substantiate this understanding, do the limits of the intellectual processes of those whom we might envisage perceiving God in the mystical sense described by others who *have* articulated their experience deny them the possibility of similar experiences? Do I have to be able to understand the background theological beliefs that underpin any perception of God I might have, and do I have to be able to say that I perceive God in order for it to be possible that I am doing so? It seems that, like mine, Alston's response would be 'no':

> [E]ven if the other grounds [of belief] must in fact have justificatory efficacy in order for MP [mystical perception] to do so, the user of MP need not know, or be justified in supposing that they do, in order that his MP based beliefs be thereby justified. Here the acquisition of justified beliefs from MP does not require that the subject himself know anything about the epistemic status of other grounds, or indeed of MP itself. (1991, p.300)

This perspective is, of course, in tune with the fundamental contention of my discussion of the spiritual experience of people with profound intellectual disabilities, namely that Christian 'background beliefs' (including those theological foundations from the historical, interpretive and biblical tradition presented above) do serve as grounds for asserting the case that people with profound intellectual disabilities might be expected to encounter God, despite and beyond the limits of their cognitive and linguistic capacities and their inability to identify and commit themselves to such theological propositions.

Religious diversity and practical rationality

One particular point of contention in relation to Alston's argument on background beliefs centres on the issue of religious diversity. He initially acknowledges (p.28) that mystical perception has been a feature of religious experience in Judaism and Islam as well as in Christianity. How, it has been asked (Justin Willard's work exemplifies this criticism), does his argument for accepting the 'perception' he describes as being of God, on the basis that it is in some aspect consistent with what is held to be true of God, stand alongside the fact that the background beliefs concerning what is true of God are often different across each of these traditions, perhaps most crucially in the significance of the person of Jesus Christ?[6] Alston does not refute the validity of the question, admitting that there is, across various faiths, 'a massive incompatibility of the output of mystical perceptual practices' (p.258).

This issue is additionally relevant to Alston's overall argument when placed within the wider context of the potential of mystical perception for generating doxastic beliefs about God – something which Alston is eager to establish. Of many criticisms of this point, Pasnau's is representative:

> The practice of mystical perception (MP) is a doxastic practice of forming beliefs about God on the basis of mystical experiences. The inputs of MP are mystical experiences, the outputs beliefs about God. Alston's assessment of the plurality of religions leads him to distinguish between varieties of mystical perception. So if Christian mystical perception (CMP) were reliable, Hindu and Moslem practices could not be reliable – the outputs of the practices are too different for each reliably to generate true beliefs. (Pasnau 1993, p.2)

It must be conceded that, in the end, Alston appears to circumvent the religious diversity issue, without overtly denying what might or might not be justifiably believed to be a perception of God within other faiths, by moving on to establish a case for the epistemic justifiability and 'practical rationality' (1991, p.168) of believing oneself to have encountered a Christian mystical experience of God on the basis that what is expressed as having been perceived is consistent with *Christian* theology of which he has personal experience and to which he has made a faith commitment (1991, p.9).

Of course, my argument is equally logically open to attack on the same grounds of religious diversity. This is inevitably the case in any discussion formulated within the broad tenets of Christian theology. If it contradicts other belief systems, it will be open to charges of non-acceptance of religious diversity. Naturally, the same applies to parallel discussions taking place within any alternative religious framework. It seems to be the existence of reports of mystical experiences across a plethora of religions which causes problems for Alston's critics, as if the phenomenon were a unique entity for the reason that it appears within

---

6   This is a brief summation of the essence of the argument made by Julian Willard in (March 2001) 'Alston's Epistemology of Religious Belief and the Problem of Religious Diversity.' *Religious Studies* 37:1, pp.59–74.

so many belief systems. There are, however, numerous common cross-religion issues of belief and experience – the afterlife, healing, the role and consequences of prayer, the accessibility of the Divine Being, to name but a few – on which divergent views are held. Religious diversity is just that and is not untenable for being just that. Once a Christian commitment is acknowledged, a scholar must surely be allowed to proceed within that context; otherwise nothing within any theological discourse would ever be worth saying. Indeed, Charry argues (2007, p.419) that confining the discussion within Christian theological parameters does not entail that spiritual experiences cannot be interpreted Christianly; 'it only serves to identify Christian experience theologically, just as theologians identify Christian revelation, Scripture, tradition and worship – that is, as sources of knowledge of the God Christians confess.' Brock is even more emphatic in claiming the legitimacy of the Christian distinctiveness of experiences which might be reported across other religious traditions, because 'the distinctive beliefs and practices of Christian faith may actually reveal features of existence different in substance from what is perceived and therefore tangible in other thought systems or faith traditions' (2009, p.9).

Neuro-scientific explanations?

Regarding the potential role of neuro-psychological forces in the construction of mystical perception, there is a current and lively debate within some parts of the scientific community in which, as Wiebe points out (2004, p.153), the contention that 'the physical sciences provide us with the conceptual resources to describe and explain all phenomena in the universe' predominates. In a fascinating paper on the subject, Lancaster sets out two conflicting positions on the relationship between science and mystical experience. 'One school of thought would have matters religious and mystical in one domain and matters physical in another; religion and science as two *nonoverlapping magesteria*' (2011, p.12; emphasis added). Refuting this viewpoint, he insists that the seemingly dualist worldview that such an understanding portrays cannot, by definition, sit easily with the worldview of science. For him, expressions of mysticism (to which he also refers as 'anomalous experience'):

> are by no means the trivia of human life; they represent the very dignity of being human. Ignoring the deep question that unifies them on the

grounds that science is not yet able to accommodate it is not only to make a false god of science but also to turn one's back on the most inspiring and transformative aspects of human experience. (p.12)

Moreover, he contends that neuro-scientific explanations of mystical experience are dependent on 'an act of faith' (p.12) correlating to that which attracts religious explanations. Fundamentally and significantly for our discussion, Lancaster's point is that mystical experience is not invalidated by neuro-scientific understandings of brain function and consciousness; rather it fits comfortably within the scope of current knowledge in this area and is therefore not to be discarded as an imaginary and non-tenable explanation of human experience.

Personal transformation: a missing element?

From a theological perspective, Johnson, refuting Alston's interpretation of his selected autobiographical accounts, is adamant that this testimony is so lacking in evidence of any divinely inspired challenge to previously held beliefs and of consequent personal transformation as to make it impossible to conceive that what has been experienced is a direct awareness of God at all. He bases his argument on two principal grounds: first, that this is not what one might expect from God, and, second, that it is contrary to what is revealed of the activity of God in Scripture. He is convinced that:

> while it might be sensible for a divine intelligence to challenge our beliefs only to the extent that we are able to bear at any moment, there is no reason to suppose that a divine intelligence would fail to challenge our beliefs at all...a powerful and caring God whose outlook on life surpasses our own would *want* to challenge us...and coax us to adopt more adequate ideas and practices. This, however, is not what happens in most modern reports of divine encounters [and this] contradicts Scripture... In sacred texts from all over the world, divine encounters are routinely described as posing challenges to people's current beliefs. (2004, p.357)

Johnson is, however, equally open to challenge on the basis that he has formed seemingly intransigent assumptions about what God should or would accomplish during the course of these encounters – something for which he offers no more evidence than do people who testify to such experiences. Having decided that God *would* do certain things, it is difficult for him prove his case that God *could not* do certain other things, should he, being God, choose to do so. Moreover, he fails to recognize the significance of the fact that one of the consistent features of the testimony of those who claim to have experienced mystical perceptions of God used by Alston (and James) is that the whole experience was uninitiated, unsought, unexpected and thus unpredictable in every sense.[7] If, then, the entire occurrence was outside of human control and solely created and directed by God, why should there exist any particular expectation of its impact on the individual? Indeed, the absence of any kind of predictability in terms of the happening and shape of mystical perceptions is a core element in the case that they occur. Why would it be unconscionable that God should offer the experience and even that it might be for him also an experience of intimacy for which he needs no justification other than that it pleases him to create it? In this context, the form, or rather the absence of form, of mystical perception – its lack of dependence on sensory and verbal means of occurring and its unpredictability of outcome – is of considerable significance. Alston (1991, p.49) is clear that we:

> know nothing of the mechanisms of [perception of God], if indeed it is proper to talk about mechanisms here; nor can we grasp any useful regularities in the conditions under which God will appear in one or another qualitatively distinct way to one's experience.

On the basis of the non-necessity of a grasp of determinable mechanisms by which a mystical perception of God might have occurred, no attempt is made here to establish any prescriptive ways in which such an experience might be brought about in people with complex and profound intellectual disabilities. As Alston argues, and on this Wainwright concurs (1981, pp.93–6), this lack of 'requisites for analysing divine appearances into phenomenological elements, cataloguing them... dimensionalizing them and so on' does not prejudice the belief in their validity since our inherent ignorance of the basic phenomenal qualities of divine appearances renders us unable to say that such qualities do not exist (1991, p.49).

Alston's and Wainwrights' views are contested by those like Draper, who argues that while the lack of regularities in such divine appearances are not evidence against their existence, 'it still doesn't entail [their] conclusion that the failure to discover such regularities does nothing to diminish the cognitive value of theistic experiences' (1992, p.151). Such

---

7   See, for example, the account cited as (5) in Alston 1991, p.14.

dissent is hardly surprising, however, in light of Draper's underlying premise of the non-existence of God, although, somewhat ironically, he advances his argument in theological terms, albeit that these appear to be simplistic and unconvincing. He insists, for example (pp.159–60), that 'God, if He does exist, does not generally intervene in ways that would improve moral character. For example, he allows all sorts of demoralizing conditions like poverty, ignorance, etc.' Christian theology might fail to recognize the mutual exclusivity of God's transforming work on the human character and the existence of suffering in the created order.

Justifiability and reasonableness

Further attempts to undermine Alston's case for the epistemological soundness of a person's mystical perception include an attack on his argument for the justifiability or reasonableness of accepting that, in these instances, a person is perceiving God. Within his perceptual construct:

> the question of whether mystical experience does count as genuine perception of God is just a question of whether it is what it seems to its subject to be…if the experience is given a perceptual construal from the start, we will at least have to take seriously the view that a claim to be perceiving God is prima facie acceptable on its merits, pending any sufficient reasons to the contrary. (1991, pp.66–7)

This aspect of his reasoning has been labelled his 'justified or innocent until proven guilty' argument; we can believe it unless we have grounds to disbelieve it. This is a major focus for dissenting voices who demand more substantial grounds to accept the reliability of a claim that one has perceived God (see Pasnau 1993; Draper 1992). Here, Alston is particularly accused of protectionism; of using a circular argument in an attempt to safeguard mystical experience from internal or external criticism. In Alston's defence, Eberle responds that 'mystical perception is not the only practice for which we can provide no non-circular support: we find ourselves in the same predicament with respect to sense perception, memory, introspection and inference' (1998, p.301).

Disposition, motivations and psychological (un?)soundness of mystics

Scepticism based on suspicions as to the temperament, psychiatric well-being or psychological predisposition of those who have relayed accounts of mystical perception is, perhaps understandably, a prominent feature of the wider debate. Swain (1988, p.468), on the basis of Alston's earlier work, accuses him of not taking into account 'relevant characteristics of the cognizer, specifically, those characteristics which determine how reliable the subject is as an information-processing mechanism. Such characteristics are relevant to ascriptions of justification and knowledge.' In response, one might ask what constitutes a conclusive basis on which reliability-determining characteristics are to be established: a psychiatric assessment, for example, or perhaps two assessments, in order to allow for the possibility that the first psychiatrist might possess dubitable reliability-determining characteristics?

In relation to historical accounts, there can no more be evidential defence against such attacks than there can be evidence for the allegations being made, especially given the obvious obstacle that opportunities for exploratory empirical research do not exist. As for cases of contemporary testimony, even here there can be no conclusive case made for either a negative or a positive judgment on what is taking place. Any negative argument concerning the subjectivity of the perceivers' construal of their experiences which postulates that a psychological hypothesis was added to a non-mystical experience is dependent on the same evidential testimony and philosophical interpretation as the issue of whether any experience actually took place at all. Thus it is impossible to establish any firm conclusions either way. Interestingly in this context, Wolterstorff concludes his *Divine Discourse* with a critique of an account of a mystical experience given by a friend who subjected herself to psychiatric examination on the basis of the extraordinary nature of the experience. He uses an argument similar to that of Alston to establish the case that it is reasonable within a theological belief framework to accept that the experience was real (1995, Chapter 15).

In addition, those who claim that the degree of personal transformation which their mystical perception has precipitated is a basis for the acceptance of its validity[8] have been susceptible to criticism on the grounds that other psycho-social factors provide equally, if not more, plausible explanations. Alston, however, argues that the converse is also true as it is impossible to justify the claim that psycho-social influences are the determining factor (1991, p.297). Concerning the possibility of future neuro-scientific or psychological discoveries being able to provide reasons to disprove the veracity of any claim to a genuine perception

---

8   Alston offers various manifestations of such evidence in Alston 1991, Chapter 8.

of God – something which Lancaster does not envisage (2011, p.13) – Mawson argues that, 'to the extent that theists who are indeterminists can hope to answer the question of whether or not a particular experience is a genuine perception of God, they must hope to do so not via neuro-scientific enquiry but via theological reflection' (2005, p.117) – a view which lies at the heart of the methodology of our discussion of the spiritual experience of people with profound intellectual disabilities.

The broader philosophical argument here relates to the nature of belief and specifically whether or not belief is a voluntary or involuntary phenomenon. Alston, among others, argues that, with minor exceptions, it is the latter – our beliefs are largely an unavoidable response to reality as we perceive it (1988, p.257). From such a position, the testimony of those who claim to have experienced mystical perception is to be justifiably accepted, since it is the experience and not their chosen interpretation of it that gives rise to their confidence in the fact of its occurrence, its content and significance, although some notable contributors to the debate[9] who agree with Alston on the general point part company with him on the issue of the significance of a perceiver's confidence.

Contradicting Alston, Mourad argues that belief can often be a voluntary act, determined by the choice of the subject which *may* be related to the pursuit of truth but may just as plausibly be related to other objectives such as reassurance or comfort. Therefore 'it seems possible to imagine cases where subjects immediately choose to believe for reasons that compete with the pursuit of truth' (2008, p.62). In a logical response, we might ask what would be gained by a mystical perceiver's intentional invention of an experience of God – what reassurance or comfort would such an invention precipitate? Indeed, for the one experiencing mystical perception, the account of it is not designed to uncover evidence for it but to describe it. Thus his argument does not preclude the validity of the proposition that mystical perception can and does occur. Nonetheless, Mourad's argument alerts us (and specifically me as author with much personal connection to the issues at the heart of this book) to the danger of excessive subjectivity. The line between believing something to be true because it might be epistemologically justifiable to do so and believing it to be true because one intrinsically wishes it to be the case is easily blurred, especially in light of the inherent complexities

---

9   Of these, Schellenberg is perhaps the most prominent. See, for example, Schellenberg, J.L. (2005) *Prolegomena to a Philosophy of Religion.* Ithaca, NY: Cornell University Press.

of making epistemological judgements on purportedly transcendent realities.

The frequency or infrequency of mystical perception

Some critics, including Draper, argue that the paucity of accounts of mystical experiences undermine any belief that they exist. He insists (1993, p.161) that 'a person's being deluded in [believing she has perceived God] this way once, is certainly some reason for thinking that person will be deluded again'. Gutting, however, directly challenges the basis on which Draper makes his claim and offers evidence that they do in fact recur (1982, pp.109ff.). Although a broader survey of such evidence is beyond the sphere of this discussion, recent examples of Wiebe's empirical work in this area (1998, 2004) suggest that even within Western Christian contexts acknowledgement of transcendent experiences of God is not as uncommon as might be generally expected, despite the cultural environment in which there is the potential danger of being considered to be psychologically unstable as a result. While Alston and many previous and subsequent commentators have selected a few notable examples of Christians who have claimed to have a mystical perception of God, it must surely be the case that not everyone is given to committing their spiritual experiences to paper, and that of those that have been recorded not many will have gained public attention or survived for posterity. Furthermore, as Hay points out (1979, pp.164–82), a body of academic empirical research in recent decades in reporting more general experiences which are perceived to be beyond the boundaries of normal sensory experience suggests that '[this] kind of experience is much more widespread in Western society than was hitherto believed'. Here he specifically identifies (p.164) consistencies in form and pattern of such experiences and his conclusions were replicated in his own study of specifically religious experience. Comparable results have emerged from other projects of a similar nature.[10]

How is this relevant to the spiritual experience of people with profound intellectual disabilities?

In drawing more general conclusions in relation to the relevance of the preceding discussion of specific aspects of Christian mysticism, I want

---

10   See Beardsworth, T. (1977) *A Sense of Presence.* Oxford: Religious Experience Unit.

first to acknowledge the work of Erinn Staley in her insightful article 'Mystical Unknowing'. In her brief but stimulating exploration of the writings of Meister Eckhart and Bonaventure, Staley seeks to identify some evidence that might support the case that people with intellectual disabilities are capable of a personal relationship with God. The common ingredient in the perspectives of these mystics, she points out (2012, p.389), is aphophaticism, which asserts the un-knowableness of God and seeks to apprehend a sense of who he is by the attempt to define who he is not. She relies on Turner's definition of such an approach 'wherein the pursuit of "learned ignorance" constitutes the theological method' (Turner 1995, p.19). Staley believes that 'for every person, regardless of cognitive function, the highest form of knowledge is unknowing, a state only reached by grace' (2012, p.394).

Eckhart's somewhat unusual definition of the intellect as something uncreated within the soul of every human being and which encounters God unmediated (1981, pp.177–81) as well as Bonaventure's position on the innate knowledge of God which does not depend on a reasoning process are indeed supportive of such a view, although, as Staley admits, other aspects of their understandings present difficulties. For example, she finds elements of Bonaventure's argument in relation to 'a movement from knowledge of that which is without, to that which is within, to that which is above' problematic in that, in this process, people with intellectual disabilities 'cannot undertake the first step, contemplation of the physical world' (Staley 2012, pp.392–3).

Staley's work is impressively painstaking in its attempt to decipher among the intricacies of these mystics' work supporting evidence for the inclusion of people with intellectual disabilities within the remit of God's embrace. Her approach has much to be commended and might initially appear to my own, particularly in relation to the possibilities of unmediated experience of God as outlined by Eckhart (Staley 2012, p.395), in addition to her general conclusions relating to the lack of grounds for the preclusion of people with profound intellectual disabilities from spiritual experience. There are, however, important distinctions between her approach and that presented in this book, and some aspects of her work present difficulties. One of these is her method of resolving the need for complex, conscious spiritual exertions towards the state of unmediated encounter with God. This resolution, she argues, can be achieved by a flexible interpretation of the sequence of movements required and a somewhat difficult understanding of what is involved wherein each step of the movement is included in the one that follows, presumably, but perhaps illogically, whether or not that step took place at all (p.393). In contrast, I am more in agreement with Swinton's contention (2010, p.146) that 'while [the contemplative's] rigorous spiritual discipline may be designed to enable her to come close to God, in reality it is not her actions that achieve this task but the actions of God through the work of the Holy Spirit'.

Significantly, however, my argument does not align itself with the fundamental elevation of the negative theologies in Swinton's and Staley's work. It is the argument of this thesis that it is in the broader theological foundations and themes of the faith tradition, and not the theoretical or practical details of aphophatic processes, nor in the act of 'detachment' as the way to union with God, which eliminates the creature–Creator distinction (Staley 2012, pp.395–6), that the affirmation they are seeking can be found. Staley rightly comments that 'the smartest human being is far more like a person with an intellectual disability than he or she is like God', but is it, as she claims, 'the unknowability of God' (p.398) that enlightens us to this, or is it the revealed Christian tradition which is permeated by a differentiation of the Infinite from the finite? Is what she identifies as the 'risk of affirming the paradox that finite human beings can know the unknowable God and speak this unspeakable truth' (p.399) really a risk at all?

Nonetheless, her idea that 'to accept the failed speech of people who are intellectually disabled as theology' is an interesting one and worthy of further exploration. The strongest part of her argument emerges in her reference to the broader foundational theological concept of the grace of God, exemplified in her quotation of the writing of Bonaventure: 'the final step of the journey into God occurs only by grace' (Staley 2012, p.393). It is my own contention that this is not only the final but the first step (and every step in between). In Staley's own words, 'if we accept that a person with a high cognitive function enters into God only by grace, then we cannot foreclose the possibility that a person with low cognitive function also enters by the same grace' (p.393). Indeed, it is important to ask why it would ever be considered that such a possibility might be foreclosed.

Significantly, however, Staley's affirmation of Swinton's recommendation of the aphophatic tradition (Swinton 2010, pp.146–8), which is, she proposes, 'a promising avenue for answering concerns about whether people who are intellectually disabled can have adequate knowledge about God, because it underscores that all human knowledge of God is partial and received, a gift of God's love' (Staley 2012, p.389), raises further issues. Undoubtedly, the incompleteness of human knowledge of God is a cornerstone of the entire theological tradition, as I have emphasized above. Yet it is in what God does to bridge the gap, not in what remains unbridged, that we find material to address such concerns. That he desires and is able to construct this bridge is something we *can* know of him because he has chosen to disclose himself by condescending to the limitations of human capacities. Furthermore, when we step aside from the detailed discussion of theological concepts and listen to Staley's words as part of the recent theological conversation about the spirituality of people with profound intellectual disabilities, the expression of these concerns and the proposition that there might be 'a promising avenue' for answering them is in itself a matter of concern. Do those of us who conceive of ourselves as having a reasonable level of intellectual ability find it necessary to seek such a promising avenue on our own behalf? Is there a latent belief that God might have a preferential option for the intellectually able?

While my exploration of the spiritual experience of people with profound intellectual disabilities has interrogated aspects of Christian mysticism to contribute to the case for understanding that such persons experience God, it has done so through the lens of the phenomenology of mystical perception, not the individual, complex theories of Christian mystics as to how such experiences might be brought about and taken to higher or deeper levels. The precise mechanisms by which the spiritual experience of people with profound intellectual disabilities might be created or sustained are not under scrutiny here, for the reasons that they are unknowable and that exploring them would not in any case further the argument. It is not being asserted here that we can know that the way in which God engages with people with profound disabilities is exactly the same as that which occurs in an experience of mystical perception or mirrors the specific, sometimes isolated instances which the accounts cited by Alston and others describe. Precisely how such divine engagement transpires in the experience of people with profound intellectual disabilities cannot be identified. Yet while these things are unknowable, the God who instigates the relationship is not. The argument from experience cannot be detached from the argument from theology. What *can* be known of God is the basis of any confidence that people with profound disabilities can know God.

Ultimately, questions of whether people with profound intellectual disabilities might be the recipients of mystical perceptions through which they might personally encounter God are theological and faith-based questions. Are we theologically justified in believing that God might facilitate any mystical perception? Agreeing with Alston, my argument is that if God exists, it is possible for human beings to perceive him; 'there is in principle no bar to this' (Alston 1991, p.9), and there is empirical evidence within the faith tradition which supports the case that they do.

In reality, there are only two potential bars for people with profound intellectual disabilities. The first is their cognitive deficit. If we conceive of this as precluding their spiritual experience, then we automatically imply a parallel deficit in God's capacity or desire to circumvent *or even use* it in order to reach into their lives. Moreover, if divine self-disclosure, potentially through mystical perception, is not a cognitively based phenomenon but a supernatural, relational one, can a certain (if indefinite) degree of intellectual capacity really be a prerequisite for its occurrence? The second potential obstacle is their humanness; if human beings can perceive God, then anyone who cannot must be less than fully a human being. Again, Rahner argues that there is something intrinsic to being human that surpasses cognitive approaches to the knowledge of God, which, he claims, 'is a transcendental knowledge because man's basic and original orientation toward mystery, which constitutes his fundamental experience of God, is a permanent existential of man as a spiritual subject... We are oriented toward God. This original experience is always present' (1978, pp.52–3).

An inability to specifically and empirically identify and describe the existence of a direct awareness of the present-ness of God in the lives of people with profound intellectual disabilities is no evidence against it. There is no reason for it not to be possible for God to be presented to anyone's experience. In Alston's words (1991, p.54), 'if God exists, there is a real possibility that experiences like the ones under consideration constitute genuine perceptions of Him'. Significantly in our context, he argues that:

> God doesn't work through natural, much less physical, means to make himself perceptible by us. Perhaps he supernaturally brings about the requisite experience... The credentials of this alleged mode of perception do not depend on our understanding of how it is effected. (1991, p.54)

Indeed, as Mawson graphically puts it, 'the "perception buck" stops with God' (2012, p.111).

Accordingly, the intrinsic and inherently immeasurable differences between finite human beings and the infinite God do not merely make the self-disclosure of the latter to the former necessarily restricted and accommodative but also supernatural and unfathomable. As Polkinghorne (in Loder 2002, p.87) insists, 'transparent moments of encounter with the sacred can neither be induced nor repeated by human contrivance, but only received'. Baillie is right to warn (1939, p.21) that '[w]e must not limit the competence of God by saying that He *cannot* reveal His will to stocks and stones'. Rutherford's lyrical writing expresses the same thought:

> The world is immense, constructed on no plan or theory which the intellect of man may grasp. The transcendent is everywhere. This is the burden of every verse. Sufficient of insufficient there is nothing more… God is great, we do not know his ways. (1885, pp.196–8)

Can we then be theologically justified in proposing that people with profound intellectual disabilities can have a spiritual life of their own? Can they access the encounter with God that finds its explanation in the written word of Scripture? In consistency with the overall argument of this work, and not only because such people cannot articulate their own experience, these questions are redirected from human beings to Christian theology and the same arguments pertain. If the content of a mystical perception is consistent with theological content of the faith tradition – that God desires relationships of intimacy with human beings; that he loves them, is inherently self-disclosing towards them; that he is infinite in power and that his ways of working are mysterious and beyond human comprehension – then we might accept this as going some way towards substantiating these claims – we could say that *such* a God would do *such* a thing. In a way which connects the current discussion to that of divine accommodation and the non-necessity of words for an encounter with God, Baillie writes (1939, p.239): 'nor can we believe that there is no other way of conceiving the approach of God to man than as the speaking of a *Word* which man is called upon to hear.' As Staley correctly argues, the 'journey into God [is the] same for all; it is a journey in which love subsumes intellect, higher forms of knowledge include lower forms, and grace alone empowers the final movement from intellect to love' (2012, p.386).

CONCLUSION

The history of disability theology has been wrought with practical and theoretical complexities. The fact that it has developed as a distinct area of theological engagement at all, alongside other liberation theologies, is an indicator of the oppression that people with disabilities have experienced, not only from political, social, medical and economic influences but from theological sources as well. Despite efforts to mitigate, re-contextualize or redeem biblical portrayals of the human experience of disability, for many people with disabilities the Bible remains a difficult, often alienating and sometimes even completely inaccessible book (Morris 2006, p.162), and without the initial efforts made by people who themselves have disabilities to grapple with these tensions and complexities, it seems unlikely that academic theology would have assigned such energy and resources to this area of enquiry as has been the case. In this unfolding process of theological engagement with the experience of disability, it is clear that intellectual disability has been at the end of a long queue; reasons for this have been explored above. Indeed, we might wonder how far along the journey of intellectual disability theology we might now be, and what direction it might have taken, had Jean Vanier not passed the institution for people with learning disabilities in the village of Trosly-Breuil each morning on his way to the train that would take him to his place of work in the University of Paris, and had he not responded with hospitality and radical commitment to Philippe and Raphael who greeted him there each day.

Yet, from tentative beginnings, important theological work in intellectual disability studies is growing, as contributions continue to emerge from diverse branches of academic theology. The understanding that people with mild to moderate intellectual disabilities are capable of enjoying and articulating something of an ongoing, personal relationship with God now seems to be well established, in significant part owing to the limited, yet important, empirical research in this area, as well as to wider theological reflection. The question of whether people whose intellectual disabilities are profound can also enjoy such a relationship with God, on the other hand, remains a matter of some ambiguity and largely unaddressed.

A 'positive theology' for people with profound intellectual disabilities?

Common themes

In this atmosphere, a search is emerging for evidence that 'will allow us to develop a positive theology with people whose lives include [profound] intellectual disabilities' and for an argument that supports such a positive theology which will 'make the point convincingly' (Swinton 2010, p.143). The object of this search is an interesting one. What is a 'positive' or, in Haslam's terms, 'life-giving' theology for people with profound intellectual disabilities; one that 'promotes their flourishing' (2011, pp.6, 9)? As is often the case in theological reflection on people whose intellectual disabilities are less severe, for some theologians and commentators it is proof of their humanity and the potential application of such proof to understandings of what it is for every human being to be made in the image of God. For others, it is the capacity to confront post-Enlightenment mindsets that emphasize individuality, intellectualism, productivity and normalization. For many, it is to reveal theological truths of radical dependence on God, and interdependence between followers of Jesus, which, it is alleged, the Church has forgotten as it has unthinkingly allowed itself to be insidiously subsumed by a secular culture. For some, it is to expand the horizons of human understandings on the nature and being of God.

It is interesting to consider what these ingredients of a 'positive theology' have in common. Undoubtedly, the most deeply embedded thread running through the entirety of this work (and this thesis) is a resolute desire to see the dignity and value of people with profound intellectual disabilities, which is already theirs as a consequence of being brought into existence by the Creator God, properly recognized by other human beings. Nonetheless, an additional commonality is worth noting. Many of the perspectives outlined above focus, albeit to varying degrees, on the *role* or *contribution* of people with profound intellectual disabilities. In each of these can be identified something of what Pailin calls 'the contributory theory of human worth' (1992, p.118), in which perceptions of the significance and purpose of the lives of people with disabilities are to some degree connected with what they make possible for others – a kind of 'performance-related' importance.

A new emphasis

While Swinton's recent empirical work presented in 'Whose Story Am I?' conforms to the same pattern, it also demonstrates a subtle, minor, yet potentially significant shift in emphasis. Like others, he uses the research to extrapolate broader exegetical and theological insights, claiming that it can offer 'a fresh way of exploring the theological contribution that the life experiences [of people with profound intellectual disabilities] have for an understanding of God, human being, and what it means to be a church'. His source for such theological reflection, however, is not just their existence or way of being in the world, but specifically their spiritual lives (Swinton *et al.* 2011, p.5), and in this respect his subject parallels that of this book.

A different method

In both 'Whose Story Am I?' and this book, the same broad issue was at the forefront of the investigation, as both its motivating factor and its source of inherent difficulty: the use and significance of human language. The issue has two interwoven elements. First is the prominent place of human language within the Christian faith tradition, and not only the language itself but the fact that the theological information for the expression of which it is a tool, takes shape in concepts, propositions, ideas, events, and stories. Second is the irrelevance of human language in the lives of people with profound intellectual disabilities and their underlying and related cognitive inability to grasp, not only linguistically communicated information but any of the concepts, propositions, ideas, events and stories that articulate and give substance to the Christian faith.

Given these challenges, in research to uncover something of the spiritual lives of people with profound intellectual disabilities, the choice of methodology seems pivotal. In the preceding discussion, I have identified significant gaps in the capacity of qualitative research methods to attain the information being sought. If the accessibility of verbal language is an indicator of and intrinsic to the problem the research is attempting to address in the first place, it is difficult to conceive of how it might form part of the solution. Participatory qualitative research in which the research subjects cannot participate lacks an essential ingredient of its authenticity; people with profound intellectual disabilities simply do not have the means to contribute to what Swinton calls a 'theological conversation' (p.6) about their spiritual lives. Attempts to disguise this reality, however highly motivated, disregard the importance of acknowledging their particular embodied experience of impairment, and substantially, if not fatally, undermine the epistemological value of any data emerging from these research projects. If people with profound intellectual disabilities were able to participate in conversations at the table of academic discussion, it might be deemed a potential source of enormous insight; it would also be a miracle. In fact, if they were capable of such input, they would not be themselves at all.

My work calls for an honest recognition that, as Tillich insists, '[a] method is a tool…which must be adequate to its subject matter…no method can claim to be adequate for every subject. Methodological imperialism is as dangerous as political imperialism' (1957, p.60). Practical theologians who understand the substantial benefits of qualitative research methods in contexts in which they are applicable, sustainable and capable of generating exciting contributions to the body of theological knowledge should nonetheless be alert to the dangers of becoming wedded to a 'one-size-fits-all' methodology. Genuine engagement with the reality of human experience is part of practical theology's particular and potentially unique contribution to theology's sources of reflection and knowledge. The use of qualitative research methods has been a significant means of developing recognition of the importance of the lived human experience. When used in the very specific context of the lives of people with profound intellectual disabilities, however, it is this foundational element that is absent. The connection with their lived experience – the actual situation from which they negotiate their place in the world – is missing. Crucially, perceptions of their experience are offered which arise as a direct result of a failure to acknowledge and accept their lives as they really are. Only when we embrace the fact that *they cannot* tell us what their inner experience is can genuine engagement with their spiritual experience begin to take place.

Dangers in practical theology

When qualitative research methodologies simply do not fit, it is possible that the admirable desire to secure the recognition of the spiritual lives of people with profound intellectual disabilities, demonstrated by researchers using this method, is leading practical theology into dubious territory. If we are to elucidate fresh theological insights on the basis of qualitative research, we must be certain that the methodology is contextually appropriate and the application of it is logically and academically sound. The quality of the data on which theological reflection is to take place must be demonstrated to be reliable so that the conversation between the research findings, the researcher and the sources of the faith tradition is reciprocally open and critical.

The conclusions reached and the theological insights gained in my critique of practical theology's use of qualitative research with people whose intellectual disabilities are profound are exclusively predicated on the inherent unsoundness of the methodology adopted, leaving the practical theologians undertaking such research in a dilemma of their own making. Having created an impossible situation for people with profound intellectual disabilities by asking them to communicate their experience when they clearly cannot do so, the research focus at times becomes blurred and, in the end, people with profound intellectual disabilities who are purported to be contributors to the conversation about their spiritual lives are forced into the position of having their spiritual experience recovered and articulated by others. On this basis, the researchers conclude that their spiritual experience is only possible within relationships with other members of a faith community. The assumptions that underpin this argument are open to debate both theologically and logically. If I cannot do something *without* your help, it is clear that I can only do something *with* your help. If, however, I *cannot say* that I can do something without your help *to say it*, it is not the case that I *cannot do* the thing without your help that I cannot say that I can do. If a person who has profound intellectual disabilities cannot have a relationship with God without the help of others, it is clear that she can only have such a relationship with the help of others. If, however, she *cannot say* that she has a relationship with God without the help of others *to say that she can*, it is not automatically the case that she *cannot have* the relationship with God without the help of others.

The theological outcome of such an assertion, as is the case with arguments from other sources of disability theology which emphasize the necessity of being the subject of loving encounters with others in order to experience God, is to exclude the majority of people with profound intellectual disabilities from any such experience. On the contrary, my argument is that the fact that some have difficulty in hearing God say that he has a meaningful personal relationship with people with profound intellectual disabilities does not mean that he is not saying it. Whether we can identify evidence for it or not does not matter. If qualitative research in the specific area of the spiritual lives of people with profound intellectual disabilities forces us to a belief that these people are incapable of a personal, individual relationship with God on the basis of their cognitive deficits and that, on the basis of this fresh insight, we must accept that all relationships with God are dependent on communal participation in a faith community, then we must ask to what extent the voice of theology has been properly heard in the conversation.

Should qualitative research be precluded in this area completely? This is certainly not what I am suggesting. Formal empirical research on the way individuals and faith communities experience the presence of people with profound intellectual disabilities should not be denied a place in the academy or the Church. Important and pioneering work in this area, including the contribution of Swinton and others at the Centre for Spirituality, Health and Disability at the University of Aberdeen, has been acknowledged here. The pursuance of such projects, however, is not the same as undertaking research which purports to 'enable people with profound intellectual disabilities to participate...at every level from design to analysis' (Swinton *et al.* 2011, p.6).

As has been consistently highlighted throughout my work, this is not merely a technical issue pertaining to the practicalities of the data-gathering. Recognition of practical theology's right to equal status within the academy, instead of being relegated to the point where so-called 'real theology' is practically applied, has been hard-fought. Therefore much care must be exerted if its reputation is not to be undermined by a lack of solidity in its research methods and outcomes. In its courageous, ongoing attempts to push the boundaries of creative approaches to gathering theological knowledge, practical theology must heed its own warnings concerning the dangers of overstepping the boundaries of theological rigour in its conversation with and accommodation to other academic disciplines and methodologies; of slipping its theological moorings, perhaps losing some degree of contact with the faith tradition out of which it is born and in which it has an indispensable role. It is crucial that practical theology continues to embrace its unique role in ways that allow space for theological thinking that is unattached to empirical research. Pattison's point on this is extremely well made: 'Contemplation, rumination, reverie, hovering attention – and perhaps even hovering inattention – need to be valued more highly as main constitutive methods in our discipline... In a way we need to internalize the dictum, "Don't just do something, stand there!"' (2007, p.285).

Authentic sources and insights

How, then, can we find a way to listen to those who, as a consequence of their wider profound intellectual disabilities, cannot speak? We cannot. The question is: does this really matter? Why stretch the qualitative research method so far as to attempt to achieve what is impossible? My work proposes one (it is not argued that it is the only) alternative methodology for eliciting the kind of knowledge about the spiritual experience of people with profound intellectual disabilities for which qualitative research projects have been searching. Rather than asking these people for information they cannot provide, or relying on assumptions made by those around them, questions can be addressed to the *source* of any spiritual experience they might have. Thus this quest for knowledge about how they might personally experience God begins in a different location – in God's self-disclosure of why and how he brings about an encounter with human beings. Here lies the essence of this research: when we are asking questions which we might, or might not, believe require to be asked concerning the spiritual lives of people with profound intellectual disabilities, the rich vein of God's self-disclosure in the sources of the faith tradition provide an appropriate focus for our attention.

This alternative approach has explored a traceable theological pattern in which God's self-disclosure might be understood as his 'methodology' for constructing relational encounters with human beings: the specific and intentional accommodation to their capacities to apprehend him. This model of divine self-disclosure lies at the heart of the history of the Judaeo-Christian tradition of revelation. God stoops to the level of finite humanity in order to welcome them into his infinite reality. As such, God's methodology for communication is multi-faceted and inevitably entirely appropriate to meeting the needs of people with profound intellectual disabilities and their incapacity to receive and apprehend information by cognitive and linguistic means. The fact of his accommodation opens a window from which a fresh perspective on their spiritual lives can be viewed. The content of the accommodation expressed in Scripture and the wider sources of faith tradition reveals reliable data from which a theological understanding of whether and how the spiritual experience of people with profound intellectual disabilities might take shape.

My work on this subject has, naturally, been less than exhaustive but, as is appropriate in any methodological approach to a discrete research area, has focussed attention on those areas in which issues of relevance to the discussion can be identified. Consequently, in addition to the theory of accommodation, further biblical material on the unpredictable activity of the Spirit, perspectives and questions arising in wider systematic theologies, and a philosophical analysis of the reasonableness of accepting evidence of a mystical, non-cognitive and non-sensory encounter with God have all contributed to the case that a profound intellectual disability is not an obstacle to an ongoing relationship with God.

Rather than concluding that people with profound intellectual disabilities experience God only by being part of a faith community or by being served by others who have capacity to articulate their own spirituality, we *can* find, within a Christian theological framework, a way of understanding them to be recipients of individual, inner and meaningful spiritual experience. Furthermore, engaging honestly with the tensions between that which God reveals to us because we *can* apprehend it and all that he does not reveal because we *cannot* offers us a safe place in which to think about these things. Between what we know of God's character and our unknowing of the mysterious ways in which he works, we find a space in which to hold, without anxiety, any questions concerning the spiritual experience of people with profound intellectual disabilities.

In her creative explication of the practice of preaching, for which she employs the metaphor of an orchestral performance, Young suggests that the performance (the homiletical presentation of the hermeneutical discoveries of the preacher) must contain some element of improvisation, most prominent in its climax or cadenza. The balance to be achieved here is, she argues, between the performer avoiding delivering a cadenza that is dull and uncommunicative and yet being 'the servant of the music – bringing out what is potentially there in the themes and harmonies of the original score. If that is not the case, the cadenza will not 'belong to the performance of this particular classic' (1990a, p.161). The contention at the end of this research is that while improvisation in the form of interpretive freedom is an aspect of the work, the theological foundations on which this alternative perspective on the spiritual experience of people with profound intellectual disabilities rests ensures that it retains its place within the classic score.

Finally, although we cannot know how it occurs or precisely what form it takes, we might allow ourselves to imagine something of how a relationship with God might be experienced in the lives of people with profound intellectual disabilities. For James, in the context of mystical experience, music is also a catalyst for reflection:

not conceptual speech but music, rather, is the element through which we are best spoken to by mystical truth… Music gives us ontological messages which non-musical criticism is unable to contradict, though it may laugh at our foolishness for minding them. (1995, pp.411–12)

It is unclear whether he is using music in a literal or metaphorical sense – perhaps it is a mixture of both – but this is an intriguing presentation of the level at which mystical experience of God chimes with something ineffable and indescribable within the human spirit.

Am I biased?

The greatest challenge, as a writer whose life is so closely interwoven with a person who has profound intellectual disabilities, is that of subjectivity. Yet it is precisely this deep connection with the research area that has rendered attaining what might be personally subjective positive outcomes whose foundations are without substance a thoroughly unenticing prospect. There would, in the end, be no comfort in reaching conclusions which, after intense scrutiny and engagement with a large, broadly based volume of theological material, were neither sustainable nor credible. Advocating that engagement with realities must not be sacrificed in the cause of creating palatable outcomes has been pivotal to the motive, content and conduct of my work. The issue then is whether I or anyone reading this finds the Christian faith tradition to be a reliable source of material, to which the response can only be that this kind of theological reflection must require a foundation of faith. There have been points in the work where personal experience has had a beneficial effect on its progress, particularly in relation to identifying unrealistic notions of the quality of the care offered to people with profound intellectual disabilities. Unreasonable perspectives on their capacity to articulate their experiences in relation to the most basic of human needs, including pain and distress, were also challenged by personal experience, as was the idealizing of the condition of vulnerability.

The inevitable theological question

In terms of the theological content at the core of the methodology of this work, the obvious question that I face is whether I am presenting a universalist perspective in relation to people with profound intellectual disabilities. It would be foolish to suggest that this is not the case. The conclusion that God accommodates himself to the extent that is necessary to draw people with profound intellectual disabilities into relationship, regardless of their cognitive deficits and inability to understand and assent to (or reject) his invitation, inevitably means that no one in this position is excluded. If there is an insistence on the necessity of intentional response to the 'good news' in terms of repentance and expression of faith, then every person with profound intellectual disabilities is excluded. If one is convinced by a doctrine of election, then some people are brought into relationship with God and some are not, regardless of their level of ability. Those who adhere to a sacramental theology that insists on infant baptism or a covenantal theology that attributes the possibility of a salvific encounter with God to the faith of the parents of a child who cannot own the faith for herself would have grounds to reject the argument of this thesis. Fundamentally, however, if one cannot accept my argument, then it can no more be accepted for one person with profound intellectual disabilities than it can for all.

Areas for further research
Developments in biblical studies

In proposing a fresh way of thinking about the spiritual lives of people with profound intellectual disabilities, this work has barely scratched the surface of the potential avenues for exploration. Tasked with investigating, understanding and articulating the accommodated revelation of God, the commitment of the academic community to the full spectrum of the condition referred to generically as intellectual disability must at least keep pace with, if not overtake, that of the secular academic community. Despite the welcome efforts of Avalos, Melcher and Schipper in bringing together biblical theologians willing to join the endeavours of interpreting what are seen as predominantly negative texts on disabilities, the primary focus remains on physical disability. As disability theologians argue for respect for various embodiments of disabilities, in the growing body of exegetical work, will serious attention be given to the spectrum of experience of intellectual disability? Do people with intellectual disabilities assume the degree of invisibility throughout the text as it might appear? Might Vanier be correct in suggesting that Lazarus, the brother of Mary and Martha, might have had an intellectual disability (2004, p.196)? While many disability theologians allude briefly to the relationship between simplicity and the fullest experience of the

Kingdom of God (Matthew 18.3), what might this actually mean for people with the most profound intellectual disabilities?

The role of the intellect

In the context of wider biblical, systematic and philosophical theology studies, there is still enormous scope for the exploration of the role of the intellect in spiritual experience, as well as for a more comprehensive investigation of the relationship between theological knowledge and spiritual experience. What might it mean, for example, that Adam and Eve are portrayed as having greater intimacy with God when they did *not* have the theological knowledge of good and evil than they did *after* they acquired it? From a contrasting perspective, Young's exposition (2014, pp.33–4) on the connection between brain functioning, personality and the soul raises controversial issues which are of potentially huge importance in discussions of the personhood and spiritual lives of people with the most profound intellectual disabilities.

The significance of words

Specifically in relation to the significance of linguistic expression in any exploration of the spiritual experience of people with profound intellectual disabilities, my work has debated one aspect of the role of words in the divine–human encounter. There is ample room here for further enquiry. What does 'word' really mean in theological terms? Does a Hebraic understanding of the relationship between word and heart have anything to contribute to this subject? Does the theological 'word' have less to do with semantic expression and more to do with relationship? What is the nature and human significance of words which are so infused with divine life and meaning that they are 'too deep to be uttered' (Romans 8.26)? Is there a place beyond words where the connection between the Spirit of God and the spirit of the human person becomes most truly alive?

Disability theology and the Church

Finally, yet of enormous importance, is the question of the relationship between disability theology and the Church. Somewhat ironically, yet perhaps inevitably, academic work that aims to change theological and ecclesial prejudice against people that disabilities, and those with intellectual disabilities in particular, has itself potential to be elitist. The reality is that this kind of academic engagement is rarely transmitted to those who live at the cutting edge of prejudicial assumptions and concomitant marginalization, or to those whose inadequate understandings and benignly oppressive practices demonstrate that they really need to hear it.

Part of the diverse work of the Centre for Intellectual Disability Theology and Ministry at Belfast Bible College, where I am employed, is to assist churches to seriously consider and develop creative strategies for inclusion of people with intellectual disabilities and their families. In the course of our engagement with these local faith communities, we speak about social and theological oppression and marginalization, the importance of inclusion and meaningful participation in faith communities and the Church's obligation of advocating for the rights of people with intellectual disabilities, including challenging a culture that would even deny their right to exist. Somewhat surprisingly, given that those in attendance clearly have sufficient pre-existing interest in the subject to bring them there in the first place, the response is invariably overwhelming. It is not the case that the audience is impressed with the eloquence or originality of the speakers, yet questions are repeatedly asked about why the Church and churches are not engaging in this kind of thinking. I was deeply moved by the tearful comment of one mother of a young man who has severe autism who asked: 'Why didn't I meet you 15 years ago?' Of course, the real question is: why is this kind of reflection, for the most part, not reaching the Church?

This small illustration of the sometimes inadequate connection between theological theory and ecclesial practice raises the challenge of how to further develop a mutually respectful, informative and perhaps transformative conversation between the academy and the Church. Those who engage in academic work in this area do so only because they are deeply committed. We must be equally committed to finding ways to release this work into the wider community of faith and to listening well as it bounces back, stimulating us to ever deeper reflection. It is not the case that disability theologians are in a position to tell churches how to treat people with intellectual disabilities, but it would be a terrible waste if channels of communication were not growing, and cross-fertilization not achieving its full potential for enlightening and energizing both study and ministry. Theological education on this subject needs to be accessible and readily available, both in formal and informal contexts. Fundamentally, there is a need for greater commitment to the ongoing, creative de-fragmentation of academy and Church, so that the ministry of the whole Church, academic theology included, might increasingly become the radically counter-cultural embodiment of the Christ of the marginalized, less frequently trailing behind socio-political agendas and instead pushing beyond the horizons of 'reasonable adjustments' to be the 'agent of change' that Gillibrand calls for (2010, pp.188–9).

In our recent training conferences, I have been sharing something of the discoveries made in the course of my own work, specifically in relation to people with profound intellectual disabilities and the theory of accommodation, and I heard it bounce back to me in the form of a question: how do we nurture the spiritual lives of people with profound intellectual disabilities? Listening to this question has provided much ongoing food for thought. Can the spiritual lives of people with profound intellectual disabilities be nourished by the ministry of other members of the Body of Christ? If God is the direct source of their spiritual experience, and awareness of the self in relation to other human beings is not an aspect of their way of inhabiting their personhood, does it matter if they are present at worship and wider gatherings of faith communities?

There appear to be some obvious responses which, nonetheless, do not constitute answers to the question. First, if my argument is accepted, whether or not people with profound intellectual disabilities have the opportunity to belong to an actual faith community cannot be decisive for their experience of God. Second, however, if they are part of a faith community, it would seem important that they are present at its gatherings, just as it is for any members. Despite anecdotal evidence of untypical reactions to being present as the community gathers to worship, what precisely they might gain from this experience is not a matter on which exact knowledge can be determined, any more than what they might lack should they not be afforded this opportunity. On the other hand, how my presence and my spiritual life might make a difference in theirs and theirs to mine seems no less puzzling or improbable than how mine might be of benefit to the person in the next pew with whom I might not personally engage at all or with whom my engagement might be less than helpful. Of course, there are obvious actions that can be taken to encourage and build up the faith of those who can understand what we say. The actions that might nurture the spiritual experience of people with profound intellectual disabilities seem less obvious. Nonetheless, the potentially invisible inner impact of engaging with them at every level in Christ-like, grace-filled ways, as we are called to do with every member of the body, does not negate the impact that accompanies such

Spirit-empowered action. Ultimately, the ministry and movement of the Spirit within and between the members of a community of believers is as much a matter of mystery in relation to the intellectually able as it is to people with profound intellectual disabilities.

Doubtless this is an important issue and, in itself, worthy of much greater exploration. The only thing that has become absolutely clear to me since being confronted by it is how, at the conclusion of this work, there are many more questions than answers. Serious research into the spirituality of people with profound and intellectual disabilities has potential to open up fresh vistas and forge new pathways of understanding. It also asks us to consider whether in some parts of the Church we have stifled our belief in the potential for continual encounter with the supernatural in the concrete reality of the human experience. Has the prism through which we expect to encounter God become too narrow? At the conclusion of a recent event at which I spoke about the spiritual lives of people with profound intellectual disabilities, I was approached by a woman in her late eighties. I wondered what she was going to say to me and was concerned that I had disturbed her theological certainties in a way that might have caused her to be upset (an indication of my own prejudicial assumptions, perhaps). Her words were extraordinary; she said, 'I never knew God was so big.' Do we rely so much on our intellectual processes in grappling with what it means to live the life of faith that the mystery of the experience of divine encounter has been diminished? Considering the possibilities of the spiritual experience of people with profound intellectual disabilities cautions us to remember that in each individual and communal place of encounter we are no more than skimming the waters of the higher ways and thoughts of God who is the reality *beyond the words* we use to hear and speak of him.

BIBLIOGRAPHY

Allik, T. (1987) 'Nature and Spirit: agency and concupisence in Hauerwas and Rahner.' *The Journal of Religious Ethics* 1:1, pp.14–32.

Alston, W. (1988) 'The Deontological Conception of Epistemic Justification' in J. Tomberlin (ed.) *Philosophical Perspectives 2: Epistemic Justification*. Alascadero, CA: Ridgeview Publishing.

Alston, W. (1989) *Divine Nature and Human Language*. Ithaca, NY: Cornell University Press.

Alston, W. (1991) *Perceiving God*. Ithaca, NY: Cornell University Press.

Anderson, H. and Foley, E. (1998) *Mighty Stories, Dangerous Rituals: Weaving Together the Human and the Divine*. San Francisco, CA: Jossey Bass.

Aquinas, T. *Summa Theologica I*, IIae.

Arnold, T. (1989) 'On Right Interpretation' in J. Drury (ed.) *Critics of the Bible 1723–1873*. Cambridge: Cambridge University Press.

Atkinson, D. and Walmsley, J. (1990) 'Using autobiographical approaches with people with learning disabilities.' *Disability and Society* 14, pp.203–16.

Augustine. *De Magistro, XI*, 36.

Augustine. *De Trinitatae*.

Augustine. *Homilies*.

Augustine (1961) *De Vera Religione*, L CSEL 77. Edited by G. Weigel. Vienna.

Augustine (1991) *On Genesis Against the Manicheans*. Translated by R. Teske. Washington, DC: Catholic University of America Press.

Augustine. *Homilies on the Gospel of John* 1.1 NPNF 1 7:7.

Avalos, H., Melcher, S. and Schipper, J. (eds) (2007) *This Abled Body: Rethinking Disabilities in Biblical Studies*. Boston, MA: Society of Biblical Literature.

Bailey, P. and Tilley, S. (2002) 'Methodological issues in nursing research: Storytelling and the interpretation of meaning in qualitative research.' *Journal of Advanced Nursing* 38:6, pp.574–83.

Baillie, J. (1939) *Our Knowledge of God*. London: Oxford University Press.

Baillie, J. (1962) *The Sense of the Presence of God*. New York, NY: Scribner's.

Barnes, C. (2004) 'Emancipatory Disability Research' in J. Swain, S. French, C. Barnes and C. Thomas (eds) *Disabling Barriers, Enabling Environments, 2nd edn*. London: Sage Publications. (Original work published 1993.)

Barnes, C. and Mercer, G. (2010) *Exploring Disability*. Cambridge: Polity Press.

Barrett, C.K. (1994) *Acts: International Critical Commentary, Vol. 1*. Edinburgh: T&T Clark.

Barth, K. (1956) *Church Dogmatics, Vol. 1.2. The Doctrine of the Word of God*. Translated and edited by G.T. Thomson and H. Knight. Edinburgh: T&T Clark.

Barth, K. (1958) *Church Dogmatics, Vol. 3.1*. Translated by J.W. Edwards, O. Bussey and H. Knight. Edinburgh: T&T Clark.

Barth, K. (1961) *Church Dogmatics, Vol. 4.1. The Doctrine of Reconciliation*. Translated and edited by G. Bromiley and T. Torrance. Edinburgh: T&T Clark.

Barth, K. (1962) *Anselm: Fides Quarens Intellectum*. Translated by I. Robertson. Cleveland, OH: World-Meridian.

Barth, K. (1967) *The Humanity of God*. London: Fontana.

Barth, K. (1969) *Church Dogmatics, Vol. 4.4. The Doctrine of Reconciliation*. Translated and edited by G. Bromiley and T. Torrance. Edinburgh: T&T Clark.

Barth, K. (2009) *Church Dogmatics, Vol. 1.1. The Doctrine of the Word of God*. Edited by G. Bromiley and T. Torrance. Translated by G. Bromiley, G.T. Thompson and H. Knight. London: T&T Clark. (Original work published 1955.)

Bartholomew, D. (2004) *Measuring Intelligence: Facts and Fallacies.* Cambridge: Cambridge University Press.

Bartholomew, C. (2009) *Ecclesiastes: Baker Commentary on the Old Testament Wisdom and Psalms.* Grand Rapids, MI: Baker Academic.

Battles, F.L. (1998) 'God was Accommodating Himself to Human Incapacity' in D. McKim (ed.) *Readings in Calvin's Theology.* Eugene, OR: Wipf & Stock.

Beardsworth, T. (1977) *A Sense of Presence.* Oxford: Religious Experience Unit.

Benin, S. (1984) 'The "cunning of God" and divine accommodation.' *Journal of the History of Ideas* 45:2, pp.179–91.

Benin, S. (1993) *The Footprints of God: Divine Accommodation in Jewish and Christian Thought.* New York, NY: State University of New York Press.

Berkouwer, G.C. (1988) *Man in the Image of God.* Grand Rapids, MI: Eerdmans. (Original work published 1962.)

Bernard, J.H. (1948) *A Critical and Exegetical Commentary on the Gospel According to St. John, Vol. 1.* Edinburgh: T&T Clark.

Betcher, S. (2007) *Spirit and the Politics of Disablement.* Minneapolis, MN: Fortress Press.

Bevans, S. (2002) *Models of Contextual Theology.* Maryknoll, NY: Orbis Books. (Original work published 1992.)

Birchenall, P. and Birchenall, M. (1986) 'Caring for mentally handicapped people: the community and the Church.' *The Professional Nurse* 1:6, pp.148–50.

Black, K. (1996) *A Healing Homiletic, Preaching and Disability.* Nashville, TN: Abingdon Press.

Boff, L. and Boff, C. (1987) *Introducing Liberation Theology.* Tunbridge Wells: Burns & Oates.

Bogdan, R. and Knopp Biklen, S. (2007) *Qualitative Research for Education: An Introduction to Theory and Methods, 5th edn.* Boston, MA: Pearson.

Bonaventure (1978) *The Soul's Journey into God: The Tree of Life, The Life of St Francis.* Translated by E. Cousins. New York, NY: Paulist Press.

Bonaventure (2002) *Itinerarium Mentes in Deum. VII.* Edited by P. Boehner and Z. Hayes. New York, NY: The Franciscan Institute, St. Bonaventure University.

Bonhoeffer, D. (1954) *Life Together.* New York: Harper and Row.

Bowen, N. (2010) *Ezekiel.* Nashville, TN: Abingdon Press.

Bray, G. (1991) 'The significance of God's image in man.' *Tyndale Bulletin* 42:2, pp.192–225.

Bray, G. (1992) *Biblical Interpretation Past and Present.* Leicester: Apollos.

Bridle, L. (2011) 'Confronting the Distortions: Mothers of Children with Down syndrome and Prenatal Testing' Accessed on 2 April 2014 at www.intellectualdisability.info/diagnosis/confronting-the-distortions-mothers-of-children-with-down-syndrome-and-prenatal-testing. (Original work published 2000 in *Interaction* 13:4, pp.26–33 by the National Council for Intellectual Disability (NCID) in Australia, revised and updated in 2011.)

Briggs, R. (2008) 'Speech–Act Theory' in D. Firth and J. Grant (eds) *Words and the Word: Explorations in Biblical Interpretation and Literary Theory.* Nottingham: Apollos.

Brock, B. (2009) 'Autism, care, and Christian hope.' *Journal of Religion, Disability & Health* 13, pp.7–28.

Brock, B. (2010) 'Supererogation and the Riskiness of Human Vulnerability' in H. Reinders (ed.) *The Paradox of Disability: Responses to Jean Vanier and L'Arche Communities from Theology and the Sciences.* Grand Rapids, MI: Eerdmans.

Bromiley, G. (1988) *International Standard Bible Encyclopaedia, Vol. 2.* Grand Rapids, MI: Eerdmans. (Original work published 1979.)

Bruce, F.F. (1972) *The Book of Acts: The New London Commentary on the New Testament.* London: Marshall, Morgan and Scott.

Bruce, F.F. (1990) *The Acts of the Apostles: Greek Text with Introduction and Commentary.* Grand Rapids, MI: Eerdmans.

Brunner, E. (1950) *Dogmatics 2, Vol. 1, The Christian Doctrine of God* (trans. O. Wyon). Philadelphia: Westminster.

Bunge, M. (ed.) (2001) *The Child in Christian Thought.* Grand Rapids, MI: Eerdmans.

Bunge, M. (2006) 'The child, religion, and the academy: developing robust theological and religious understandings of children and childhood.' *The Journal of Religion* 86:4, pp.549–79.

Burrell, G. and Morgan, G. (1979) *Sociological Paradigms and Organisational Analysis.* Aldershot: Ashgate.

Calvin, J. (1844) *Institutes of the Christian Religion, Vol. 1.* Translated by H. Beveridge. Edinburgh: Calvin Translation Society.

Calvin, J. (1948) *Commentaries of the First Book of Moses Called Genesis, Vol. 1.1.* Translated by J. King. Grand Rapids, MI: Eerdmans.

Campbell, C. (1995) 'Between text and sermon.' *Interpretation: A Journal of Bible and Theology* 49:4, pp.394–8.

Carr, A. (1973) 'Theology and experience in the thought of Karl Rahner.' *The Journal of Religion* 53, pp.359–76.

Carson, D. (1986) 'Recent Developments in the Doctrine of Scripture' in D. Carson and J. Woodbridge (eds) *Hermeneutics, Authority and Canon.* Grand Rapids, MI: Zondervan.

Carson, D. (2005) *Being Conversant with the Emergent Church.* Grand Rapids, MI: Zondervan.

Caspary, A. (2012) 'The Patristic Era: Early Christian Attitudes Towards the Disfigured Outcast' in J. Swinton and B. Brock (eds) *Disability in the Christian Tradition: A Reader.* Grand Rapids, MI: Eerdmans.

Chan, S. (1995) *Spiritual Theology.* Leicester: InterVarsity Press.

Charlton, J. (2000) *Nothing About Us Without Us: Disability Oppression and Empowerment.* Berkeley, CA: University of California Press.

Charry, E. (1997) *By the Renewing of Your Minds.* New York, NY: Oxford University Press.

Charry, E. (2007) 'Experience.' In J. Webster, K. Tanner and I. Torrance (eds) *The Oxford Handbook of Systematic Theology.* Oxford: Oxford University Press.

Chase, F.H. (1902) *The Credibility of the Acts of the Apostles.* London: Macmillan.

Chi-fung S.S. (2014) 'What does it mean to be saved? Evangelicalism and People with Severe Intellectual Disabilities.' Unpublished thesis, University of Aberdeen,

Chiovitti, R.F. and Piran, N. (2003) 'Rigour and grounded theory research.' *Journal of Advanced Nursing* 44:4, pp.427–35.

Chrysotome, St Jean (1970) *Sur l'incomprehensibilité de Dieu: Homélies I–V* (SC 28bis), 2nd edn. Edited by A.M. Malingrey. Paris: Les Éditions du Cerf.

Clines, D. (1968) 'The image of God in man.' *Tyndale Bulletin* 19, pp.53–103.

Cobb, M., Puchlaski, C. and Rumbold, B. (eds) (2012) *Oxford Textbook on Spirituality in Health Care.* New York, NY: Oxford University Press.

Coleman, L. (2010) 'Stigma: An Enigma Demystified' in L. Davis (ed.) *Disability Studies Reader.* London: Routledge.

Corbin, J. and Strauss, A. (2008) *Basics of Qualitative Research: Techniques and Procedures for Developing Grounded Theory*, 3rd edn. Thousand Oaks, CA: Sage.

Corker, M. and Shakespeare, T. (eds) (2000) *Disability/Postmodernity: Embodying Disability Theory.* London: Continuum.

Creamer, D.B. (2009) *Disability and Christian Theology: Embodied Limits and Constructive Possibilities.* Oxford: Oxford University Press.

Davis, L. (1995) *Enforcing Normalcy: Disability, Deafness and the Body.* London: Verso.

Davis, L. (ed.) (2010) *The Disability Studies Reader.* London: Routledge.

Demarest, B. (1992) General Revelation: Historical Views and Contemporary Issues. Nashville, TN: Zondervan.

Denzin, N. and Lincoln, Y. (eds) (1998) *The Landscape of Qualitative Research: Theories and Issues.* Thousand Oaks, CA: Sage.

Denzin, N. and Lincoln, Y. (eds) (2000) *Handbook of Qualitative Research.* Thousand Oaks, CA: Sage.

de Sales, St Francis, *Treatise on the Love of God, Book 4.* Accessed on 5 June 2014 at www.catholictreasury. info/books/on_love_of_God/index.php.

Devries, D. (2001) '"Be Converted and Become as Little Children": Friedrich Schleiermacher on the religious significance of childhood' in M. Bunge (ed.) *The Child in Christian Thought.* Grand Rapids, MI: Eerdmans.

Dibelius, M. (1956) *Studies in the Acts of the Apostles.* Translated by M. Ling. London: SCM Press.

Dickson, J.N.I. (2009) 'Nourishing the Spirit of Persons with Down Syndrome.' Unpublished paper presented at the World Down Syndrome Conference, Dublin, 2009.

Dodd, C. (1936) *The Apostolic Preaching and its Developments.* London: Hodder and Stoughton.

Dowling, S., Manthorpe, J. and Cowley, S. (2007) 'Working on person-centred planning: from amber to green light?' *Journal of Intellectual Disabilities* 11:1, pp.65–82.

Draper, P. (1992) 'God and perceptual evidence.' *International Journal for Philosophy of Religion* 32:3, pp.149–65.

Duce, P. and Strange, D. (2001) *Keeping Your Balance: Approaching Theological and Religious Studies.* Leicester: InterVarsity Press.

Dunn, J. (1996) *The Acts of the Apostles.* Peterborough: Epworth Press.

Eberle, C. (1998) 'The autonomy and explanation of mystical perception.' *Religious Studies* 34:3, pp.299–316.

Edwards, J. (1994) 'The Miscellanies' entry nos. a–z, aa–zz, 1–500, *The Works of Jonathan Edwards, Vol. 13.* Edited by T. Schafer. New Haven, CT: Yale University Press.

Egan, H. (1997) 'Introduction to Karl Rahner' in B. Gillette (trans.) *The Need and Blessing of Prayer.* Collegeville, MD: The Liturgical Press.

Egan, H. (2013) 'The mystical theology of Karl Rahner.' *The Way* 52:2, pp.43–62. Accessed on 22 October 2013 at www.theway.org.uk/Back/522Egan.pdf.

Eiesland, N. (1994) *The Disabled God: Towards a Liberatory Theology of Disability.* Nashville, TN: Abingdon Press.

Endberg-Pedersen, T. (2012) '*Logos* and *Pneuma* in the Fourth Gospel' in D. Aune and F. Breck (eds) *Greco-Roman Culture in the New Testament: Studies Commemorating the Centennial of the Pontifical Bible Institute.* Leiden: Brill.

Fairburn, P. (1859) 'True and False Accommodation; or the Influence that should be allowed to Prevailing Modes of Thought in Fashioning the Views and Utterances of the Sacred Writers' in P. Fairburn, *Hermeneutics Manual.* Philadelphia, PA: Smith, English and Co. Accessed on 20 June 2012 at http://faculty.gordon.edu/hu/bi/ted_hildebrandt/digitalcourses/mathewson_hermeneutics/mathewson_hermenetucis_texts/fairbairn_patrick_hermeneutical_manual_files/fairbairn_patrick_hermeneutical_manual.pdf.

Farley, E. (1983) *Theologia: The Fragmentation and Unity of Theological Education.* Philadelphia, PA: Fortress Press.

Ford, D. (2005) 'Wilderness Wisdom or the Twenty-First Century: Arthur, L'Arche, and Christian History' in R. Sugirtharajah (ed.) *Wilderness: Essays in Honour of Frances Young.* London: Continuum.

Fuller, R. (1963) *Interpreting the Miracles.* Philadelphia, PA: Westminster.

Funkenstein, A. (1986) *Theology and the Scientific Imagination from the Middle Ages to the Seventeenth Century.* Princeton, NJ: Princeton University Press.

Gadamer, H.G. (1981) *Truth and Method.* London: Sheed and Ward.

Garland-Thomson, R. (1997) *Extraordinary Bodies: Figuring Disability in American Society and Culture.* New York, NY: Columbia University Press.

Garland-Thomson, R. (2002) 'Integrating disability, transforming feminist theory.' *NWSA Journal* 14:3, pp.1–32.

Gates, B. and Beacock, C. (eds) (1997) *Dimensions of Learning Disability.* London: Tyndall Balliere.

Gates, B. (1997) 'The Nature of Learning Disability' in B. Gates and C. Beacock (eds) *Dimensions of Learning Disability.* London: Tyndall Balliere.

Gaventa, B. (eds) (1986) *From Darkness to Light: Aspects of Conversion in the New Testament.* Philadelphia, PA: Fortress Press.

Gaventa, W. and Coulter, D. (eds) (2001) *The Theological Voice of Wolf Wolfensberger.* New York, NY: Routledge.

Gillibrand, J. (2010) *Disabled Church – Disabled Society: The Implications of Autism for Philosophy, Theology and Politics.* London: Jessica Kingsley Publishers.

Gilson, M.É. (1924) *The Philosophy of St Thomas Aquinas.* Edited by G.A. Elring, translated by E. Bullough. Cambridge: W. Heffer.

Goble, C. (2004) 'Dependence, Independence and Normality' in J. Swain, S. French, C. Barnes and C. Thomas (eds) *Disabling Barriers, Enabling Environments, 2nd edn.* London: Sage Publications. (Original work published 1993.)

Godet, F. (1969) *Commentary on the Gospel of John, Vol. 1.* Grand Rapids, MI: Zondervan. (Originally published 1893.)

Gooding, D. (1990) *True to the Faith: A Fresh Approach to the Acts of the Apostles.* London: Hodder and Stoughton.

Goodley, D. and Rapley, M. (2000) 'Changing the Subject: Postmodernity and People with "Learning Difficulties"' in T. Shakespeare and M. Corker (eds) *Disability/Postmodernity: Embodying Disability Theory.* London: Continuum.

Goodley, D. (2010) *Disability Studies: An Interdisciplinary Introduction*. London: Sage.

Gorringe, T. (2001) *The Education of Desire: Towards a Theology of the Senses*. London: SCM Press.

Graham, E., Walton, H. and Ward, F. (2005) *Theological Reflection: Methods*. London: SCM Press.

Gray, B. and Jackson, R. (eds) (2002) *Advocacy and Learning Disabilities*. London: Jessica Kingsley Publishers.

Gregory of Nyssa (19580 *Ad Eusthathium de sancta trinitae* in *Gregorii Nysseni Opera*, vol. 3.1 EUS. Edited by F Mueller. Leiden: Brill.

Gregory of Nyssa, *Answer to Euonimus' Second Book, NPNF 2*.

Grudem, W. (1994) *Systematic Theology*. Leicester: InterVarsity Press

Gutting, G. (1982) *Religious Belief and Religious Skepticism*. Notre Dame, IN: University of Notre Dame Press.

Hall, D.J. (1986) *Imaging God: Dominion as Stewardship*. Grand Rapids, MI: Eerdmans.

Haraway, D. (1991) *Simians, Cyborgs and Women*. New York, NY: Routledge.

Hargreaves, J. (1990) *A Guide to Acts*. London: SPCK.

Harré, R. and van Langenhove, L. (1999) *Positioning Theory*. Oxford: Blackwell.

Harshaw, J. (2010) 'Prophetic Voices, Silent Words: The Prophetic Role of Persons with Profound Intellectual Disabilities in Contemporary Christianity.' *Practical Theology* 3, pp.311–329.

Haslam, M. (2011) *A Constructive Theology of Intellectual Disability: Human Beings, Mutuality and Response*. London: Fordham University Press.

Hauerwas, S. (2001) *The Hauerwas Reader*. Durham, NC: Duke University Press.

Hauerwas, S. (2005) 'The Retarded and the Criteria for the Human' in J. Swinton (ed.) *Critical Reflections on Stanley Hauerwas' Theology of Disability*. New York, NY: Routledge.

Hawkesworth, M. (2006) 'Contending Conceptions of Science and Politics' in P. Schwartz-Shea and D. Yanow (eds) *Interpretation and Method: Empirical Research Methods and the Interpretive Turn*. New York, NY: M.E. Sharpe Publishing.

Hay, D. (1979) 'Religious experience amongst a group of post-graduate students – a qualitative study.' *Journal for the Scientific Study of Religion* 18:2, pp.164–82.

Hay, D. (2006) *The Spirit of the Child*. London: Jessica Kingsley Publishers.

Hay, D. and Nye, R. (1996) 'Investigating children's spirituality: the need for a fruitful hypothesis.' *International Journal of Children's Spirituality*, pp.6–16.

Headlam, A. (1934) *Christian Theology*. Oxford: Cheltenham.

Heitzenrater, R. (2001) 'John Wesley and Children' in M. Bunge (ed.) *The Child in Christian Thought*. Grand Rapids, MI: Eerdmans.

Herrnstein, R. and Murray, C. (1996) *The Bell Curve: Intelligence and Class Structure in American Life*. New York, NY: Free Press Paperbacks.

Hinsdale, M.A. (n.d.) '"Infinite openness to the infinite": Karl Rahner's contribution to modern Catholic thought on the child', pp.1–49. Accessed 7 February 2014 at www.academia.edu/3605641.

Holley, K. and Colyar, J. (2009) 'Rethinking texts: narrative and the construction of qualitative research.' *Educational Researcher* 38:9, pp.680–6.

Holt, B. (1997) *A Brief History of Christian Spirituality*. Oxford: Oxford University Press.

Hubbard, R. (2010) 'Abortion and Disability: Who Should and Should Not Inhabit the World' in L. Davis (ed.) *Disability Studies Reader*. London: Routledge.

Hughes, P.E. (1989) *The True Image: The Origin and Destiny of Man in Christ*. Grand Rapids, MI: Eerdmans.

Hull, J. (2003) 'The broken body in a broken world: a contribution to a Christian doctrine of the person from a disabled point of view.' *Journal of Religion, Disability and Health* 7:4, pp.5–23.

Hulme, K. (1983) *The Bone People*. London: Picador.

Imhof, P. and Biallowons, H. (1986) *Karl Rahner in Dialogue*. New York: Crossroad.

Imhof, P. and Biallowons, H. (eds) (1991) *Faith in a Wintry Season: Conversations and Interviews with Karl Rahner in the Last Years of His Life*. New York, NY: Crossroad.

James, W. (1995) *The Variety of Religious Experience: A Study in Human Nature. The Gifford Lectures 1901–1902*. Edited by W. Proudfoot. New York, NY: Touchstone/Simon and Schuster. (Original work published 1982.)

Jensen, P. (2002) *The Revelation of God*. Leicester: InterVarsity Press.

Johnson, R. (2004) 'A missing element in reports of divine encounters.' *Religious Studies* 40:3, pp.351–60.

Kairos Forum (2012) 'Knowing "how" but not "why"; knowing "why" but not "how".' Research Report: Accessed on 29 November 2013 at www.thekairosforum.com/content/resources.

Keddie, G. (2001) *John Vol. 1.1.* Darlington: Evangelical Press.

Kilby, K. (2007) *The SPCK Introduction to Karl Rahner.* London: SPCK.

Lancaster, L. (2011) 'The cognitive science of consciousness, mysticism and psi.' *International Journal of Transpersonal Studies*, pp.11–21. Accessed on 1 August 2013 at www.transpersonalstudies.org/ ImagesRepository/ijts/Downloads/Lancaster.pdf.

Larkin, W. (1995) *Acts: IVP New Testament Commentary Series.* Downer's Grove: InterVarsity Press.

Le Pichon, X. (2010) 'Sign of Contradiction' in H. Reinders (ed.) *The Paradox of Disability: Responses to Jean Vanier and L'Arche Communities from Theology and the Sciences.* Grand Rapids, MI: Eerdmans.

Lieve, O. (2014) 'Experience, biography, autism, love and Christian hope.' Accessed on 29 May 2014 at www.academia.edu/7452224/Experience_biography_autism_ love_and_Christian_ho-pe.

Lincoln, Y. and Guba, E. (1985) *Naturalistic Enquiry.* London: Sage.

Lindars, B. (1972) *The Gospel of John.* London: Marshall, Morgan & Scott.

Loder, T. (2002) *The Haunt of Grace.* Philadelphia, PA: Innisfree Press.

Louth, A. (1981) *The Origins of the Christian Mystical Tradition.* Oxford: Oxford University Press.

Luther, M. (1958) *Luther's Works, Vol.4: Dialogues.* Edited by J. Pelikan. St Louis, MO: Concordia.

Luther, M. (1963) *Luther's Works, Vol. 48: Letters.* Translated and edited by G. Krodel. Philadelphia, PA: Fortress Press.

Maimonides, M. (1963) *The Guide of the Perplexed, Vol.1.* Translated by S. Pines. Chicago, IL: University of Chicago Press.

Markus, R.A. (1957) 'St Augustine on Signs' in *Phronesis II.*

Marshall, H. and Petersen, D. (eds) (1998) *Witness to the Gospel: The Theology of Acts.* Grand Rapids, MI: Eerdmans.

Mawson, T.J. (2005) 'How can I know I've perceived God?' *International Journal for Philosophy of Religion* 57:2, pp.105–21.

McCloughry, R. and Morris, W. (2002) *Making a World of Difference: Christian Reflections on Disability.* London: SPCK.

McFague, S. (1993) *The Body of God: An Ecological Theology.* Minneapolis, MN: Fortress Press.

McGinn, B. (1991) *History of Western Christian Mysticism, 3 vols.* London: SCM Press.

McGinn, B. and McGinn, P.F. (2003) *Early Christian Mystics.* New York, NY: Crossroads.

McGrath, A. (1993) *Reformation Thought: An Introduction.* Oxford: Blackwell.

McHugh, J. (2009) *A Critical and Exegetical Commentary on John 1–4.* London: T&T Clark.

McIntosh, M. (1998) *Mystical Theology.* Oxford: Blackwell Publishing.

McKeown, J. (2008) *Genesis: Two Horizons Old Testament Commentary.* Grand Rapids, MI: Eerdmans.

McLeod, J. (2001) *Qualitative Research in Counselling and Psychotherapy.* London: Sage.

McNair, J. (2010) *The Church and Disability.* Create Space Independent Publishing.

Meister Eckhart (1981) *The Essential Sermons, Commentaries, Treatises and Defense.* Translated by E. Colledge and B. McGinn. Mahwah, NJ: Paulist Press.

Merton, T. (1972) *Seeds of Contemplation.* Hertfordshire: Anthony Clarke Books.

Middleton, R. (2005) *The Liberating Image: The Imago Dei in Genesis 1.* Grand Rapids, MI: Brazos Press.

Migliore, D. (2004) *Faith Seeking Understanding: An Introduction to Christian Theology.* Grand Rapids, MI: Eerdmans.

Milbank, J. (1990) *Theology and Social Theory: Beyond Reason.* Oxford: Blackwell.

Moltmann, J. (1996) 'Liberate Yourselves by Accepting One Another' in N. Eiesland and D. Saliers (eds) *Human Disability in the Service of God.* London: Routledge.

Monteith, G. (2005) *Deconstructing Miracles: From Thoughtless Indifference to Honouring Disabled People.* Glasgow: Covenanters Press.

Morris, J. (1991) *Pride Against Prejudice.* London: Women's Press.

Morris, J. (1992) 'Personal and political: a feminist perspective in researching physical disability.' *Disability, Handicap and Society* 7:2, pp.157–66.

Morris, L. and Morris, J. (1972) *The Gospel According to John.* London: Marshall, Morgan and Scott.

Morris, W. (2006) 'Does the Church Need the Bible? Reflections on the Experiences of Disabled People' in D. Bates, G. Durka and F. Schweitzer (eds) *Education, Religion and Society: Essays in Honour of John M. Hull.* Abingdon: Routledge.

Morris, W. (2008) *Theology Without Words: Theology in the Deaf Community*. Aldershot: Ashgate.

Morris, W. (2013) 'Transforming able-bodied normativity: the wounded Christ and human vulnerability.' *Irish Theological Quarterly* 78:3, pp.231–43.

Mourad, R. (2008) 'Choosing to believe.' *International Journal for Philosophy of Religion* 63:1.3, pp.55–69.

Murray, T. (1996) *The Worth of a Child*. Berkeley and Los Angeles, CA: University of California Press.

Narayanasamy, A. (1996) 'Spiritual Dimensions of Learning Disability' in B. Gates and C. Beacock (eds) *Dimensions of Learning Disability*. London: Tyndall Balliere.

Natoli, J., *et al.* (2012) 'Prenatal Diagnosis of Down Syndrome: A Systematic Review of Termination Rates (1995–2011).' *Prenatal Diagnosis* 32:3, pp.142–153.

Newell, C. (2007) 'Disabled theologies and the journeys of liberation to where our names appear.' *Feminist Theology* 15:3, pp.322–45.

Norris, F. (1991) *Faith Gives Fullness to Reasoning: The Five Theological Orations of Gregory Nazanzien*. Translated by L. Wickham and F. Williams. Leiden: Brill.

Nouwen, H. (1997) *Adam: God's Beloved*. Maryknoll, NY: Orbis Books.

Nyatanga, L. (2003) 'Professor Peter Birchenall: The Man and the Leader.' *Nurse Education Today* 23:5, pp.321–2.

Ochberg, R. (2003) 'Teaching Interpretation' in Josselson, R., Lieblich, A. and McAdam, D. (eds) *Up Close and Personal: The Teaching and Learning of Narrative Research*. Washington, DC: American Psychological Association.

Oliver, M. (1983) *Social Work with Disabled People*. Basingstoke: Macmillan.

Oliver, M. (1990) 'The Individual and Social Models of Disability.' Paper presented at Joint Workshop of the Living Options Group and the Research Unit of the Royal College of Physicians, 23 March 1990. Accessed on 9 October 2012 at http://disability-studies.leeds.ac.uk/files/library/Oliver-in-soc-dis.pdf.

Oliver, M. (1996) *Understanding Disability*. London: Macmillan.

Oliver, M. (2004) 'If I Had a Hammer: The Social Model in Action' in J. Swain, S. French, C. Barnes and C. Thomas (eds) *Disabling Barriers, Enabling Environments, 2nd edn*. London: Sage Publications. (Original work published 1993.)

Origen, *Against Celsus*, V.XVI.

Orye, L. (2014) 'Experience, Biography, Autism, Love and Christian Hope.' Available at www.academia.edu/7452224/Experience_biography_autism_love_and_Christian_hope.

Pailin, D. (1992) *A Gentle Touch*. London: SPCK.

Parsons, M. (2005) 'The character of the lame man in Acts 3–4.' *Journal of Biblical Literature* 124, pp.295–312.

Pasnau, R. (1993) 'Justified until proven guilty: Alston's new epistemology.' *Philosophical Studies: An International Journal for Philosophy in the Analytic Tradition* 72:1, pp.1–33.

Pattison, S. (2007) *The Challenge of Practical Theology*. London: Jessica Kingsley Publishers.

Perrin, D. (1981) *Studying Christian Spirituality*. London: Routledge.

Pink, A. (1975) *Exposition of the Gospel of John, Vol. 1*. Grand Rapids. MI: Zondervan.

Polkinghorne, J. (1991) 'Science and the Spiritual Quest.' Unpublished conference paper, Berkeley, California.

Post, S. (2010) 'Drawing Closer: Preserving Love in the Face of "Hypercognitive" Values' in H. Reinders (ed.) *The Paradox of Disability: Responses to Jean Vanier and L'Arche Communities from Theology and the Sciences*. Grand Rapids, MI: Eerdmans.

Poulain, A. (1950) *Graces of Interior Prayer*. Translated by L. Yorke Smith and J.V. Bainvel. London: Routledge & Kegan Paul.

Priestly, M. (2003) *Disability: A Life Course Approach*. Cambridge: Polity Press.

Quinn, P. (2001) 'Can God speak? Does God speak?' *Religious Studies* 37:3, pp.259–69.

Rahner, K. (1961) 'Concerning the Relationship Between Nature and Grace.' In *Theological Investigations, Vol. 1*. Translated by C. Ernst. Baltimore, MD: Helicon.

Rahner, K. (1967) 'The Ignatian Mysticism of Joy in the World' in *Theological Investigations, Vol. 3*. Translated by K. Kruger and B. Kruger OFM. Baltimore, MD: Helicon Press.

Rahner, K. (1971) 'Ideas for a Theology of Childhood' in *Theological Investigations, Vol. 8. Further Theology of the Spiritual Life 2*. Translated by D. Bourke. London: Darton, Longman and Todd.

Rahner, K. (1978) *Foundations of Christian Faith*. New York, NY: Seabury Press, 1978.

Rahner, K. (1979) 'Religious Enthusiasm and the Experience of Grace' in *Theological Investigations, Vol. 16.* Translated by David Moreland. New York, NY: Seabury.

Rahner, K. (1981) 'Mystical Experience and Mystical Theology' in *Theological Investigations, Vol. 17.* Translated by M. Kohl, London: Darton, Longman and Todd.

Rahner, K. (1982) *Theological Investigations, Vol. 15.* Translated by David Bourke. New York, NY: Crossroads.

Rahner, K. (1982) 'The New Claims Which Pastoral Theology Makes Upon Theology as Whole.' in *Theological Investigations, Vol. 11.* Translated by D. Bourke. New York, NY: Crossroad.

Rahner, K. (1983) 'Experiencing the Spirit' in *The Practice of Faith: A Handbook of Contemporary Spirituality.* Edited by K. Lehman and A. Raffelt. New York, NY: Crossroad.

Rahner, K. (1994) *Hearer of the Word: Laying the Foundations for a Philosophy of Religion.* New York, NY: Continuum.

Rahner, K. (1997) *The Need and Blessing of Prayer.* Translated by B. Gillette. Collegeville, MN: The Liturgical Press.

Rahner, K. (1999) *Encounters with Silence.* South Bend, IN: St Augustine's Press.

Ramm, B. (1870) *Protestant Biblical Interpretation.* Grand Rapids, MI: Baker.

Ramshaw, E. (1987) *Ritual and Pastoral Care.* Philadelphia, PA: Fortress Press.

Reimer, K. and Furrow, J. (2001) 'A qualitative exploration of relational consciousness in Christian children.' *International Journal of Children's Spirituality* 6:1, pp.7–23.

Reinders, H. (2008) *Receiving the Gift of Friendship: Profound Disability, Theological Anthropology, and Ethics.* Grand Rapids, MI: Eerdmans.

Reinders, H. (ed.) (2010) *The Paradox of Disability: Responses to Jean Vanier and L'Arche Communities from Theology and the Sciences.* Grand Rapids, MI: Eerdmans.

Reynolds, T. (2008) *Vulnerable Communion: A Theology of Disability and Hospitality.* Grand Rapids, MI: Brazos Press.

Ritschl, A. (1990) *The Christian Doctrine of Justification and Reconciliation.* Edinburgh: T&T Clark.

Roid, G. (2003) *Stanford-Binet Intelligence Scales, 5th edn.* Scarborough, ON: Nelson Education.

Rorty, R. (1980) *Philosophy and the Mirror of Nature.* Princeton, NJ: Princeton University Press.

Rowland, C. (2007) 'Liberation Theology' in J. Webster, K. Tanner and I. Torrance (eds) *The Oxford Handbook of Systematic Theology.* Oxford: Oxford University Press.

Rumbold, B. (2012) 'Models of Spiritual Care' in M. Cobb, C. Puchalski and B. Rumbold, *Spirituality in Health Care.* Oxford: Oxford University Press.

Rutherford, M. (1885) *Mark Rutherford's Deliverance.* London: Trubner and Co.

Saliers, D. and Eiesland, N. (1996) *Human Disability in the Service of God.* London: Routledge.

Sandelowski, M. (2008) 'The problem of rigour in qualitative research.' *Advances in Nursing Science* 8:3, pp.27–37.

Sanders, F. (2007) 'The Trinity' in J. Webster, K. Tanner and I. Torrance (eds) *The Oxford Handbook of Systematic Theology.* Oxford: Oxford University Press.

Sarna, N.H. (1989) *Genesis: JPS Torch Commentary.* New York, NY: Jewish Publication Society.

Schalock, R., Borthwick-Duffy, S.A., Bradley, V., Buntinx, W. *et al.* (2010) *Intellectual Disability: Definition, Classification, and Systems of Supports, 11th edn.* Washington, DC: American Association on Intellectual and Developmental Disabilities.

Schalock, R., Luckasson, R. and Shogren, K. (2007) 'The renaming of mental retardation: understanding the change to the term intellectual disability.' *Intellectual and Developmental Disabilities* 45: 2, pp.116–24.

Schellenberg, J.L. (2005) *Prolegomena to a Philosophy of Religion.* Ithaca, NY: Cornell University Press.

Schneiders, S. (1991) *The Revelatory Text.* San Francisco, CA: Harper.

Schneiders, S. (2002) 'Biblical Spirituality.' *Interpretation* 56:2, pp.133–142.

Schwartz-Shea, P. and Yanow, D. (eds) (2006) *Interpretation and Method: Empirical Research Methods and the Interpretive Turn.* New York, NY: M.E. Sharpe Publishing.

Scott, J. and Larcher, J. (2002) 'Advocacy with People with Communication Difficulties' in B. Gray and R. Jackson (eds) *Advocacy and Learning Disabilities.* London: Jessica Kingsley Publishers.

Seisenberger, M. (1911) *Practical Handbook for the Study of the Bible.* New York, NY: Wagner.

Shakespeare, S. and Raymond-Pickard, H. (2006) *The Inclusive God: Radical Theology for an Inclusive Church.* Norwich: Canterbury Press.

Shakespeare, T. (1998) 'Choices and rights: eugenics, genetics and disability equality.' *Disability and Society* 13:5, pp.665–81.

Sheldrake, P. (1995) *Spirituality and History*. London: Darton, Longman and Todd.

Sheldrake, P. (2011) *Spirituality and Theology: Trinity and Truth*. London: Darton, Longman and Todd.

Shepherd, A. (1966) 'One Body' in P. Hunt (ed.) *Stigma: The Experience of Disability*. London: Geoffrey Chapman.

Shildrick, M. (2012) *Dangerous Discourses of Disability, Subjectivity and Sexuality*. London: Palgrave Macmillan.

Silverman, D. (2005) *Doing Qualitative Research, 2nd edn*. London: Sage.

Silverman, D. (2011) *Interpreting Qualitative Data, 4th edn*. Thousand Oaks, CA: Sage.

Smith, K. (2011) *The Politics of Down Syndrome*. Winchester: Zero Books.

Sparks, K. (2008) *God's Word in Human Words: An Evangelical Appropriation of Critical Biblical Scholarship*. Grand Rapids, MI: Baker Academic.

Spencer, S. (2004) *Journeying through Acts: A Literary–Cultural Guide*. Peabody, MA: Hendrickson.

Spitz, L. (2001) *The Protestant Reformation, 1517–1599*. St Louis, MO: Concordia.

Staley, E. (2012) 'Intellectual disability and mystical unknowing: contemporary insights from Medieval sources.' *Modern Theology* 28:3, pp.385–401.

Stanley, L. and Wise, S. (1983) *Breaking Out: Feminist Consciousness and Feminist Research*. London: Routledge.

Steinmetz, M. (2012) 'Thoughts on the experience of God in the theology of Karl Rahner: gifts and implications.' *Lumen et Vita* 2, pp.1–14.

Stortz, M.E. (2001) 'Where or When Was Your Servant Innocent? Augustine in Childhood' in B. Bunge (ed.) *The Child in Christian Thought*. Grand Rapids, MI: Eerdmans.

Swain, J., French, S., Barnes, C. and Thomas, C. (eds) (2004) *Disabling Barriers, Enabling Environments, 2nd edn*. London: Sage Publications. (Original work published 1993.)

Swain, M. (1988) 'Internalistic Externalism' in *Philosophical Perspectives 2, Epistemology*, pp.461–73.

Swain, S. (2011) *Trinity, Revelation and Reading*. London: T&T Clark.

Swinton, J. (1997) 'Restoring the image: spirituality, faith and intellectual disability.' *Journal of Religion and Health* 36:1, pp.21–7.

Swinton, J. (2001) 'Building a Church for Strangers: Theology, Church and Learning Disabilities' Accessed on 1 April 2016 at https://www.abdn.ac.uk/sdhp/documents/buildingachurchforstrangers.pdf.

Swinton, J. (2002) 'A space to listen: meeting the spiritual needs of people with learning disabilities.' *Learning Disability Practice* 5:2, pp.95–8.

Swinton, J. (2004) 'The Body of Christ Has Down syndrome.' Accessed on 1 April 2016 at www.abdn.ac.uk/sdhp/documents/The_Body_of_Christ_Has_Down_Syndrome.pdf.

Swinton, J. (ed.) (2005) *Critical Reflections on Stanley Hauerwas' Theology of Disability: Disabling Society, Enabling Theology*. London: Routledge.

Swinton, J. (2010) 'Known by God' in H. Reinders (ed.) *The Paradox of Disability: Responses to Jean Vanier and L'Arche Communities from Theology and the Sciences*. Grand Rapids, MI: Eerdmans.

Swinton, J. (2012) 'Reflections on autism and love: what does love look like?' *Practical Theology* 5:3, pp.259–78.

Swinton, J. and Brock, B. (eds) (2007) *Theology, Disability and the New Genetics*. London: Continuum.

Swinton, J. and Brock, B. (eds) (2012) *Disability in the Christian Tradition: A Reader*. Grand Rapids, MI: Eerdmans.

Swinton, J. and Mowat, H. (2006) *Practical Theology and Qualitative Research*. London: SCM Press.

Swinton, J., Mowat, H. and Baines, S. (2011) 'Whose Story Am I? Redescribing profound disability in the Kingdom of God.' *Journal of Religion, Health and Disability* 15, pp.5–19.

Swinton, J., Gangemi, C., Tobanelli, M. and Vincenzi, G. (2013) 'Enabling Communities to meet People with Learning Disabilities and respond effectively to their expressed Spiritual and Religious Needs: A Participatory Action Research Approach.' The Kairos Forum. Accessed on 12 January 2014 at http://thekairosforum.com.

Tataryn, T. and Truchan-Tataryn, M. (2013) *Discovering Trinity in Disability: A Theology for Embracing Difference*. Toronto, ON: Novalis.

Temple, W. (1947) *Readings in St. John's Gospel*. London: Macmillan.

Temple, W. (2003) *Nature, Man and God: The Gifford Lectures, 1932–34*. Whitefish, MT: Kessinger Publishing. (Original work published 1934.)

Teresa of Avila, *The Interior Castle, Fifth Abode*. In *Oeuvres*, translated by Bouix, iii.

Tertullian, *De virginibus velandis*.

Thiselton, A. (2000) *The New International Greek Testament Commentary: The First Epistle to the Corinthians*. Grand Rapids, MI: Eerdmans.

Thiselton, A. (2006) *1 Corinthians: A Shorter Exegetical and Pastoral Commentary*. Grand Rapids, MI: Eerdmans.

Tillich, P. (1957) *Systematic Theology, Vol. 1*. Chicago, IL: University of Chicago Press. (Original work published 1951.)

Tillich, P. (1978) *Systematic Theology, Vol. 2*. London: SCM Press. (Original work published 1951.)

Thomas, C. and Corker, M. (2000) 'A Journey around the Social Model' in M. Corker and T. Shakespeare (eds) *Disability/Postmodernity: Embodying Disability Theory*. London: Continuum.

Torrance, T. (1957) *Calvin's Doctrine of Man*. Grand Rapids, MI: Eerdmans.

Towner, W.S. (2005) 'Clones of God: Genesis 1.26–8 and the image of God in the Bible.' *Interpretation* 59, pp.241–56.

Turner, D. (1995) *The Darkness of God: Negativity in Christian Mysticism*. Cambridge: Cambridge University Press.

Union of the Physically Impaired Against Segregation and the Disability Alliance (1997) 'Fundamental Principles of Disability.' Accessed on 13 November 2014 at www.leeds.ac.uk/disability-studies/archiveuk/UPIAS/UPIAS.pdf.

Vacant, A., Mangenot, E., Amann, E., Loth, B. and Michel, A. (1908) *Dictionnaire de Theologie Catholique, Vol. 1*, col. 2041. Letouzey at Ané.

Vainio, O. (2012) *Engaging Luther: A New Theological Perspective*. New York, NY: Cascade Books.

Van Bemmelin, P. (1998) 'Divine accommodation in revelation and Scripture.' *Journal of Adventist Theological Society* 9:1–2, pp.221–9.

Vanier, J. (2004) *Drawn Into the Mystery of Jesus Through the Gospel of John*. Ottawa, ON: Novalis.

Vanier, J. (2006) *Community and Growth*. London: Darton, Longman and Todd.

Vanier, J. (2012) *L'Arche, An Ark for the Poor, rev. edn*. Toronto, ON: Novalis. (Original work published 2004.)

Vanier, J. (2013) *The Heart of L'Arche: A Spirituality for Everyday*. London: SPCK.

Von Balthasar, H.U. (1994) *Theo-Drama: Theological Dramatic Theory, Vol. 4: The Action*. Translated by G. Harrison. San Francisco, CA: Ignatius.

Vorgrimler, H. (1986) *Understanding Karl Rahner: An Introduction to His Life and Thought*. London: SCM Press.

Wainwright, W. (1981) *Mysticism*. Madison, WI: University of Wisconsin Press.

Walmsley, J. (2002) 'Principles and Types of Advocacy' in B. Gray and R. Jackson (eds) *Advocacy and Learning Disabilities*. London: Jessica Kingsley Publishers.

Walmsley, J. and Johnson, K. (2003) *Inclusive Research with People with Learning Disabilities. Past, Present and Future*. London: Jessica Kingsley Publishers.

Ward, P. (2008) *Participation and Mediation: A Practical Theology for the Liquid Church*. London: SCM Press.

Warren, M.A.C. (1963) *Introduction to the Work of John V. Taylor: The Primal Vision: Christian Presence Amid African Religion*. Philadelphia, PA: Fortress Press.

Watt, J. (2002) 'Calvinism, childhood, and education: the evidence from the Genevan Consistory.' *The Sixteenth Century Journal* 33:2, pp.439–56.

Webb, S, (2006) 'In whose image?' *Books and Culture* 12:4, pp.10–11.

Webber, R. (1999) *Ancient Future Faith: Rethinking Evangelicalism for a Postmodern World*. Grand Rapids, MI: Baker Books.

Webb-Mitchell, B. (1993) *God Plays Piano Too: The Spiritual Lives of Disabled Children*. New York, NY: Crossroad.

Webster, J., Tanner, C. and Torrance, I. (eds) (2007) *The Oxford Handbook of Systematic Theology*. Oxford: Oxford University Press.

Wechsler, D. (2003) *Wechsler Intelligence Scale for Children*. San Antonio, TX: Psychological Corporation.

Wechsler, D. (2008) *Wechsler Adult Intelligence Scale, 4th edn*. San Antonio, TX: Psychological Corporation.

Weiss Block, J. (2002) *A Copious Hosting: A Theology of Access for People with Disabilities*. London: Continuum.

Welker, M. (2007) 'The Holy Spirit' in J. Webster, K. Tanner and I. Torrance (eds) *The Oxford Handbook of Systematic Theology*. Oxford: Oxford University Press.

Wendell, S. (1997) *The Rejected Body: Feminist Philosophical Reflections on Disability*. London: Routledge.

Wesley, J. (1831) 'The Doctrine of Original Sin, Part III, Sec. II' in *The Works of the Rev. John Wesley, Vol. 9*. New York, NY: J. Emory and B. Waugh.

Westcott, F. (1886) *Christus Consummator*. London.

White, A.D. (1920) *A History of the Warfare of Science with Theology in Christendom, Vol. 1*. New York, NY: Appleton.

Whitmore, T, (1997) 'Children: An Undeveloped Theme in Catholic Theology' in M. Ryan and T. Whitmore (eds) *The Challenge of Global Stewardship: Roman Catholic Responses*. South Bend, IN: University of Notre Dame Press.

Wiebe, P. (1998) *Visions of Jesus: Direct Encounters from the New Testament to Today*. Oxford: Oxford University Press.

Wiebe, P. (2004) *God and Other Spirits*. Oxford: Oxford University Press.

Wigner, D. (2007) 'Clarity in the midst of confusion: defining mysticism.' *Perspectives in Religious Studies* 3, pp.331–45.

Willard, J. (2001) 'Alston's epistemology of religious belief and the problem of religious diversity.' *Religious Studies* 37:1, pp.59–74.

Williams, S. (2007) *The Shaming of the Strong: The Challenge of an Unborn Life*. Vancouver, BC: Regent College Publishing.

Willimon, W. (1988) *Acts: Interpretation Series*. Atlanta, GA: John Knox Press.

Willis, P. (1981) *Learning to Labor: How Working Class Kids Get Working Class Jobs*. New York, NY: Columbia University Press.

Winter, J. (2003) 'The development of the disability rights movement as a social problem solver.' *Disability Studies Quarterly* 23:1, pp.33–61.

Witherington III, B. (1998) *The Acts of the Apostles: A Socio-Rhetorical Commentary*. Grand Rapids, MI: Eerdmans.

Wolfson, H, (J1961) 'Extradeical and intradeical interpretations of Platonic ideas.' *Journal of the History of Ideas* 22:1, pp.3–32.

Wolterstorff, N. (1995) *Divine Discourse: Philosophical Reflections on the Claim that God Speaks*. Cambridge: Cambridge University Press.

World Health Organization (WHO) *International Statistical Classification of Diseases and Related Health Problems, 10th Revision ICD-10*, Chapter 5: 'Mental and Behavioural Disorders, F70–F79 Mental Retardation.' Accessed on 1 April 2016 http://apps.who.int/classifications/icd10/browse/2016/en#/F70-F79.

Wynn, K. (2007) 'The Normate Hermeneutic and Interpretations of Disability within the Yahwistic Narratives' in H. Avalos, S. Melcher and J. Schipper (eds) *This Abled Body: Rethinking Disabilities in Biblical Studies*. Boston, MA: Society of Biblical Literature.

Yanow, D. (2006) 'Thinking Interpretively: Philosophical Presuppositions and the Human Sciences' in P. Schwartz-Shea and S. Yanow (eds) *Interpretation and Method: Empirical Research Methods and the Interpretive Turn*. New York, NY: M.E. Sharpe Publishing.

Yong, A. (2007) *Theology and Down Syndrome: Reimagining Disability in Late Modernity*. Waco, TX: Baylor University Press.

Yong, A. (2011) *The Bible, Disability and the Church: A New Vision of the People of God*. Grand Rapids, MI: Eerdmans.

Young, F. (1985) *Face to Face*. London: Epworth Press.

Young, F. (1990a) *The Art of Performance: Towards a Theology of Holy Scripture*. London: Darton, Longman and Todd.

Young, F. (1990b) *Face to Face: A Narrative Essay in the Theology of Suffering*. Edinburgh: T&T Clark.

Young, F. (2013) *God's Presence: Current Issues in Theology*. New York, NY: Cambridge University Press.

Young, F. (2014) *Arthur's Call: A Journey of Faith in the Face of Severe Learning Disability*. London: SPCK.

SUBJECT INDEX

AUTHOR INDEX

CPI Antony Rowe
Chippenham, UK
2019-02-06 14:08